STUDIO GHIBLI
The Complete Works

INTRODUCTION

This book takes a close look at every Studio Ghibli film,* from *Nausicaä of the Valley of the Wind* to the brand-new *Earwig and the Witch*. The *Earwig and the Witch* section is particularly detailed, featuring an interview with director Goro Miyazaki, a summary, character introductions, and a look at how the film was created. Then, following a history and chronology of Studio Ghibli itself, producer Toshio Suzuki shares his thoughts on *Earwig and the Witch* and the future of Ghibli.

The Complete Works is stuffed with content to enhance your enjoyment of the Ghibli world and to offer new ways of looking at these films: pages exploring particular scenes through themes like "flight" and "eating"; profiles of Studio Ghibli's directors, plus their thoughts at the time of each film's production; book and DVD recommendations for those who want to dig deeper into Ghibli's films; and an index to take you straight to your favorite Ghibli characters.

HOW TO READ THIS BOOK

Here's how to read the pages dedicated to each film, with *Nausicaä of the Valley of the Wind* as an example:

- ■ Title and year of release
- ■ Description
- ■ Credits
- ■ Plot summary
- ■ Work on which the film was based (not included for Ghibli originals)
- ■ Posters created for the film's release
- ■ Newspaper advertisements from the time of release

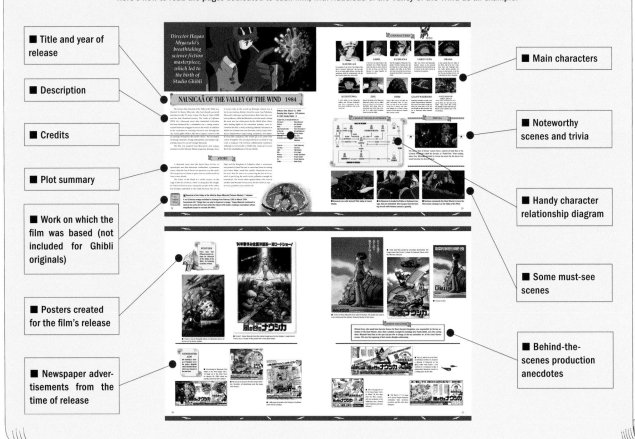

- ■ Main characters
- ■ Noteworthy scenes and trivia
- ■ Handy character relationship diagram
- ■ Some must-see scenes
- ■ Behind-the-scenes production anecdotes

*The films featured in this book come from the "List of Studio Ghibli Works" given on the Studio Ghibli website. Short films and other works not listed there are not included here either.

CONTENTS

EARWIG AND THE WITCH

Interview with Director Goro Miyazaki

From toon shading to full 3DCG— creating appealing characters

Goro Miyazaki made his directorial debut with the 2006 film *Tales from Earthsea*. After his second film, 2011's *From Up on Poppy Hill*, he left Studio Ghibli to direct the animated series *Ronja, the Robber's Daughter* for NHK. Now he has returned to create Studio Ghibli's first full 3DCG work, *Earwig and the Witch*. Here he speaks about the challenges and difficulties of working on the film, and about his plans for the future.

■ Goro Miyazaki working on *Earwig*.

Depicting Earwig's mother, who doesn't appear in the novel

—How did the *Earwig and the Witch* project begin?
[Producer Toshio] Suzuki handed me the book *Earwig and the Witch*, and said, "How about doing this?" That's how it got started (laughs).

—What were your initial thoughts about turning *Earwig and the Witch* into an animated film?
I'd been working on a CG series called *Ronja, the Robber's Daughter* (2014-2015), so I was already thinking about doing a full 3DCG project next, and *Earwig* seemed like it might be the perfect choice. Most of it takes place in one house, after all, and there are only a few characters. So my first thought was that if we really gave it our all, we could do it in full 3DCG. And, having worked on *Ronja, the Robber's Daughter,* I felt like CG could be used very effectively to depict everyday life, maybe even more so than hand-drawn animation. Depicting all of a girl's movements in an appealing way struck me as a worthwhile challenge.

—How did you put together the story?
I asked Keiko Niwa, who also worked on the script for *From Up on Poppy Hill* (2011), to develop a story based on the novel. With this as the starting point, I fleshed out the details, then restructured the story while doing the storyboards. We worked on imageboards and rough sketches at the same time.

—Did you struggle with anything during that process?
There was a lot of trial and error, partly because the original

story is pretty simple, and we wanted to add some flashier elements. I tried including all twelve witches, I tried adding a completely new setting…but I ended up ditching it all, because the more I added, the more we moved away from my goal of portraying the charm of this one individual girl. The one element I did decide to add was Earwig's mother, who doesn't appear in the novel. I thought she was the key to understanding how you could end up with a girl like Earwig. But coming up with a version of the mother that made sense was an arduous process. Ordinarily you'd start by showing a witch riding a broom to the home for children and leaving her baby there or something. But that didn't feel right. She had to be such an unusual, non-conformist witch that twelve other witches would be after her. That's how I came up with the idea of putting her on a motorcycle.

—You worked with Katsuya Kondo on the character designs for *From Up on Poppy Hill* and *Ronja, the Robber's Daughter* as well. Why did you tap him this time around?
I didn't even consider working with anyone else on the character design, for a number of reasons. One is that Katsuya's characters have an appealing grace to them. Another is that his drawings have a strong sense of form, so the flat pictures can be turned into 3D models without losing any of their charm.

—For *Ronja, the Robber's Daughter*, you used a technique called "toon shading" to create CG art that resembles cel animation. For *Earwig*, you opted for the full 3DCG approach that Pixar and other studios use.

■ Earwig as drawn by Goro Miyazaki.

Toon shading is a much better choice for a TV series, where you have to crank out a lot of episodes. Because of the smaller volume of data, it's cheaper and the postprocessing is easier. Still, with toon shading I can't shake the feeling that circumstances are forcing us to use computers when we really want to be using hand-drawn animation. Using toon shading to cut costs for a TV series is a perfectly valid choice, but for Ghibli's first 3DCG movie, it didn't feel like an option to me. I can't say what the reception will be like, but as a creator, I wanted to challenge myself to do the movie in full 3DCG.

The animators' personalities made Earwig more expressive

—How did you as the director see the character of Earwig?
The female characters in Diana Wynne Jones's novels run the gamut from good to bad, but they all have a strong sense of self. That's why they're so compelling. Her work has that twisted, dark British humor. It's never straightforward, and that's part of the appeal. Earwig isn't a pure, well-behaved, beautiful "ideal" heroine. In the novel, too, Earwig manipulates people into doing things for her so she can get what she wants. I expect some people might even find her off-putting. But it's not like she has it easy. Even stuck at the home for children, she's always firing on all cylinders and acting to realize her desires. She's strong enough to hold onto her self-respect.
—It must have been quite a task to bring out Earwig's charm on screen.
The animators' personalities really came through in Earwig, and this made her very expressive. We had female animators from overseas on the production team this time around, and the accumulation of individuality from all those different people and countries made Earwig's character that much richer. I like how the involvement of lots of people resulted in an Earwig with so many different expressions and facets—serious, irresponsible, lovable, obnoxious.

Last but not least, Kokoro Hirasawa gave us the perfect voice for Earwig. Once that was added in, Earwig's personality became complete.
—The film's setting has the feel of a small town in the English countryside. Did you use Diana Wynne Jones's hometown of Bristol as an inspiration?

Bristol is actually a pretty big city, comparable to a port town like Kobe or Hakodate, and I didn't envision the town where Earwig lived as being that urban. Still, I wanted it to be a town that a Japanese person would recognize as English. There aren't that many outdoor scenes in *Earwig*, but such as they are, I wanted them to evoke England. I asked a few of the staff to go location scouting around the countryside in the Cotswolds. If you head south from London and follow the coastline, then head up toward the Cotswolds, you see rows of low hills, meadows, fields, forests—the kind of landscape we think of as quintessentially English.
—What does the future hold for you?
Right now I'm working on Ghibli Park, which is scheduled to open in 2022. I don't have any specific film projects on the docket, but given the opportunity, I'd like to keep exploring the expressive possibilities of CG. I was able to make *Earwig* in 3DCG because the number of settings and characters was limited, but I'm thinking about how to use 3DCG with a slightly wider world. CG suddenly becomes a whole lot harder when you introduce a plethora of locations and characters. I'm trying to come up with ways to overcome these challenges and create a story within a more expansive CG world.
—Do you have any stories or themes in mind?
I don't know yet, but I *would* like to work on stories geared towards children. Our view of the world has been completely upended due to COVID-19. We tried to fool ourselves into believing the world would stay the same forever, but now it feels like it's in the throes of furious change. It's the children, not us adults, who are going to live through these extraordinary times, and I want to do what I can to support them. Children are bundles of possibility and hope, and I'm asking myself how I can create stories that will help them move through the world with enough flexibility to remain true to themselves and maintain their self-respect, to be resourceful and comfortably leap over the hurdles that present themselves.

Interview: Chikashi Saito
September 2, 2020

Illustration: Goro Miyazaki

Ghibli's first full 3DCG film tells the story of the clever, lovable heroine Earwig

EARWIG AND THE WITCH 2020

On December 30, 2020, NHK General TV broadcast Studio Ghibli's first-ever feature produced in full 3DCG: *Earwig and the Witch*, directed by Goro Miyazaki, which had already garnered worldwide attention as one of four animated films among the 56 Official Selection titles for the Cannes Film Festival in June of that year.

The film is based on the last book published during the lifetime of Diana Wynne Jones, author of *Howl's Moving Castle*. The protagonist, Earwig, is a clever girl who manipulates everyone around her into doing what she wants. Goro Miyazaki directed the film, based on a proposal by director Hayao Miyazaki and producer Toshio Suzuki, who were fond of the novel.

Goro Miyazaki had previously won an International Emmy Kids Award for *Ronja, the Robber's Daughter*, which aired on NHK from 2014-2015. For that series he used a 3DCG technique called toon shading, which emulates the feel of cel animation. This experience showed him the potential of computer animation, and he decided to produce *Earwig* in full 3DCG.

During the production, Miyazaki struggled with how to depict Earwig herself. "Making people do what you want" essentially means "manipulating" them, and he worried that she could come off as unlikeable. But Earwig doesn't trick people, or try to get the upper hand without making any effort of her own; she's an independent girl who makes herself and everyone around her happy—and so another strong heroine joins the Ghibli ranks.

Air date: December 30, 2020
Theatrical release: August 27, 2021
Running time: Approx. 83 minutes
© 2020 NHK, NEP, Studio Ghibli

Based on the Novel by ········· Diana Wynne Jones
Planning ························· Hayao Miyazaki
Screenplay ······················ Keiko Niwa
                                 Emi Gunji
Director ························· Goro Miyazaki
Producer ························· Toshio Suzuki
Music ···························· Satoshi Takebe
Original Character and
Setting Design ·················· Miho Satake
Character Design ················ Katsuya Kondo
CG Supervisor ··················· Yukinori Nakamura
Animation Supervisor ············ Tan Se Ri
Art Director ····················· Yuhki Takeuchi
Chief Executive Producers ······· Isao Yoshikuni
                                 Keisuke Tsuchihashi
Executive Producers ············· Koji Hoshino
                                 Kiyofumi Nakajima
Theme song ······················ Sherina Munaf
Animation Production ············ Studio Ghibli
Production ······················ NHK
                                 NHK Enterprises
                                 Studio Ghibli

Earwig ··························· Kokoro Hirasawa
Bella Yaga ······················ Shinobu Terajima
The Mandrake ···················· Etsushi Toyokawa
Thomas ··························· Gaku Hamada
Earwig's Mother ················· Sherina Munaf

STORY

Earwig, raised in a home for children since the time she was a baby, enjoys an easy life making everyone around her do as she wishes. She has never wanted to be adopted, but one day a gaudy woman and a tall man called the Mandrake come to take her away. "My name is Bella Yaga," the woman says. "I'm a witch. I brought you here because I need another pair of hands." Earwig negotiates with the woman, asking that in exchange for her help the woman teach her magic. But all Bella Yaga does is work her like a slave. The Mandrake, for his part, is always out of sorts. Earwig, faced with not getting her way for the first time in her life, starts to fight back.

The Original Novel

◆ ***Earwig and the Witch* by Diana Wynne Jones, 2011**
◇ Japanese edition translated by Kaoruko Tanaka and illustrated by Miho Satake (Tokuma Shoten)

A children's book by the author of *Howl's Moving Castle*. The drawings by Miho Satake, whom the author named as "my favorite illustrator in the world," depict a wonderfully expressive Earwig who doesn't try to make herself look cute. Hayao Miyazaki raved about what he called "a thoroughly lovely book."

CHARACTERS

EARWIG

A 10-year-old girl with a talent for manipulating the people around her into doing what she wants.

EARWIG'S MOTHER

Pursued by the twelve witches in her coven, she leaves Earwig in the care of a home for children and disappears.

BELLA YAGA

A witch who makes her living selling dubious spells. She goes to the home for children to find an assistant, and adopts Earwig.

THE MANDRAKE

Bella Yaga's housemate. Always out of sorts, his catchphrase is "Don't disturb me." He loses control when he gets angry.

THOMAS

Bella Yaga's familiar. She requires him to create her spells, but he hates them, and always tries to run away from her.

CUSTARD

Earwig's best friend at the home for children. He can't visit her because he's terrified of the Mandrake.

MATRON

The Matron of the home for children. She dotes on Earwig.

ASSISTANT MATRON

The easygoing Assistant Matron of the home for children. She has worked with the Matron for a very long time.

DEMONS

Imps that serve the Mandrake. They bring food from some unknown place at his command.

BEHIND THE SCENES

Goro Miyazaki attempted to make Earwig's face fully expressive by bringing the exaggerated and symbolic expressions typical of Japanese manga and hand-drawn animation to 3DCG.

CHARACTER RELATIONSHIPS

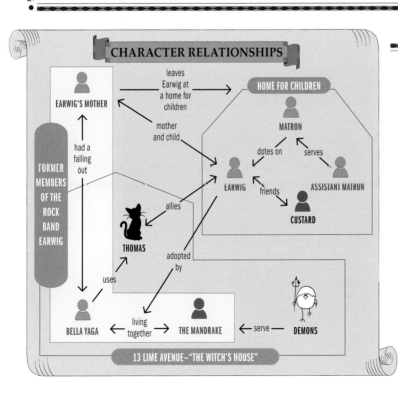

BEHIND THE SCENES

Tons of tasty-looking food appears in *Earwig*. To achieve this, the animators scanned actual dishes and created 3D models from them, then added details by hand to make the food look even more delicious.

Understanding Earwig's Charms
A peek inside her day-to-day life

Everyone who knows Earwig loves her—because being with her makes them happy. Let's see how she spent her time at the home for children, and what her life is like after Bella Yaga adopts her.

The home for children where Earwig grew up

■ Earwig was left on the doorstep as a baby.

■ Earwig appeals to the Matron's softer side to explain why the children left their beds in the middle of the night.

■ Earwig and Custard are best friends. Even though they're polar opposites, he's the only one at the home for children Earwig can open up to.

■ After Sally asks her to write a love letter on her behalf, Earwig says, "Don't worry, I rewrote the whole thing and put it in the mail. You should be getting a lovey-dovey reply tomorrow!"

■ Earwig loves the cook's shepherd's pie. Undaunted by his grumpiness, she waltzes into the kitchen and asks, "Are we having shepherd's pie for lunch today?"

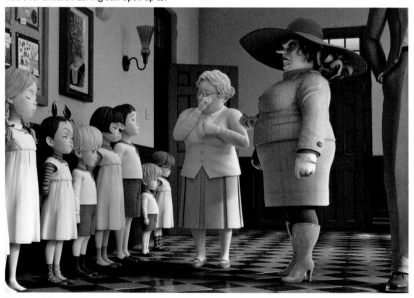

■ A suspicious-looking couple shows up at the home for children. Earwig grimaces so she won't get chosen, as she always tells Custard to do, but the woman in the red hat says, "We'll take this one," and adopts Earwig.

13 Lime Avenue—"The Witch's House"

■ Earwig's new home. The witch Bella Yaga has made sure Earwig can't open the windows or doors.

■ Bella Yaga, who adopted Earwig to help with her work, warns her not to disturb the Mandrake for any reason.

■ Dying to learn magic, Earwig sneaks peeks at Bella Yaga's notebook.

■ In the middle of the night, Earwig secretly looks up a spell to protect herself, as Thomas the black cat looks on.

■ Certain words are required to make the spell work. Repeating after Thomas, Earwig begins to chant...

■ Earwig hits on the idea of attaching new hands to Bella Yaga, who's always complaining that she "needs another pair of hands."

■ The Mandrake brings a snack to Earwig, who's been left alone in Bella Yaga's workshop.

■ Earwig tries to make fried bread for the Mandrake, but dumps a ton of oil into the pan and startles him.

■ Earwig's plan is a huge success! New hands sprout out from Bella Yaga's forehead and rear end.

■ In the Mandrake's room, Earwig tells him her wishes.

■ Before she knows it, Earwig has the life she wants in her new home.

THE MAKING OF *EARWIG AND THE WITCH*

What went into the creation of *Earwig and the Witch*, Studio Ghibli's first full 3DCG film? Let's look at a scene from Bella Yaga's workshop to get a glimpse of the process.

STORYBOARDS

A storyboard is like a blueprint that includes details of how the characters will move and what they'll say. *Earwig* was made from storyboards drawn by director Goro Miyazaki.

	Dialog	Action Notes
	アーヤ「『ドッグショーで優勝する呪文』?」 ベラ・ヤーガ (off→on)「あら、もちろんですわ。——(次カットにこぼし)	アーヤ、ノートを覗きこみながら、訝しげに呟き、

C302
1

04:00

CHARACTERS

First comes character creation. In the beginning, rough drawings, designs, and a catalog of expressions are drawn on paper, just as with hand-drawn animation. Then the characters are rendered in 3D using a computer.

1. CHARACTER DRAWING

Earwig as drawn by Goro Miyazaki. Everything starts here.

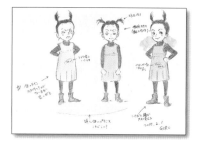

2. CHARACTER DESIGN

Based on the director's drawings, character designer Katsuya Kondo puts together a comprehensive design.

3. EXPRESSION SHEET

Kondo details a variety of facial expressions for each character.

4. CHARACTER MODELING

A three-dimensional character is constructed in the computer based on Kondo's designs.

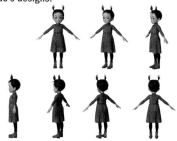

5. ADDING SKELETAL STRUCTURE

Bones and ligaments are added to the 3D characters so they can be moved freely.

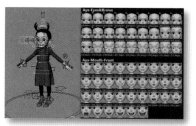

6. FACIAL TEST

The characters are put through a variety of postures and expressions to ensure there are no problems.

10

BACKGROUNDS

Backgrounds like Earwig's room are first drawn on paper to solidify the vision. The big difference between 3DCG and traditional hand-drawn animation is that the rooms themselves will then be constructed as three-dimensional spaces.

1. IMAGEBOARD

Goro Miyazaki's imageboard of Bella Yaga's workshop. This is the guideline on which the final background will be based.

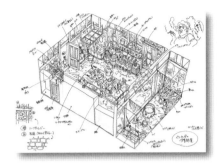

2. SET DESIGN

A sketch drawn by the director, depicting in detail how the room should look when rendered in CG.

3. PRODUCTION DESIGN

Based on the imageboard and set design, background artist Yuhki Takeuchi draws Bella Yaga's workshop as a reference for the CG staff. The design drawing for the shelves that cover one wall includes notes on details like wooden box handles and the amount of dust.

4. CG BACKGROUND

The CG version of Bella Yaga's workshop, based on everything from imageboard to production design. Created to enable filming from any angle.

PROPS

Bella Yaga's workshop, the main setting for the story, is filled with objects. Each item in this room will ultimately be rendered in 3D, but the process begins with a design drawing. Bella Yaga's spell book, which plays a critical role in the story, started as a design drawing, which can be seen below.

■ Most of the tools used by Earwig and Bella Yaga are implements for cooking or chemistry experiments. CG is able to make the items look realistic and slightly dirty.

LAYOUT & ANIMATION

Based on the storyboards, Earwig is placed in front of a preliminary background to check her movements and see what props and parts of the setting will appear in the shot.

FINAL CUT

Props in the background that weren't fully drawn in the storyboard are refined during the CG rendering process.

■ Design drawing detailing the notebook's thickness, cover, and contents.

■ For the pages that appear in close-up, Yuhki Takeuchi carefully added stains and scribbled handwriting.

What is ジブリ Studio Ghibli?

What kind of animation studio is Studio Ghibli? We look back on its history.

スタジオジブリ
STUDIO GHIBLI

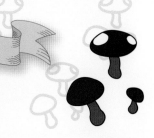

STUDIO GHIBLI'S HISTORY

GHIBLI'S BEGINNINGS AND PREHISTORY

Studio Ghibli was established after the box-office success of *Nausicaä of the Valley of the Wind*, directed by Hayao Miyazaki and released in 1984. Tokuma Shoten, the publisher that produced *Nausicaä*, played a central role in establishing the studio in 1985 for the production of *Castle in the Sky*. Since then, Ghibli has mainly produced animated feature films for theatrical release, centered around directors Hayao Miyazaki and Isao Takahata. A "ghibli" is a hot wind that blows through the Sahara Desert. The name was given to a type of Italian reconnaissance plane during World War II, and Miyazaki, an aircraft aficionado, used it as the name of the studio, reportedly with the intention of "stirring up a whirlwind in the domestic animation industry."

Takahata and Miyazaki met more than fifty years ago while working at Toei Doga (now Toei Animation), which produced feature-length animated films. They worked together on a number of successful features, including Takahata's 1968 directorial debut *The Little Norse Prince Valiant*, but the rise of television during this era curtailed production of animated as well as live action theatrical films. They were forced to move into television, where they produced masterpieces like the series *Heidi, A Girl of the Alps* (1974), *Marco, From the Apennines to the Andes* (1976), and *Conan, The Boy in Future* (1978). They were painfully aware, however, of the budgetary and scheduling limitations of television as a medium, which ultimately provided the impetus for establishing Ghibli. They wanted a place of their own where they could pour their energy into each project, dedicating the time and money necessary to produce auteur-driven features with the realistic, high-quality animation they envisioned. Ghibli would be that place, and its history reflects the preservation of that philosophy in the face of the dual tasks of achieving commercial success and running a studio.

No one involved with Ghibli at the outset imagined that it would last this long. In the beginning, the idea was that if a film succeeded, they would make another one. If a film failed, that would be the end of it. To mitigate that risk, Ghibli didn't hire employees; rather, it pulled together a staff of about seventy for each film, disbanding the group after production was finished. They rented a single floor of a building in Kichijoji, Tokyo. It was actually Takahata who came up with this operating principle. He was the producer on *Nausicaä of the Valley of the Wind*, and his talent for the practical side of the business was on display from the get-go. Toshio

Suzuki, who would later take on an important role as a producer at Ghibli, was also involved from the start. Suzuki met Takahata and Miyazaki in the late seventies when he was an editor at Tokuma Shoten's animation magazine *Animage*. They became close, and discussed creative work with one another. While still working as deputy editor- (and later editor-) in-chief of *Animage*, Suzuki was deeply involved in the film adaptation of *Nausicaä of the Valley of the Wind* and the founding of Studio Ghibli. By that time, he was already taking on the role of something like a producer.

Like *Nausicaä of the Valley of the Wind*, Studio Ghibli's first film was produced by Isao Takahata and directed by Hayao Miyazaki: *Castle in the Sky*, released in 1986 to great acclaim.

THE JAPANESE FILM INDUSTRY TAKES NOTICE OF GHIBLI

The next films Ghibli produced were *My Neighbor Totoro*, directed by Hayao Miyazaki, and *Grave of the Fireflies*, directed by Isao Takahata. These two films were produced at the same time and released as a double feature in April 1988. The simultaneous production of two feature films put a serious strain on the studio, but they decided this was their only shot at these two projects, so they forged ahead despite the difficulties.

Ghibli's goal was to make high-quality movies, and maintaining and developing the company was secondary. This was a major difference between Ghibli and most other enterprises, and the double-feature project of *My Neighbor Totoro* and *Grave of the Fireflies* was only possible because of this philosophy. The films had lackluster box-office openings, partly because they weren't released during the summer, but both received widespread critical acclaim. *My Neighbor Totoro* swept that year's Japanese film awards (in competition against live action films as well), while *Grave of the Fireflies* won rave reviews as a literary masterpiece. Thanks to these two projects, Studio Ghibli became famous in the Japanese film world.

Ghibli's first big box-office success was the Miyazaki-helmed *Kiki's Delivery Service* in 1989. It was the year's top domestic film, seen by 2.64 million people. Distribution revenue and audience turnout were literally an order of magnitude higher than Ghibli's previous films. This was partially thanks to the power of the film itself, of course, but Nippon TV also joined the production committee, and their big advertising push was a major factor in its success, a positive feedback loop which has continued to this day.

A CHANGE IN DIRECTION AND THE CONSTRUCTION OF A NEW STUDIO

After wrapping up *Kiki's Delivery Service*, Ghibli began production on *Only Yesterday*, directed by Takahata. In tandem with this, Ghibli made its staff full-time employees as of November 1989, and switched from an unstable system of piecework pay to fixed salaries, with the goal of doubling compensation. They also launched an animation trainee system and began recruiting new employees annually, as Miyazaki had proposed moving toward a corporate structure and production system with greater continuity in order to continue producing high-quality animation. Around the same time, Toshio Suzuki, who had already been doing the substantive work of a producer, moved from Tokuma Shoten to work exclusively for Studio Ghibli, and went on to produce almost every subsequent Ghibli feature.

Only Yesterday was released in 1991, and became the number-one domestic film as well. That year Ghibli also accomplished the two goals Miyazaki had set: doubling salaries and hiring new employees. Production expenses also began to soar, however—personnel comprises the bulk of animation production costs, so doubling salaries meant almost doubling those costs. The only way to cover the significant increase in production expenses was to attract a larger audience by advertising more deliberately and strategically. After *Only Yesterday*, Toshio Suzuki led the charge for Ghibli to set its own policies and direct its own advertising. Having formal employees also meant that salaries had to be paid every month. Ghibli had painted themselves into a corner—they had to keep the films coming continuously, and as such they threw themselves into the production of Miyazaki's *Porco Rosso* while work on *Only Yesterday* was still underway.

Along with the production of *Porco Rosso*, Miyazaki worked on building a new studio. He believed that by creating a better environment they could attract and nurture talent and create quality films. The new studio in Koganei, Tokyo was completed in summer of 1992, during the theatrical run of *Porco Rosso*, and the company moved from Kichijoji. Miyazaki created the basic design for the building, Ghibli's first dedicated home. Additional buildings were built nearby—Studio 2 in 1999, Studio 3 in 2000, and Studio 5 in 2010—making Kajinocho in Koganei the headquarters of Studio Ghibli.

Porco Rosso was the number-one box-office hit in Japan among *all* films released that year, including foreign ones. From this point on, most Ghibli features would reach number one for domestic films, and some would hit number one for all films domestic and foreign.

In 1993, Ghibli purchased two large computer-controlled animation stands and launched their long-desired camera department. This is how Ghibli grew to become a studio with all necessary departments, from animation to background art to ink and paint to camera. A process-based division of labor is more advantageous if efficiency is the top priority, and indeed most Japanese animation companies operate that way. It was another sign of valuing quality above all else, as close coordination at a shared location should further increase production quality.

Ghibli also added a publishing department in 1993 and a merchandising department in 1994, now working not only on film production, but bringing related jobs in-house as well. This was not only beneficial for revenue, but represented, again, an expression of their desire to ensure work quality. 1993 also saw the production of Ghibli's first TV movie, *Ocean Waves*, directed by Tomomi Mochizuki. It was the first Ghibli animation directed by someone other than Takahata and Miyazaki, and most of the staff were young as well. While *Ocean Waves* achieved a measure of critical success, it also presented challenges as it ran significantly over budget and behind schedule.

GHIBLI SETS RECORDS WITH *PRINCESS MONONOKE* AND *SPIRITED AWAY*

Young animators who had been hired under the trainee system and cut their teeth at Ghibli did the majority of the drawing for Takahata's 1994 film *Pom Poko*. This also featured Ghibli's first introduction of CG, which was used for just three scenes but would eventually lead to the creation of Ghibli's CG department. For *Whisper of the Heart* (1995), Miyazaki wrote the screenplay and created the storyboards in addition to acting as general producer, while Yoshifumi Kondo, who had previously worked as supervising animator on Takahata and Miyazaki productions, made his directorial debut. It was a new lineup that would usher in subsequent films from younger directors.

The next Ghibli film, 1997's *Princess Mononoke*, was the first in five years to be directed by Miyazaki himself. It was unparalleled in content and scale, with an initial budget of ¥2 billion (later increased), a three-year production timeline, and full-scale implementation of CG. It became a massive hit, far exceeding the expectations of everyone involved: the film's run continued into the next year and reached an audience of 14.2 million, bringing in ¥19.3 billion, surpassing *E.T.* and breaking all Japanese box-office records along the way. *Princess Mononoke* went beyond the bounds of film to become a social phenomenon, featured across all media and garnering widespread attention for Studio Ghibli. It met acclaim when it was released in theaters in the U.S. in 1999 and France in 2000 through a Disney affiliate, and was subsequently released in many countries around the world, kicking off full-scale overseas distribution for Ghibli.

After wrapping production on *Princess Mononoke*, Ghibli's ink and paint and camera departments took the plunge, going completely digital. Takahata's 1999 film *My Neighbors the Yamadas* was Ghibli's first all-digital release, using not a single cel of traditional animation.

Spirited Away was released in July 2001. It broke all previous records, running for almost a full year and bringing in an audience of 23.8 million. With revenue of ¥30.8 billion, it beat out the previous record set by *Titanic* to become the greatest box-office smash of all time (at the time) in Japan. Video and DVD sales topped 5.5 million units. The film was also highly acclaimed overseas, becoming the first animated film ever to win a Golden Bear at the 52nd Berlin International Film Festival in 2002. The following year, it won the Oscar for Best Animated Feature at the 75th Academy Awards. It was a huge box-office hit in places like France, South Korea, Taiwan, and Hong Kong as well, securing overseas recognition for Hayao Miyazaki and Studio Ghibli.

THE CREATION OF THE GHIBLI MUSEUM AND FURTHER GROWTH

During the production of *Spirited Away*, Miyazaki was also working on the creation of a museum, and in October of 2001, Ghibli Museum, Mitaka opened its doors. Just as he had when directing *Porco Rosso*, Miyazaki succeeded in simultaneously completing these two projects. Of course, it was impossible for an individual to actually design and open the museum on his own; a large staff including the museum's first managing director, Goro Miyazaki, came together to turn his plan into a reality.

Studio Ghibli as it exists today was virtually complete with the 2001 release of *Spirited Away* and the opening of the Ghibli Museum, Mitaka. The following year, Ghibli released a double feature, both by younger directors: Hiroyuki Morita's *The Cat Returns* and Yoshiyuki Momose's *the GHIBLIES episode 2*. In 2003, the Event Division (now the Business Development Division) was established to handle exhibitions, which would become a new communication medium for Ghibli works. November 2004 saw the release of Hayao Miyazaki's *Howl's Moving Castle*. Initially planned for a summer 2004 release, a four-month production delay made it Ghibli's first New Year's movie. And for the first time, Studio Ghibli entered a film into festival competition in advance of its Japanese release, receiving a Golden Osella at the 61st Venice International Film Festival. The film had a worldwide release, establishing Ghibli as an international presence.

Studio Ghibli became independent from Tokuma Shoten in 2005, but its activities remained essentially unchanged. *Tales from Earthsea* was released in 2006, Goro Miyazaki leaving his position as managing director of the Ghibli Museum to make his feature film directorial debut. The theme song from Hayao Miyazaki's 2008 film *Ponyo on the Cliff by the Sea* was a big hit, and, in sync with the film's content, Ghibli opened a company nursery school that same year.

THE PRESENT, AND THE FUTURE

After the release of *Ponyo on the Cliff by the Sea*, Hayao Miyaza-

ki drafted a plan for the future, and announced internally that Ghibli would produce two films helmed by young directors in the next three years. He had it in mind to spend the subsequent two years on his own next film, so in practice this was something of a five-year plan. *Arrietty*, Hiromasa Yonebayashi's directorial debut, was released in 2010, and *From Up on Poppy Hill*, the second film directed by Goro Miyazaki, was released in 2011. Hayao Miyazaki contributed to the planning for both films and co-wrote the screenplays. And, just as planned, the summer of 2013 saw the release of his own *The Wind Rises*. This was the first time since *Nausicaä of the Valley of the Wind* that Miyazaki had directed an adaptation of his own manga, and the first time he had based his characters on real people and depicted a real war.

Isao Takahata, for his part, had been planning to film *The Tale of the Bamboo Cutter* since around 2005, and although there were complications, *The Tale of The Princess Kaguya* was officially selected as his next work—thus Ghibli was working on two films simultaneously for the first time in years. They rented an office near JR Higashi Koganei Station for the project, then an entire building at the beginning of 2012, establishing the temporary Studio 7 there until the film was completed. *The Tale of The Princess Kaguya* was released in November 2013, marking the first time since the release of *Grave of the Fireflies* and *My Neighbor Totoro* twenty-five years earlier that Takahata and Miyazaki had released films in the same year, putting Studio Ghibli front and center on the world stage once again.

Yonebayashi's second film, *When Marnie Was There*, was released in 2014. Like *Arrietty*, it was an animated adaptation of a British children's book, with the setting moved to Japan. 2016 saw the release of *The Red Turtle*, a Japanese/French co-production directed by Michael Dudok de Wit, with Isao Takahata serving as artistic producer. In 2017, Ghibli began production on Hayao Miyazaki's next film, *Kimitachi wa Do Ikiruka* (*The Boy and the Heron*), in earnest. They reconstituted the production department, which had been dissolved after *When Marnie Was There* was completed due to the suspension of feature-length productions. Isao Takahata passed away in 2018, and his memorial service was held at the Ghibli Museum.

Goro Miyazaki's *Earwig and the Witch*, Ghibli's first full 3DCG film, was broadcast on NHK General TV at the end of 2020 and released in theaters in August of 2021. Hayao Miyazaki has been working diligently on *Kimitachi wa Do Ikiruka* (*The Boy and the Heron*), and in 2022, phase 1 of Ghibli Park is scheduled to open at the Aichi Earth Expo Memorial Park in Nagakute, Aichi Prefecture.

As it gradually expands even today, Studio Ghibli remains true to its mission of creating quality animated films.

by Studio Ghibli

A STUDIO GHIBLI TIMELINE

3/11/1984	*Nausicaä of the Valley of the Wind* released
June 1985	Studio Ghibli Co., Ltd. established in Kichijoji, Musashino City, Tokyo
8/2/1986	*Castle in the Sky* released
April 1987	Studio 2 established for simultaneous production of two feature films
4/16/1988	*My Neighbor Totoro* and *Grave of the Fireflies* released as double feature
April 1988	Having fulfilled its function, Studio 2 closes
7/29/1989	*Kiki's Delivery Service* released
November 1989	Staff made full-time employees Animation trainee system and regular new hiring begin
7/20/1991	*Only Yesterday* released
7/18/1992	*Porco Rosso* released
August 1992	Studio Ghibli relocates to new company building in Koganei, Tokyo (current Studio 1)
December 1992	*What is This?** commercial (Design proposal and planning: Hayao Miyazaki) broadcast for Nippon TV's 40th Anniversary *The Blue Seed* commercial (Dir: Hayao Miyazaki) broadcast for Nippon TV's 40th Anniversary
5/5/1993	*Ocean Waves* broadcast
July 1993	Ghibli installs two large-scale computer-controlled animation stands Camera department established in April, begins filming in August
August 1993	Studio Ghibli's publishing department releases its first book, *What is a Movie? - A look at SEVEN SAMURAI and MADADAYO** by Akira Kurosawa and Hayao Miyazaki
April 1994	Studio Ghibli's Product Planning Department established Character merchandise planning and development brought in-house
7/16/1994	*Pom Poko* released
April 1995	"Higashi Koganei Workshop" courses in animation direction begin, led by Isao Takahata
June 1995	CG department established
7/15/1995	*Whisper of the Heart* released. Shown with *On Your Mark* (Dir: Hayao Miyazaki)
July 1996	Parent company Tokuma Shoten enters into film and video partnership with Disney
August 1996	"Everything Ghibli! Studio Ghibli Original Art Exhibition"* held at the Mitsukoshi Museum in Shinjuku
October 1996	Tokuma Shoten establishes Tokuma International to oversee its international affairs. This will later become Studio Ghibli's International Division
February 1997	Website started the previous year is revamped, and a *Princess Mononoke* production log is added
April 1997	"Friday road SHOW!" opening (Original Story: Hayao Miyazaki; Dir: Yoshifumi Kondo) begins broadcast
June 1997	Ghibli merges with Tokuma Shoten to become Studio Ghibli Company, a division of Tokuma Shoten Co., Ltd.
7/12/1997	*Princess Mononoke* released
October 1997	*Princess Mononoke* surpasses *E.T.* to set a new Japanese box-office record
6/26/1998	*Making of Princess Mononoke** VHS goes on sale (DVD released later)
September 1998	"Higashi Koganei Workshop II" courses in animation direction begin, led by Hayao Miyazaki
October 1998	Museo D'Arte Ghibli company established in preparation for the opening of the Ghibli Museum, Mitaka
November 1998	Isao Takahata receives a Medal with Purple Ribbon from the Japanese government
April 1999	Studio Ghibli Studio 2 completed
July 1999	"Everything Ghibli! Studio Ghibli Original Art Exhibition"* held at Takashimaya Museum in Nihonbashi (moved from Takamatsu, where it began in March) to celebrate the release of *My Neighbors the Yamadas*
7/17/1999	*My Neighbors the Yamadas* released
October 1999	Company name changed to Studio Ghibli, a division of Tokuma Shoten Co., Ltd.
March 2000	Studio Ghibli Studio 3 completed
4/29/2000	*Princess Mononoke—English dubbed version with Japanese subtitles* released
12/7/2000	*Ritual* (Dir: Hideaki Anno), the first film from Ghibli's Studio Kajino banner, shown at the Tokyo Photographic Art Museum
June 2001	"Hayao Miyazaki—Genealogy of Manga Animated Films 1963-2001"* exhibit opens at the Tokyo Photographic Art Museum
7/20/2001	*Spirited Away* released
10/1/2001	Ghibli Museum, Mitaka opens Ghibli Museum original short "The Whale Hunt" (Dir: Hayao Miyazaki) released
November 2001	*Spirited Away* beats out *Titanic* to set a new Japanese box-office record
1/3/2002	Ghibli Museum original short "Koro's Big Day Out" (Dir: Hayao Miyazaki) released
February 2002	*Spirited Away* wins the Golden Bear at the 52nd Berlin International Film Festival
7/20/2002	*The Cat Returns* (Dir: Hiroyuki Morita) released. Shown with *the GHIBLIES episode 2* (Dir: Yoshiyuki Momose)
10/1/2002	Ghibli Museum original short "Mei and the Baby Cat Bus" (Dir: Hayao Miyazaki) released
January 2003	Ghibli's publishing department begins publishing monthly booklet *Neppu*
March 2003	*Spirited Away* wins the Oscar for Best Animated Feature at the 75th Academy Awards
June 2003	"Studio Ghibli Models Exhibition" opens at the Museum of Contemporary Art, Tokyo Ghibli's Event Division established
8/2/2003	*Kirikou and the Sorceress* (Dir: Michel Ocelot) released. Studio Ghibli contributed to the Japanese dubbed version, marking their first contribution to a foreign animated film
3/6/2004	Studio Ghibli co-produces *Ghost in the Shell 2: Innocence* (Dir: Mamoru Oshii; Produced by Production I.G)
September 2004	*Howl's Moving Castle* wins a Golden Osella at the 61st Venice International Film Festival
11/20/2004	*Howl's Moving Castle* released
March 2005	"Satsuki and Mei's House" (Original Story: Hayao Miyazaki; Production: Goro Miyazaki) built as part of the 2005 World Exposition, Aichi, Japan
April 2005	Ghibli becomes independent from Tokuma Shoten, reestablishing itself as Studio Ghibli Inc. "The circus exhibition of the 'Howl's Moving Castle'" opens at the Museum of Contemporary Art, Tokyo
September 2005	Hayao Miyazaki wins a Golden Lion for Lifetime Achievement at the 62nd Venice International Film Festival
11/16/2005	*Everything Ghibli! Special Short-Short,** a DVD of all Ghibli short films and commercials to date, is released
1/3/2006	Ghibli Museum original shorts "House Hunting," "The Day I Bought a Star," and "Mon Mon the Water Spider" (all Dir: Hayao Miyazaki) released

7/7/2006	*The Night of Taneyamagahara** (Dir: Kazuo Oga) DVD goes on sale
7/29/2006	*Tales from Earthsea* released
December 2006	NTV Big Clock designed by Hayao Miyazaki* completed and unveiled at Nippon TV headquarters in Shiodome
7/4/2007	*Iblard Time** (Dir: Naohisa Inoue) Blu-ray and DVD go on sale
July 2007	Studio Ghibli participates in the planning and production of exhibit "Kazuo Oga—Ghibli's Image Artisan" at the Museum of Contemporary Art, Tokyo
October 2007	Toshio Suzuki's "Sweating Ghibli" begins broadcasting on Tokyo FM and Japan FM network
February 2008	Koji Hoshino appointed president
	Toshio Suzuki steps down as president, appointed producer and executive director of Studio Ghibli
April 2008	Ghibli's company nursery school "The House of Three Bears" opens
	Ghibli Museum staff become full-time employees
7/19/2008	*Ponyo on the Cliff by the Sea* released
July 2008	Studio Ghibli participates in the planning and production of "Studio Ghibli Layout Designs Exhibition" at the Museum of Contemporary Art, Tokyo
October 2008	"Yoshie Hotta Exhibition: The turbulent times as depicted by Studio Ghibli" opens at Kanagawa Museum of Modern Literature, sponsored by Studio Ghibli
April 2009	"Ghibli West," a short-term project to develop new talent, begins at the Toyota Motor Corporation Honsha Plant in Toyota, Aichi Prefecture
12/8/2009	*Making of Ponyo** Blu-ray and DVD go on sale
1/3/2010	Ghibli Museum original short "A Sumo Wrestler's Tail" (Dir: Akihiko Yamashita) released
June 2010	Office near JR Higashi Koganei Station's south exit rented for the production of *The Tale of The Princess Kaguya*
	Studio Ghibli Studio 5 completed
7/17/2010	*Arrietty* released
July 2010	Studio Ghibli participates in the planning and production of exhibit "*Arrietty* x Yohei Taneda" at the Museum of Contemporary Art, Tokyo
August 2010	"Ghibli West" project ends. Staff transfers to Koganei
11/20/2010	Ghibli Museum original short "Mr. Dough and the Egg Princess" (Dir: Hayao Miyazaki) released
6/4/2011	Ghibli Museum original short "Treasure Hunting" (Directing Animator: Takeshi Inamura) released
7/16/2011	*From Up on Poppy Hill* released
February 2012	Studio 7 begins operation. *The Tale of The Princess Kaguya* staff move in
July 2012	Studio Ghibli participates in the planning and production of "Museum Director Hideaki Anno's Tokusatsu Special Effects Museum: Craftsmanship of Showa and Heisei Eras Seen Through Miniatures" at the Museum of Contemporary Art, Tokyo
	Exhibit features short film "A Giant Warrior Descends on Tokyo" (Planning and Screenplay: Hideaki Anno; Dir: Shinji Higuchi) produced by Studio Ghibli
November 2012	Hayao Miyazaki selected as a Person of Cultural Merit
March 2013	Studio Ghibli plans and supervises "Studio Ghibli Models Exhibition" at Lagunasia in Laguna Gamagori
May 2013	Forest of Ghibli, their first official site for smartphones, launches on au phones
7/20/2013	*The Wind Rises* released
November 2013	Ghibli documentary *The Kingdom of Dreams and Madness* (Presented by Dwango; Dir: Mami Sunada) released
11/23/2013	*The Tale of The Princess Kaguya* released

January 2014	Having fulfilled its function, Studio 7 closes
June 2014	Isao Takahata receives the Cristal d'honneur at the Annecy International Animation Film Festival
July 2014	Studio Ghibli participates in the planning and production of exhibit "Yoshifumi Kondo" at the Niigata Bandaijima Art Museum
	"Studio Ghibli Models" exhibit opens at the Edo-Tokyo Open Air Architectural Museum
7/19/2014	*When Marnie Was There* released
July 2014	"*When Marnie Was There* x Yohei Taneda" exhibit opens at the Edo-Tokyo Museum
November 2014	Hayao Miyazaki receives the Honorary Oscar for Lifetime Achievement from the Board of Governors for the Academy of Motion Picture Arts and Sciences
12/3/2014	*Isao Takahata and His "Tale of The Princess Kaguya"* Blu-ray and DVD go on sale
April 2015	France makes Isao Takahata an Officer of the Order of Arts and Letters
September 2015	Studio Ghibli participates in the planning and production of "Ghibli Expo—From *Nausicaä* to *Marnie*" at the Aichi Earth Expo Memorial Park
May 2016	Studio Ghibli sets up official LINE account
July 2016	Studio Ghibli participates in the planning and production of "Ghibli Expo—From *Nausicaä* to *The Red Turtle*" at the Tokyo City View Observation Deck at Roppongi Hills
9/17/2016	*The Red Turtle* released
July 2017	Internal explanation meeting held for *Kimitachi wa Do Ikiruka* (*The Boy and the Heron*) (Dir: Hayao Miyazaki); production begins
August 2017	Studio Ghibli participates in the planning of "Studio Ghibli—Toshio Suzuki—Magic of Words" exhibit at the Fudenosato Kobo in Hiroshima
November 2017	Kiyofumi Nakajima appointed president
	Koji Hoshino appointed chairman
3/21/2018	Ghibli Museum original short "Boro the Caterpillar" (Dir: Hayao Miyazaki) released
4/5/2018	Isao Takahata dies at the age of 82
April 2019	Studio Ghibli provides special cooperation for the "Toshio Suzuki and Studio Ghibli" exhibit at Kanda Myojin Hall
May 2019	Aichi Prefecture, Studio Ghibli, and Chunichi Shimbun Co., Ltd. sign basic agreement for Ghibli Park
July 2019	Studio Ghibli participates in the planning of "Takahata Isao: A Legend in Japanese Animation" at the National Museum of Modern Art, Tokyo
7/17/2019	*Everything Ghibli! Special Short-Short 1992-2016** Blu-ray and DVD go on sale
December 2019	Kabuki play *Nausicaä of the Valley of the Wind* debuts at the Shinbashi Enbujo theater
12/30/2020	Studio Ghibli's first full 3DCG film *Earwig and the Witch* (Dir: Goro Miyazaki) broadcast on NHK General TV
January 2021	Kiyofumi Nakajima appointed executive director of the Ghibli Museum
	Koji Hoshino appointed chairman and president
8/27/2021	*Earwig and the Witch* released
9/30/2021	"Hayao Miyazaki" exhibit opens as the inaugural temporary exhibition at the new Academy Museum of Motion Pictures in Los Angeles
Fall 2022	Ghibli Park phase 1 scheduled to open

As of Jan 2022
*English title provisional

INTERVIEW
WITH PRODUCER TOSHIO SUZUKI

Earwig and the Witch and Ghibli's future

After completing *When Marnie Was There* in 2014, Studio Ghibli suspended feature-length production and shut down its production department. But it started a new chapter with the 2016 release of *The Red Turtle*, and in 2017 Hayao Miyazaki ramped up production on his next film, *Kimitachi wa Do Ikiruka* (*The Boy and the Heron*). In 2020, Ghibli released the NHK co-production *Earwig and the Witch*. Other ongoing projects include Ghibli Park, currently under construction in Aichi Prefecture. We spoke with producer and executive director Toshio Suzuki about Studio Ghibli's future.

■ Toshio Suzuki has remained busy even during the pandemic. Shown here in front of an *Earwig and the Witch* poster.

Making *Earwig and the Witch*

—First off, let's talk about *Earwig and the Witch.* The original novel was written by Diana Wynne Jones, also the author of *Howl's Moving Castle.* Had you always been interested in adapting *Earwig* for film?

Well, Tokuma Shoten sends me and Miya-san (Hayao Miyazaki) their newest children's books every month, and *Earwig and the Witch* was one of the ones they sent us. Miya-san's so dedicated, he looks through all of them.

Right off the bat, Miya-san was completely enthralled by Earwig herself. He rushed over with the book, all excited, and said, "Read this!" When I did, I thought the story was a bit short, but in fact good.

At this point Miya-san was already developing *Kimitachi wa Do Ikiruka* (*The Boy and the Heron*), but now he was fired up about making a movie of *Earwig* as well. Torn between the two, he asked me which one he should do, and I said, "Let's go with *Kimitachi.*" We decided to keep *Earwig* on hold, and make the film somewhere down the line if the chance presented itself.

—How did Goro Miyazaki end up directing it?

After Goro wrapped up the TV series *Ronja, the Robber's Daughter,* he was busy working on plans for the Ghibli Park we're building in Aichi Earth Expo Memorial Park. But he also wanted to make a film. One day when we'd been discussing various plans, Miya-san popped by Goro's office because the Ghibli Park project was on his mind. I wasn't there, but apparently he asked Goro if he wanted to make a movie, and told him about *Earwig.* Goro came to talk to me about it, so I said, "Just try reading it. I'm for it, too." That's how the project got started.

—Goro ended up falling for the book as well?

Earwig must have clicked for him as a character. I mean, Miya-san and Goro are both kind of like her. Earwig's a little obnoxious in the way she twists adults around her little finger. I wrote the tagline "I'm not at anybody's mercy" for this film, and that perversity of hers, well, it's just like a certain father and son. At least that's what I thought. Apparently, when I wasn't around, Goro said, "I based Earwig on Suzuki-san" (laughs).

Anyway, Goro brought a lot of confidence to this film from start to finish. Because he was depicting himself. He must have felt like he wanted to be freed from outside restraints and do it his own way. The only thing he asked me to do was read over the storyboards.

—People are talking about the fact that this is Ghibli's first full 3DCG project. *Ronja, the Robber's Daughter* was also 3DCG, but it was done using toon shading (a technique to make CG resemble hand-drawn animation). Why did Ghibli make the bold decision to use full 3DCG for this film?

I'm the one who urged him to try using real CG. Everyone's convinced the Japanese will only go for cel animation, but I wondered if that was true. There had been some pieces incorporating 3DCG, sure, but no one had ever gone all the way with it. So I figured Ghibli should take the first shot.

—Did the 3DCG production go smoothly?

The team really did a great job. I only made one suggestion: that this wasn't a plot-driven movie, it was all about showing off the characters. In other words, everything depended on Earwig's expressions. When I said this, Goro seemed confident. I found out later that he felt like he'd pulled together a really excellent staff.

—A lot of CG animators from other countries were involved, right?

A Malaysian animator named Tan Se Ri agreed to work on the film, and brought in a really amazing multinational team of skilled animators from Indonesia, Singapore, Malaysia, France, etc. Without a doubt, this team's work would surpass anything Japanese CG had accomplished before, and could even rival American CG, I convinced myself.

When Goro started *Earwig and the Witch,* he said, "This is going to be my last film." But by the end he was saying he wanted to make a couple more. That's because of this team. He felt that with them, he could make more fun works.

—Having seen the finished film, what's your honest opinion?

It's unequivocally the best thing Goro's ever done. The reaction at the staff screening was even better than before.

And Miya-san has always had something critical to say about Goro's work, but for once it was nothing but praise.

It's rare for a project to go this well. So I'm urging Goro to make a sequel.

—It was a surprise to see the film released on broadcast TV through NHK. What was the thinking behind this?

The Japanese film industry has changed a lot in the last few years. Projects are scarce and the industry is withering. I thought it would be difficult to get people interested if we suddenly released *Earwig and the Witch* under those circumstances. That's when the idea of broadcasting it on TV first popped into my head. I thought it would be an interesting experiment, so I approached an NHK producer I know about it, and he got on board. Ghibli ending up co-producing the film with NHK.

—COVID has made theatrical releases tricky, and companies like Disney are debuting their new films on streaming services. What do you think about these developments?

Our generation grew up seeing movies on the big screen, so we're still attached to theaters. But the reality is that there are other ways to watch movies now. We already had TV, video, DVD, and now here comes streaming. Some people are watching movies on tiny smartphone screens. It isn't a bad thing to have more viewing options; I think it's interesting to have a mix. I don't know what will happen, but after showing *Earwig and the Witch* on TV, there are a number of other directions I'd like to try taking things in.

■ Producer Toshio Suzuki talks about his desire to continue trying different things after the television broadcast of *Earwig and the Witch.*

The Future of Studio Ghibli ✻

—Can you talk about Hayao Miyazaki's new movie, *Kimitachi wa Do Ikiruka* (*The Boy and the Heron*)? How far along is production?

We're finally finished with about half—60 minutes out of about a two-hour film. Animation for Ghibli films usually proceeds at a pace of about five minutes a month, but this time we were only doing about a minute per month, initially. Our pace has picked up now, but it will probably take another three years to finish the film.

—I'm sure there were times that work was suspended or people had to work remotely because of COVID. What impact did that have on production?

Actually, our productivity increased thanks to remote working. When someone works at home, they can't see how other people are doing. No one wanted to hold everyone else up, so they worked really hard to meet their quotas. It really brought home to me that that kind of concern is where Japanese industriousness comes from.

Even when the staff were all working from home, Miya-san would come to the studio every day and check the key animation. I think he saw it as an opportunity to catch up on his own work, but the staff kept cranking out key animation, so his plan was foiled (laughs).

—I'm curious also about the Ghibli Park that Goro Miyazaki is working on. What will it be like?

When you go to European or American cities, you have huge parks in the middle of the city, like Hyde Park in London and Central Park in New York. I think that's the sort of thing we're aiming for. Ghibli Park will be in Nagakute in Aichi Prefecture, not in the middle of a city, but we're trying to make it the real deal. It's not a "theme park."

■ Illustration of the Hill of Youth area of Ghibli Park, with elevator building. The above right illustration is the artist's rendering of the Ghibli's Grand Warehouse area.

—Is the idea to have a Ghibli exhibition facility on the former site of the Expo?

Yes, that's the idea. Construction is going well so far, and phase 1 is slated to open in fall of 2022. But there's this guy named Hayao Miyazaki who can't just sit back and hope for the best with his son's work (laughs). He's so competitive. He's thinking up ideas day and night to put his own stamp on Ghibli Park.

—Because of COVID, the Ghibli Museum was closed for a while,

and is now limiting entry. It seems to be continually trying to adapt to the situation.

In Ghibli's world, COVID has impacted the museum the most. It's been really tough. While the museum's started to let some visitors in, it hasn't been able to completely re-open. I think we'll have to operate on a small scale for the time being.

We wanted to do something for the fans while the museum was closed, though, so we've tried all kinds of things, including posting a *Ghibli Museum Video Diary* on YouTube. We're also planning new merchandise just for the museum. We'd like to create things that harken back to the Showa Period, like a Ghibli Museum Notebook inspired by the "Boy Detective Notebook" that was popular when I was a kid, or reissues of old *Animage* magazine supplements.

■ The Ghibli Museum, which has limited entry due to COVID, is posting a *Ghibli Museum Video Diary* on YouTube. This video features Toshio Suzuki.

—Ghibli made the decision to disband its production department in 2014, but it seems to have shifted into a completely different mode when Hayao Miyazaki returned to directing. What does the future hold for this reactivated Studio Ghibli?

Ghibli exists because of the work. If we didn't make films, we wouldn't be Studio Ghibli. We're working on developing a new hand-drawn project as a follow-up to Goro's *Earwig and the Witch* and Hayao Miyazaki's *Kimitachi wa Do Ikiruka* (*The Boy and the Heron*). Miya-san and I are both acting as producers, and preparations are already underway. And I'm sure once things settle down with Ghibli Park, Goro will start thinking about his next CG project.

—That's a lot of projects! What will this new hand-drawn film be about?

I can't get into the details yet, but the screenplay is already written and we're trying to persuade a new director to come on board. The release is a long way off, but I think you'll have something to look forward to.

Interview: Kan Yanagibashi   Photos: Shoko Mizuno
This interview took place on September 17, 2020

1984

1986

1988

1988

1989

1991

1992

1993

1994

1995

1995

1997

1999

2001

2002

STUDIO GHIBLI
The Complete Works

2002

2004

2006

2008

2010

2011

2013

2013

2014

2016

Director Hayao Miyazaki's breathtaking science fiction masterpiece, which led to the birth of Studio Ghibli

NAUSICAÄ OF THE VALLEY OF THE WIND 1984

The feature film *Nausicaä of the Valley of the Wind* was directed by Hayao Miyazaki, who had already garnered attention for the TV series *Conan, The Boy in Future* (1978) and his first theatrical feature, *The Castle of Cagliostro* (1979). Set a thousand years after industrial civilization has been destroyed by a calamitous war, a young woman named Nausicaä struggles to revive the world. In addition to the excitement of watching Nausicaä soar through the sky on her glider Mehve, the story inspires viewers with its message of hope for the Earth's future. The succession of strange creatures, flying contraptions, and unique supporting characters are all vintage Miyazaki.

The film was adapted from Miyazaki's own manga, serialized in the Tokuma Shoten magazine *Animage*. Since it focuses only on the events up through volume two, it has its own ending, distinct from the comic. Isao Takahata, Miyazaki's colleague and friend since their Toei days, acted as producer, while Joe Hisaishi wrote the music, setting the sonic tone for subsequent Studio Ghibli films. Many other leading lights of the animation industry were involved in the film as well, including Mitsuki Nakamura of *Mobile Suit Gundam* fame (art director), *Galaxy Express 999*'s Kazuo Komatsubara (supervising animator), and Hideaki Anno (key animator), who would go on to create *Neon Genesis Evangelion*. The actual production was done by Top Craft, a company with overseas collaboration experience. Although not technically a Ghibli film, *Nausicaä*'s success led to the establishment of Studio Ghibli.

Release date: March 11, 1984
Running time: Approx. 116 minutes
© 1984 Studio Ghibli - H

Original Story, Screenplay Written and Directed by	Hayao Miyazaki
Producer	Isao Takahata
Music	Joe Hisaishi
Supervising Animator	Kazuo Komatsubara
Art Director	Mitsuki Nakamura
Color Design	Michiyo Yasuda
Production	Top Craft
Production Committee	Tokuma Shoten Hakuhodo

Nausicaä	Sumi Shimamoto
Lord Yupa	Goro Naya
Asbel	Yoji Matsuda
Mito	Ichiro Nagai
Kushana	Yoshiko Sakakibara
Kurotowa	Iemasa Kayumi
Jihl	Masato Tsujimura
Obaba	Naoko Kyoda

STORY

A thousand years after the Seven Days of Fire, an apocalyptic war that destroyed civilization, a poisonous forest called the Sea of Decay has spread across the earth. This fungal forest is home to giant insects, and humankind lives in fear of both.

The Valley of the Wind is a small country on the edge of the Sea of Decay, ruled by King Jihl. His daughter Nausicaä lives in peace among the people of the valley, but becomes embroiled in the battle between the city of Pejite and the Kingdom of Tolmekia when a mysterious and powerful Giant Warrior is unearthed from its resting place below Pejite. Amid this conflict, Nausicaä uncovers the truth: that the insects are protecting the Sea of Decay, which is purifying the earth of the pollution wrought by humankind. She stands alone against those who want to use the Giant Warrior to burn away the Sea of Decay and its insect guardians once and for all.

The Original Manga

◆ *Nausicaä of the Valley of the Wind* by **Hayao Miyazaki (Tokuma Shoten), 7 volumes**

A sci-fi/fantasy manga serialized in *Animage* from February 1982 to March 1994. Fascinated with "things that can only be depicted in manga," Hayao Miyazaki continued to work on the series for ten years after the release of the anime, creating a masterpiece whose magnificent scope far exceeds the film's.

CHARACTERS

NAUSICAÄ

The daughter of Jihl, king of the Valley of the Wind. A talented "wind-user," she flies with the aid of her trusty glider Mehve, and has the mysterious ability to communicate with the giant insects others fear and loathe.

ASBEL

A boy from the royal family of the industrial city of Pejite. Nausicaä saves him from an insect attack in the Sea of Decay, and after they discover its secret together, he becomes her ally.

KUSHANA

The 4th daughter of King Vai of Tolmekia, Princess Kushana lost her left hand to an insect attack. She occupies the Valley of the Wind, and tries to burn the Sea of Decay using the Giant Warrior stolen from Pejite.

LORD YUPA

Jihl's best friend and Nausicaä's teacher. Known as the greatest swordsman in the Sea of Decay, he is forever on the road seeking an answer to its mysteries.

OBABA

A wise woman from the Valley of the Wind, said to be over a hundred years old. Although blind, she makes herbal remedies and passes on the legends of the Valley. She can read the air itself, and understand the Ohm's thoughts.

KUROTOWA

A staff officer in the Tolmekian military and Princess Kushana's aide. Born a commoner, he harbors secret ambitions even as he serves her.

JIHL

King of the Valley of the Wind and Nausicaä's father. Once a skilled wind-user himself, he has become bedridden after being beset by poisonous mist in the Sea of Decay. He is killed when Tolmekian troops invade the Valley.

OHM

Kings of the insects, the Ohm are giant arthropods with 14 eyes. They are said to be the masters of the Sea of Decay, and whenever humans try to burn it away, swarms of Ohm appear to destroy their country or town.

GIANT WARRIORS

Doomsday machines created by the ancient mega-industrial civilization. They burned everything to the ground during the Seven Days of Fire and were thought to all be fossilized, but one is discovered intact beneath Pejite.

5 OLD MEN OF THE CASTLE
(MUZU, MITO, GIKKURI, GOL, NIGA)

Led by Mito, the "old men of the castle" serve there after having lost mobility in their limbs with age, thanks to the poisonous gas in the Sea of Decay.

CHARACTER RELATIONSHIPS

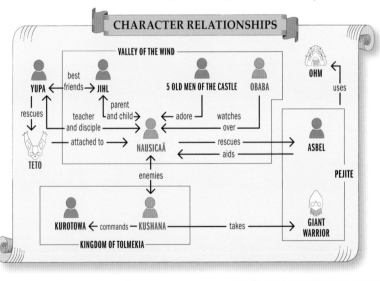

TRIVIA

The name "Sea of Decay" comes from a system of tidal flats in the Crimean Peninsula called the Syvash, or "Putrid Sea." After reading about this, Miyazaki decided to borrow the name for the forest that would become the Sea of Decay.

■ Nausicaä can calm berserk Ohm using an insect whistle.

■ As Nausicaä is headed to Pejite as Kushana's hostage, they are ambushed. She escapes from the burning aircraft with Kushana aboard a gunship.

■ Kushana commands the Giant Warrior to burn the Ohm swarm closing in on the Valley of the Wind.

POSTERS

There were four different poster designs for *Nausicaä of the Valley of the Wind*, all featuring exclusive artwork.

■ Poster 2 was by Yoshiyuki Takani, an illustrator famous for his box art for plastic models.

■ Poster 1. Hayao Miyazaki drew the original image based on the designer's rough sketch. There is also a version of this poster with a dark green border.

NEWSPAPER ADS

Ads featuring a close-up of Nausicaä ran in the papers alongside ads for *Sherlock Hound*, which was released at the same time.

■ Advertising for *Nausicaä of the Valley of the Wind* began with a 1/3-page ad in the Tokyo *Times* on January 18, 1984, about two months before the film's release.

■ This ad ran on January 26 in the *Yomiuri Shimbun*. Hereafter, all advertising used the image from Poster 3.

■ A full-page ad carried in the February 16 edition of the *Yomiuri Shimbun*.

■ Daiei used this poster for secondary distribution. The image came from Poster 3, drawn by Yoshiyuki Takani when the film was released.

■ Korean poster.

■ Drawn by Hayao Miyazaki to be used in theaters, this poster was used as a gift and became the primary *Nausicaä* poster in later years.

BEHIND THE SCENES

Hideaki Anno, who would later become famous for *Neon Genesis Evangelion*, was responsible for the key animation of the Giant Warrior. Anno, then a student, brought his drawings into Studio Ghibli, and after seeing them, Miyazaki hired him on the spot and put him in charge of the key animation for all the Giant Warrior scenes. This was the beginning of their master-disciple relationship.

■ This ad, which ran in the *Yomiuri Shimbun* on March 6, featured a drawing of Nausicaä on her glider taken from Poster 3 and overlaid on a triangular design. It emphasized Nausicaä herself as a selling point for the film.

■ This 1/6-page ad ran in the local Tokyo *Times* on March 16, five days after the film's release, and was exclusive to the Yokohama area. Several more Yokohama-only ads followed.

■ This March 17 1/3-page ad in *Sports Nippon* featured comments from audience members and film critic Koyo Udagawa.

Finally up and running, Studio Ghibli's first official feature is a rollicking airborne action adventure

CASTLE IN THE SKY 1986

Following on the heels of *Nausicaä of the Valley of the Wind*, Hayao Miyazaki's next film would be Studio Ghibli's first official release: *Castle in the Sky*, a dramatic action-adventure story intended for everyone from elementary school children to adults. Inspired in part by *Gulliver's Travels*, the story concerns the legendary floating island Laputa. The protagonists are Pazu, a boy who dreams of finding Laputa, and Sheeta, a girl descended from Laputa's royal family. Thrown into the mix are the gutsy air pirate captain Dola and her sons, and the villainous Muska, who covets Laputa's technology. The old-fashioned setting has a whiff of the 19th century and features a string of exciting action sequences bursting with unique mechanical contraptions, like the insectoid flaptters and the massive flying battleship *Goliath*. There is pathos in the robot soldier who guards the decaying gardens of the abandoned Laputa, and Hayao Miyazaki brings unique depth and emotion to the excitement of action animation. Like *Nausicaä of the Valley of the Wind*, the film won the Ofuji Noburo Award for an outstanding work of animation at the Mainichi Film Awards. It also ranked at the top of many movie magazines' top ten lists. Still popular today, *Castle in the Sky* is a hot topic on social media every time it airs on TV.

For this film, Ghibli began its tradition of casting veteran television and stage actors like Kotoe Hatsui (Dola) and Minori Terada (Muska) alongside the other voice actors.

Release date: August 2, 1986
Running time: Approx. 124 minutes
© 1986 Studio Ghibli

Original Story, Screenplay Written and Directed by	Hayao Miyazaki
Producer	Isao Takahata
Music	Joe Hisaishi
Supervising Animator	Tsukasa Tannai
Art Directors	Toshio Nozaki / Nizo Yamamoto
Color Design	Michiyo Yasuda
Song "Kimi wo Nosete (Carrying You)" Performed by	Azumi Inoue
Production	Studio Ghibli
Production Committee	Tokuma Shoten

Pazu	Mayumi Tanaka
Sheeta	Keiko Yokozawa
Dola	Kotoe Hatsui
Muska	Minori Terada
Uncle Pom	Fujio Tokita
General	Ichiro Nagai
Boss	Hiroshi Ito
Boss's Wife	Machiko Washio

STORY

Long ago, the people of Laputa raised a large island into the sky using a giant Levitation Crystal, and ruled over the lands below with their superior scientific knowledge. Seven hundred years have passed since that time, and Laputa is now only a legend.

Pazu, an impoverished boy who works in a mine, dreams of completing his late father's quest to find the lost island of Laputa. One night, a girl literally falls from the sky into Pazu's arms—slowly, protected by the Levitation Crystal in her pendant. She is Sheeta, heir to the throne of Laputa. Together they set off, Pazu protecting Sheeta all the while from the government agents and air pirates who are after the Levitation Crystal and Laputa's treasures.

PAZU

An honest, cheerful boy who works at the mines as an apprentice mechanic. He has lived on his own since being orphaned at a young age, but after meeting Sheeta he embarks on an adventure to find Laputa.

SHEETA

Sheeta's real name is Princess Lucita Toelle Ur Laputa, rightful heir to the throne of Laputa. She wears a pendant set with a Levitation Crystal, which she inherited from her mother.

DOLA

Captain of the airship *Tiger Moth* and boss of the air pirates. Her gang, a crew of ten including her three sons, has its sights set on Laputa's treasures.

DOLA'S SONS
(HENRI, CHARLES, LOUIS)

Three burly men who are very much mama's boys at heart. They dote on their "Mama" Dola, who named them all after French kings, and are also Sheeta's biggest fans.

MUSKA

A member of the government agency that kidnapped Sheeta, he is in fact also a descendent of the Laputian royal family whose real name is Romuska Palo Ur Laputa. He is plotting to revive the kingdom of Laputa.

MOTORO

A member of the Dola Clan, Motoro is an elderly engineer who works in the *Tiger Moth*'s engine room.

UNCLE POM

An old mining expert and acquaintance of Pazu's who knows everything there is to know about the mines.

GENERAL

A soldier in charge of the exploration of Laputa. He accompanies Muska aborad the giant airship *Goliath*, but there's no love lost between the two.

BOSS (DUFFY)

One of the miners in Slag Ravine, and Pazu's boss. Strict when it comes to work, he's nevertheless kind to the orphaned Pazu.

ROBOT SOLDIER

A semi-organic robot created by the people of Laputa, it reacts to Levitation Crystals and is loyal only to Laputians. In addition to soldiers, there are also gardener robots that tend the grounds of Laputa.

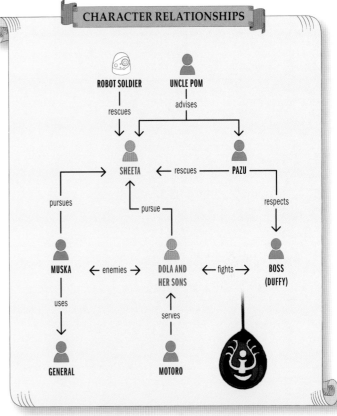

ROBOT SOLDIER — rescues → SHEETA
UNCLE POM — advises → SHEETA / PAZU
SHEETA ← rescues — PAZU
MUSKA — pursues → SHEETA
DOLA AND HER SONS — pursue → SHEETA
PAZU — respects → BOSS (DUFFY)
MUSKA ← enemies — DOLA AND HER SONS — fights → BOSS (DUFFY)
MUSKA — uses → GENERAL
DOLA AND HER SONS ← serves — MOTORO

■ After Sheeta literally falls from the sky into Pazu's arms, their adventure begins.

■ "Will you let me join you, Ma'am?" asks Pazu. "I need to save Sheeta." Dola obliges.

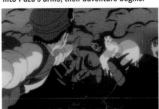

■ With Dola's help, Pazu rescues Sheeta from Muska's clutches.

■ Drawn into a low-pressure system called the Dragon's Lair, Pazu and Sheeta find themselves in the gardens of Laputa.

TRIVIA

Dola, who is both a mother and a pirate, was inspired by Hayao Miyazaki's own mother. Prone to illness, she was confined to her bed from the time Miyazaki was six until he was fifteen, but she shared Dola's force of will. "She had four boys," Miyazaki explains, "but my three brothers and I were no match for her."

POSTERS

The Japanese posters focused on Pazu and Sheeta, while foreign versions featured Laputa more prominently.

■ Poster 1 used an exclusive drawing of Pazu and Sheeta in the air.

■ Poster 3 used the tagline "One day, a girl fell from the sky…" to give a mystical feel to Pazu and Sheeta's first encounter.

NEWSPAPER ADS

As with *Nausicaä of the Valley of the Wind*, ads for *Castle in the Sky* started running about two months before the film's release.

■ This June 25 ad from the *Yomiuri Shimbun* used the image from Poster 3 as the centerpiece, surrounding it with stills from memorable scenes.

■ This full-page ad in the June 10, 1986 edition of the *Mainichi Shimbun* used the image from Poster 1, but the beauty of the background didn't come through in black and white, so other drawings were used for future ads.

■ This *Yomiuri Shimbun* ad from July 25, approximately one week before the film's release, emphasized audience reactions to sneak previews: "The screening room was awash with love and excitement surpassing even *Nausicaä of the Valley of the Wind*."

■ Imageboard by Hayao Miyazaki.

■ French poster.

■ Korean poster.

■ Italian poster.

■ German poster.

■ Alternate Italian poster.

■ Norwegian poster.

■ This *Asahi Shimbun* ad from July 28, five days before the film's release, was structured around the image from Poster 3.

■ The ad in the *Asahi Shimbun* on August 1, the day before the release, announced an "on-stage appearance and bonus gift," and revealed that the first showings in the Tokyo metropolitan area would start at 8:40 a.m.

BEHIND THE SCENES

During development, the working title for *Castle in the Sky* was *Pazu and the Secret of the Levitation Crystal*. Pazu was the name of a sailor Hayao Miyazaki had come up with in his student days, while the name Sheeta came from the Japanese pronunciation of the "theta" symbol he had learned about in math class.

■ The *Yomiuri Shimbun* ad for August 8, about a week after the film's release, completely replaced the copy used in previous advertisements.

A fantasy about two children and the mysterious forest spirits they encounter

MY NEIGHBOR TOTORO 1988

Hayao Miyazaki's theatrical feature *My Neighbor Totoro* is about two young sisters, Satsuki and Mei, who find themselves surrounded by nature when they move to a suburb on the outskirts of Tokyo. There they meet Totoro, a forest spirit only visible to children, and have a series of strange and wonderful experiences. The characters were based on sketches Miyazaki had made in his downtime back when he was working in TV. The story is set in the late 1950s, before televisions were commonplace in Japanese households. This nostalgic world is bolstered by the pastoral summer landscapes and other beautiful backgrounds. The scene in which Satsuki rushes around looking for Mei, in particular, exploits the expressive possibilities of animation to their fullest, using changes in the color of the sky and clouds to show the passage of time. This was

art director Kazuo Oga's first time working on a Studio Ghibli film, and he would become an essential member of the Ghibli team thereafter.

Totoro was initially released as part of a double feature with Isao Takahata's *Grave of the Fireflies*. It went on to achieve great acclaim and win many awards, including the Mainichi Film Ofuji Noburo Award. The compelling creatures and human characters like Granny, voiced by veteran actor Tanie Kitabayashi, continue to be just as popular today as they were when the film was released. Totoro himself became Studio Ghibli's logo, and the Cat Bus has become a beloved source of toys and merchandise. The songs "Hey Let's Go" and "My Neighbor Totoro" also came to be sung in kindergartens and elementary schools across Japan, and they remain well-loved to this day.

Release date: April 16, 1988
Running time: Approx. 86 minutes
© 1988 Studio Ghibli

Original Story, Screenplay Written
and Directed by ·············· Hayao Miyazaki
Producer ························· Toru Hara
Music ·························· Joe Hisaishi
Supervising Animator ········· Yoshiharu Sato
Art Director ···················· Kazuo Oga
Color Design ················ Michiyo Yasuda
Songs "Sampo (Hey Let's Go)" and
"Tonari no Totoro (My Neighbor Totoro)"
Performed by ·················· Azumi Inoue
Production ··················· Studio Ghibli
Production Committee ········ Tokuma Shoten

Satsuki ···················· Noriko Hidaka
Mei ······················· Chika Sakamoto
Father ···················· Shigesato Itoi
Mother ··················· Sumi Shimamoto
Granny ················· Tanie Kitabayashi
Totoro ····················· Hitoshi Takagi

STORY

The film takes place in a Tokyo suburb in the 1950s. One sunny day in May, sisters Satsuki and Mei move into a ramshackle old house with their father so that their mother, currently in the hospital, can come home to fresh, clean air. As they're moving in, the two girls are thrilled and excited to spot fuzzy black dust sprites called Dust Bunnies. Have they moved into a haunted house?!

One day, when Satsuki is at school and her father is busy with work, Mei is playing outside by herself. In the course of her explorations she meets Totoro, a strange creature who has resided in Japan since an-

cient times. Totoro eventually reveals itself to Satsuki as well, and so begins a series of wondrous and delightful encounters for the sisters.

CHARACTERS

SATSUKI

A lively, cheerful sixth grader. Stepping up in place of her mother, who is in the hospital, the responsible Satsuki does the housework and takes care of her little sister. She sends letters to her mother to keep her apprised of what's going on at home.

MEI

Satsuki's spirited 4-year-old sister. In contrast to her reasonable older sibling, Mei has a stubborn streak and can be very insistent. Highly curious, she becomes completely absorbed in whatever interesting things she finds.

FATHER
(TATSUO KUSAKABE)

A scholar of anthropology, Tatsuo commutes to a university in Tokyo where he teaches as an adjunct professor. Satsuki and Mei love their dad, who says, "It was always my dream to live in a haunted house."

MOTHER
(YASUKO KUSAKABE)

Hospitalized with an illness, Yasuko is recuperating and wants to get back to her family as soon as possible. A clever, intelligent woman, Satsuki and Mei feel safe just being around her.

GRANNY

Kanta's grandmother, and caretaker of the Kusakabes' new home. She looks after Satsuki and Mei as best she can while their mother is in the hospital.

KANTA

Satsuki's classmate, who lives on the farm next door. He's constantly curious about Satsuki, but can't bring himself to interact with her normally.

DUST BUNNIES

Little black creatures shaped like chestnut burrs. They prefer dark places and take up residence in unoccupied homes, covering them in soot and dust.

CAT BUS

A bus-shaped cat Totoro and his companions ride in. The Cat Bus is invisible to most people, though they can feel the whirlwind as it goes by. With its twelve legs, the Cat Bus can run across both sky and sea.

TOTORO

A mysterious spirit who has resided in Japan since before the arrival of humankind, he eats nuts and acorns and lives a peaceful life in the forest. Totoro is the name Mei gives him.

CHARACTER RELATIONSHIPS

KANTA — grandmother → GRANNY   TOTORO   CAT BUS

classmates   takes care of   helps   helps

SATSUKI ← sisters → MEI

parents and children   discover

FATHER · MOTHER

DUST BUNNIES

■ Satsuki and Mei ride with their father to visit their mother in the hospital.

■ Playing in the yard alone, Mei spots a strange creature and chases after it...

■ The Cat Bus takes the children to the hospital, where they look down into their mother's room from a tree branch.

■ Satsuki and Mei have fun with Totoro, flying through the sky and playing ocarinas in the branches of a tree.

TRIVIA

Totoro's name is an abbreviation of "Tokorozawa ni iru tonari no obake" (the monster-next-door in Tokorozawa). Hayao Miyazaki was inspired to create the character by a scene from Kenji Miyazawa's "The Acorns and the Wildcat," where a squeaking acorn sits at the feet of a dazed wildcat.

POSTERS

The posters for *My Neighbor Totoro* feature Totoro and a girl who combines Satsuki and Mei's characteristics, some of which are exclusive images.

■ Poster 2 has Totoro and the girl in the center, surrounded by stills from the film, some of which are playfully placed upside down.

■ Poster 1, drawn especially for theaters, is the most common Totoro poster.

■ This limited-edition poster for people who bought advance tickets boasts an exclusive drawing, featuring Totoro both flying through the sky on a top, and riding the Cat Bus.

■ Italian poster.

■ French poster for the 30th anniversary rerelease.

■ Finnish poster.

■ Chinese poster.

■ Alternate Italian poster.

■ Korean poster.

■ Alternate Korean poster.

■ Third Korean poster.

BEHIND THE SCENES

Art director Kazuo Oga used sepia and chrome green in almost every scene to give the film a cohesive feel. Mixing these two shades into both exterior and interior scenes gives a sense of being in the "same world," even when the action moves indoors.

Isao Takahata's tragic film about a brother and sister during wartime helped boost Studio Ghibli's reputation

GRAVE OF THE FIREFLIES — 1988

The first film adaptation of Akiyuki Nosaka's semi-autobiographical Naoki-Prize winning short story, Isao Takahata's *Grave of the Fireflies* is the tale of 14-year-old Seita and his 4-year-old sister Setsuko struggling to survive in Kobe during the final months of the Second World War. Takahata thoroughly researched the period in order to recreate wartime conditions as accurately as possible, right down to the structure of the incendiary bombs that reduced the city to cinders. He also cast 5-year-old Ayano Shiraishi as Setsuko, in an endeavor to help audiences engage more naturally with the story. Instead of having her move her mouth to match the animation, her voice was recorded first and the drawings were matched to her movements, with the other voice actors working off her lines. Character designer and supervising animator Yoshifumi Kondo and the rest of the animation staff also observed children at daycare centers to use as reference for Setsuko's movements.

This pursuit of realism gave the completed film a raw and vivid feel—not only for those who had experienced the war, but for later generations as well. The opening, in which the siblings lead the audience into the story, makes full use of the unique power of film, while the final scene, in which the modern cityscape floats into view before the two characters, expresses Takahata's intended theme: that the current peace is built upon the wars of the past. *Grave of the Fireflies* was released as part of a double feature with *My Neighbor Totoro*, and though it was not a big hit at the time, it went on to win children's film awards around the world and boost Studio Ghibli's global reputation.

Release date: April 16, 1988
Running time: Approx. 88 minutes
© Akiyuki Nosaka/Shinchosha, 1988

Original Story ···················· Akiyuki Nosaka
Screenplay Written and
Directed by ························ Isao Takahata
Producer ····························· Toru Hara
Music ······························· Michio Mamiya
Character Design and
Supervising Animator ········· Yoshifumi Kondo
Layout Assistant and
Supervising Animator ········· Yoshiyuki Momose
Art Director ························ Nizo Yamamoto
Character Color Design ······· Michiyo Yasuda
Song "Home, Sweet Home"
Performed by ······················ Amelita Galli-Curci
Production ·························· Studio Ghibli
Production Committee ········· Shinchosha

Seita ································ Tsutomu Tatsumi
Setsuko ···························· Ayano Shiraishi
Mother ······························ Yoshiko Shinohara
Widow ······························ Akemi Yamaguchi

STORY

It is 1945, and the Second World War is still raging. B-29s rain bombs down on Seita and Setsuko's hometown of Kobe, transforming it into a burned-out wasteland. The siblings, who lose their mother in an air raid, go to live with a widowed relative. As the war drags on, food becomes scarce and she begins to treat Seita and Setsuko as nothing but a nuisance. The children use the money their mother left them to buy a charcoal brazier and plates so they can enjoy a modest meal with what little food they can get their hands on, but later they leave the widow's house and begin living in an abandoned bomb shelter beside a pond.

At night they catch fireflies by the edge of the pond and release them inside their mosquito nets. The fireflies illuminate the darkness with a beautiful, unearthly light. But the siblings can't continue to play house forever, and their situation becomes more and more desperate.

The Original Story

◆ Grave of the Fireflies by Akiyuki Nosaka (Shincho Bunko)

Akiyuki Nosaka based this short story, part of a collection that won the 58th Naoki Prize, on his own wartime experiences. Nosaka had a special attachment to this story and believed it was unfilmable, but after seeing the images from the Ghibli film, Nosaka said, "I'm in awe of what animation can do."

SEITA

A 14-year-old boy who loses his mother in an air raid while his father, a Japanese navy lieutenant, is at sea. Believing his father will come back someday, Seita takes the best care he can of his little sister.

SETSUKO

4-year-old Setsuko was happy at first to live in a bomb shelter with her older brother, but her spirits start to wane as food begins to run out.

MOTHER

Seita and Setsuko's mother has a weak heart, and is headed to the air raid shelter ahead of her children when she is killed in the massive air raid of June 1945.

WIDOW

A distant relative of Seita and Setsuko's who lives in Nishinomiya. She takes in the two children after they lose their mother, but the relationship gradually becomes strained.

CHARACTER RELATIONSHIPS

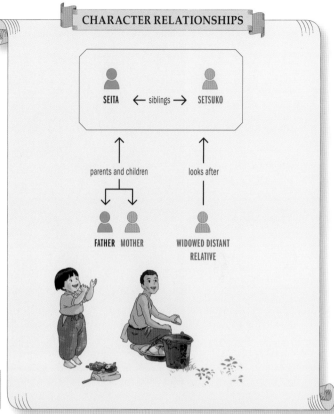

SEITA ← siblings → SETSUKO

parents and children

looks after

FATHER   MOTHER

WIDOWED DISTANT RELATIVE

■ Seita and Setsuko appear at the beginning of the film to lead viewers into the story.

■ As air raid sirens blare across the city, Setsuko's mother fastens an air-raid hood around her neck. This is their last moment together.

■ Seita and Setsuko take a bath in their new neighborhood. Seita makes Setsuko smile with a washcloth.

■ On the train home from the bank after withdrawing their mother's savings, Seita tells Setsuko they can do whatever they need to with this money.

■ Seita and Setsuko, now living in a bomb shelter, catch fireflies and release them in their mosquito net.

■ Seita lies beneath the glow of the fireflies with Setsuko. He tells her about a naval review he once saw, and thinks about their father, who is off at war.

■ In the morning, the fireflies are dead. Thinking of their mother, Setsuko digs a hole and makes a grave for the fireflies.

■ Seita, alone now, recalls the days he spent with Setsuko.

TRIVIA

In the scene where Seita recalls going to the beach with his mother, the shadow of her parasol has a pinkish hue. Michiyo Yasuda, the color designer (who chooses all the colors used in the film), created this shade based on a book of Monet paintings Isao Takahata gave her to use as a reference.

■ The image for Poster 1 was created with the "michiyuki" travel scene from kabuki and other traditional art forms in mind.

POSTERS

The posters used Shigesato Itoi's tagline: "At 4 and 14, they tried to survive."

■ Poster 2 added dots of light representing fireflies, balls of fire representing incendiary bombs, and a smattering of stills from the movie to the image from Poster 1.

NEWSPAPER ADS

The newspaper ads for *Grave of the Fireflies* ran alongside ads for *My Neighbor Totoro*, which was released simultaneously, with the tagline "We're here to bring you something you left behind."

■ This ad ran in the February 19, 1988 edition of the *Seikyo Shimbun*, about a month before ads were placed in general newspapers, and included the announcement that Min-On Concert Association tickets would be accepted.

■ For the February 24 *Grave of the Fireflies* ad in the *Seikyo Shimbun*, the image from Poster 2 was used to communicate some of the content of the film.

■ The March 25 ad from the *Yomiuri Shimbun* dedicated a large amount of space to announcing the availability of limited advance tickets that came with telephone cards.

■ Special poster for people who purchased advance tickets. The faint black silhouette floating above the characters is a B-29, and the orange flecks of lights in the sky represent incendiary bombs.

FROM STUDIO GHIBLI CREATORS OF *Ponyo* & SPIRITED AWAY
25TH ANNIVERSARY RELEASE

"One of the most beloved of all family films"
Roger Ebert

"Belongs on any list of the greatest war films ever made"
Roger Ebert

A FILM BY HAYAO MIYAZAKI
MY NEIGHBOUR
TOTORO

A FILM BY ISAO TAKAHATA
GRAVE OF THE
FIREFLIES

IN CINEMAS TOGETHER FOR THE FIRST TIME MAY 24

■ UK poster for the 25th anniversary rerelease of *Grave of the Fireflies* and *My Neighbor Totoro*.

BEHIND THE SCENES

To accurately portray the era and heighten the film's sense of realism, director Isao Takahata and the production staff researched everything from the structure of incendiary bombs to B-29 flight paths, candy tins, gramophones, and the route from Hankyu Sannomiya Station to Mikage Public Hall. They even sketched the 4-year-old daughter of a staff member to use as reference for drawing Setsuko.

■ In the April 8 *Asahi Shimbun* ad, new stills were added for both films.

■ This ad ran in the *Mainichi Shimbun* on April 15, the the day before the films were released, and replaced the previous tagline with "Tomorrow, we finally bring the whole country what it left behind!"

■ The *Yomiuri Shimbun*'s review featured prominently in this ad in the *Mainichi Shimbun*, published April 28, almost two weeks after the films were released.

GHIBLI DRAWS
CITIES AND BUILDINGS

Ghibli films are set against a backdrop of striking buildings and settlements. For live action films, staff go location scouting before shooting to find the perfect settings, and the same is true for animation. Even though many Studio Ghibli films are fantasy, they still use location scouting to create settings and provide references for backgrounds. This sort of meticulous preparation helps lend Ghibli's films an air of realism.

■ Slag Ravine, where Pazu and Sheeta flee for help.

■ The gardens of Laputa, abandoned and in ruin.

■ The flying island of Laputa.

Castle in the Sky

Laputa is a flying island created by a once-glorious technological civilization. Now abandoned and lying in ruins, it has become a world of otherwise extinct animals and robotic gardeners. Pazu's home of Slag Ravine is a mining town with houses, refineries, and a railroad built along steep cliffs.

■ The interior of the bathhouse, where Chihiro gets a job.

Spirited Away

Hayao Miyazaki based the bathhouse where Sen (Chihiro) works and the surrounding town in part on the Edo-Tokyo Open Air Architectural Museum. The bathhouse is divided into several levels, from the top floor where Yubaba lives to the boiler room at the bottom, and boasts everything from medicinal baths to banquet rooms.

■ The wizard Cob's castle.

■ Yubaba's bathhouse.

■ Ashitaka works the bellows with the women.

■ The fortress-like Iron Town.

Princess Mononoke

Iron Town, ruled by Lady Eboshi, represents a type of iron-sand refining town that flourished before the importation of Western technology. Lady Eboshi founded it in part to protect women and outcasts, and they manufacture ironware and hand cannons in defiance of the feudal lord's power.

■ Hort Town, the port where Arren meets Therru.

Tales from Earthsea

The dark wizard Cob lives in an enormous castle with many towers, its silhouette eerie in the night but beautiful under the light of the sun. Claude Laurent's paintings served as a reference for the design of Hort Town, the port where Arren and Therru meet.

Nausicaä of the Valley of the Wind

Nausicaä's home, the Valley of the Wind, is an agricultural land whose windmills are powered by the winds off the acid lakes. The people live in harmony with nature, all the while guarding against the incursion of insects and poison from the Sea of Decay. The world also includes the industrial city of Pejite, and the military kingdom of Tolmekia, which uses materials and technology gleaned from the ruins of the Seven Days of Fire.

■ Koriko, the town where Kiki decides to live. It's packed with cars and people around the clock tower.

■ Locals come to relax in the square where Kiki sits, unable to find a place to stay.

■ The area around the clock tower, one of Kiki's favorite places.

Kiki's Delivery Service

As part of her training to be a witch, Kiki leaves home for the town of Koriko, which was modeled on the Swedish capital of Stockholm and on Visby, a town on Gotland Island in the Baltic Sea. Director Hayao Miyazaki called on his previous experiences traveling overseas to create the scenery, which is meant to evoke the feel of medieval Europe.

■ The Hotel Adriano, run by Madam Gina.

■ The hotel garden where Madam Gina enjoys alone time.

■ The hotel restaurant, where Madam Gina and Porco talk about the past. Old photos line the walls.

Porco Rosso

Madam Gina runs the Hotel Adriano, which lies amid the waters of the Adriatic Sea. In addition to a bar and restaurant, the hotel is equipped with an aeronautical beacon and piers to moor boats and seaplanes. It also provides a hangout for air pirates, including the Mamma Aiuto gang of outlaws.

■ The city of Kochi, where the story is mainly set.

■ Kochi Castle, one of the city's biggest tourist attractions. After a class reunion, the main characters look up at it together.

Ocean Waves

The depictions of Kochi and its castle were based on actual locations. Rikako and Taku's school, in particular, was a faithful reproduction of a high school in the city. The use of dialect along with this background art added local color to the film.

■ The front entrance to the main characters' high school.

Whisper of the Heart

Mukaihara, where Shizuku lives, is modeled after the area along a private railway line in western Tokyo. Centered around the antique shop on the hill, it was designed with the differing elevations of an Italian hilltop town in mind. This, combined with Naohisa Inoue's drawings for the fantasy world that appears in Shizuku's story, give the scenery an overall sense of the exotic.

■ World Emporium, the antique shop owned by Seiji's grandfather, where Shizuku encounters Baron.

■ Iblard, the setting for the story Shizuku writes.

■ Shizuku gets a panoramic view of town from the hill as she heads to the library after school.

The Wind Rises

■ Fujimi Kogen Sanatorium, where Nahoko goes to be treated for tuberculosis.

Jiro dreams of becoming an aircraft designer, and goes to work at Mitsubishi Internal Combustion in Nagoya, Aichi Prefecture. The staff used documents from the time to create period-appropriate scenery, including the area around Nagoya Station and the bank where the bank run occurs. The sanatorium where Jiro's wife Nahoko recovers was also a real place.

■ Nagoya Station, where Jiro arrives to start work at Mitsubishi Internal Combustion.

The Cat Returns

Haru goes to the Cat Bureau, located on a plaza in another world connected to a crossroads in this one. Initially human-sized, Haru suddenly finds herself the same size as Baron. The Cat Castle where Haru is taken is surrounded by a maze, and the walls are decorated with motifs of fish, a cat's favorite food.

■ The otherworldly plaza where the Cat Bureau is located.

■ The Cat Kingdom, where Haru is taken. In the distance lies the castle of the Cat King.

From Up on Poppy Hill

The clubs at Konan Academy, Umi and Shun's school, are located in an old building nicknamed the "Latin Quarter" (after the student area in Paris). Equipment and documents are piled up in each room like geological strata, and the interior is very much like a labyrinth. After a massive clean-up, people see the building in a completely new light.

Kiki struggles to become a full-fledged witch in Studio Ghibli's first major hit

KIKI'S DELIVERY SERVICE   1989

Based on the novel by multi award-winning children's author Eiko Kadono, *Kiki's Delivery Service* was the first Ghibli project brought in from an outside company. It was originally conceived as a short, so at first Hayao Miyazaki planned to produce the film and write the screenplay, but leave the directing to someone younger. As he worked on the screenplay, however, his vision for the story expanded and he decided to direct it himself. Initially he planned to end the film with Kiki tearing up at Madame's gift, but associate producer Toshio Suzuki wanted something more climactic, so they added the scene where Kiki saves Tombo from a dirigible accident.

Kiki's tale depicts the life of the average girl who moves from the country to the city, and magic—her ability to fly on a broomstick—is merely one of her talents, fundamentally no different from the art student Ursula's talent for painting. Meeting Ursula sparks Kiki to reexamine her own life, a theme Miyazaki would later revisit in his screenplay for *Whisper of the Heart* (1995).

From beginning to end, it's the detailed portrayal of 13-year-old apprentice witch Kiki's emotions that draws the viewer in, revealing a new side of Hayao Miyazaki beyond the science fiction and adventure. Tie-ins with Yamato Transport and cooperation from TV stations were part of a massive publicity campaign for the film's release, which brought 2.64 million people into theaters, an absolutely unprecedented audience for an animated film.

Release date: July 29, 1989
Running time: Approx. 102 minutes
© 1989 Eiko Kadono - Studio Ghibli - N

Original Story ···················· Eiko Kadono
Produced, Screenplay Written and
Directed by ···················· Hayao Miyazaki
Associate Producer ··········· Toshio Suzuki
Music ································· Joe Hisaishi
Music Direction ················ Isao Takahata
Character Design ·············· Katsuya Kondo
Supervising Animators ········ Shinji Otsuka
                                  Katsuya Kondo
                                  Yoshifumi Kondo
Art Director ······················ Hiroshi Ono
Color Design ···················· Michiyo Yasuda
Songs "Rouge no Dengon (A Message Left in
Lipstick)" and "Yasashisa ni Tsutsumaretanara
(Wrapped in Gentleness)"
Performed by ···················· Yumi Arai
Production ······················· Studio Ghibli
Production Committee ········ Tokuma Shoten
                                  Yamato Transport
                                  Nippon Television Network

Kiki / Ursula ···················· Minami Takayama
Jiji ································· Rei Sakuma
Kokiri ····························· Mieko Nobusawa
Osono ····························· Keiko Toda
Tombo ····························· Kappei Yamaguchi
Barsa ····························· Hiroko Seki
Okino ····························· Koichi Miura
Madame ··························· Haruko Kato

STORY

Kiki has just turned 13, the age at which apprentice witches must leave home and spend a year in an unfamiliar town. Under the light of a glorious full moon, Kiki sets off with her black cat Jiji in tow. By morning she has arrived in the bustling seaside town of Koriko.

The owner of a bakery lets her stay in the spare room, and Kiki helps out in the shop while starting a "delivery service" using her only magical skill, the ability to fly on a broomstick. She has plenty of travails, dropping things and struggling to deliver a package only to get a negative reaction from the recipient, but she matures through her experiences and interactions with the people she meets.

The Original Novel

◆ ***Kiki's Delivery Service* by Eiko Kadono (Fukuinkan Shoten), 6-book series with 2 special volumes**

The magnum opus by children's author Eiko Kadono, winner of the 2018 Andersen Award. In the later volumes, Kiki matures into a woman through work, love, and new meetings and partings.

KIKI

A 13-year-old witch whose only magical ability is the power of flight. Hoping to become a full-fledged witch, she goes to the town of Koriko to begin her training. She isn't thrilled that witches have to wear black.

JIJI

A black cat born around the same time as Kiki. Raised together, they're able to communicate, and Jiji goes along with Kiki as her somewhat sarcastic traveling companion.

TOMBO

A 13-year-old boy who lives in Koriko. He dreams of flying and is drawn to Kiki, whom he befriends.

KOKIRI

Kiki's 37-year-old mother. A card-carrying witch who can not only fly, but makes medicines for the townspeople.

OKINO

Kiki's 40-year-old father, a folklorist who studies witches and fairies. He is a doting and affectionate parent.

OSONO

The pregnant, 26-year-old owner of the Gütiokipänjä bakery. Osono is a caring person who takes to Kiki, and lets her stay in a spare room at the bakery.

OSONO'S HUSBAND

Osono's 30-year-old husband. A taciturn baker who rises early every morning to bake the bread.

URSULA

An 18-year-old art student who lives and paints in a shack in the woods. A straight shooter, she becomes Kiki's closest confidant.

MADAME

A kind, elegant old woman who lives in a big house with a blue roof. After Madame hires Kiki to make a delivery, they become friends.

BARSA

A maid who has worked for Madame for many years.

OKINO · KOKIRI   TOMBO   MADAME ← serves — BARSA

interested in   worries about

parents and child

KIKI ← companions → JIJI

supports   helps

OSONO — husband and wife → OSONO'S HUSBAND

URSULA

■ As a witch who just turned thirteen, Kiki must leave her hometown for a year as part of her training.

■ In the seaside town of Koriko, she meets a boy her age named Tombo. They ride together on his bicycle.

■ Kiki runs into a storm while out on a delivery.

■ A sudden gust of wind sends the dirigible shooting into the sky. Tombo is in danger, and Kiki must rescue him...

Ursula's drawing is based on a woodblock print called *The Ship that Flies Over the Rainbow*, made by the special needs students at Hachinohe Minato Junior High School. The original print lacks the girl modeled on Kiki that appears in Ursula's version.

■ For Poster 2, the original tag-line "Sometimes I felt sad, but now I'm fine" was changed to "Sometimes I feel sad, but I love this town."

POSTERS

Two posters were created for *Kiki's Delivery Service*, both featuring the heroine.

■ Poster 1 shows Kiki minding the bakery, based on a scene from the film. Reflections in the glass create a sense of depth and three-dimensionality.

■ The first ad ran in the *Yomiuri Shimbun* on April 28, 1989, about three months before the film's release, and the day advance tickets went on sale.

NEWSPAPER ADS

These ads used the images from the posters, with the title in big letters to help it stand out.

■ The illustration from Poster 2 was used for this June 22 ad in the *Yomiuri Shimbun*, with copy to match the image.

■ The June 29 *Asahi Shimbun* ad featured a pre-view invitation and tie-ins with the release of related books and music. The soundtrack was released on cassette and LP as well as CD.

■ Korean poster.

■ Italian poster.

■ French poster.

■ Finnish poster.

■ Norwegian poster.

BEHIND THE SCENES

There are female characters of all ages in the film, all of whom can be seen to represent grown-up versions of Kiki—it's as if Kiki becomes Ursula, then Osono, then her mother Kokiri, and finally Madame. This is also why the same voice actress, Minami Takayama, played both Kiki and Ursula.

■ In order to help cement the film's image, the ads went back to featuring the illustration from Poster 1 about a month before the film's release. This ad from the July 21 *Yomiuri Shimbun* is one such example.

■ The ad that ran on August 18 in the *Yomiuri Shimbun* featured a third illustration, a still of Kiki and Jiji taken from the film. To connect the ad with Yumi Arai's song "Wrapped in Kindness," the word "kind" was used in the accompanying copy.

■ This Tokyo *Times* ad from July 22, one week before the film's release, used a horizontal layout and added a still of the heroine and an introduction to the story alongside the main image.

■ Later ads, like this one from the September 1 *Mainichi Shimbun*, mentioned audience numbers and the film's long run to emphasize that the film was a massive hit.

43

A tale of self-discovery told with a combination of two different animation styles

ONLY YESTERDAY   1991

For *Only Yesterday,* director Isao Takahata put his own spin on the manga written by Hotaru Okamoto and illustrated by Yuko Tone, and based on Okamoto's own experiences as a fifth-grader in 1966. 27-year-old Taeko, who works in a corporate office, goes to visit her relatives in Yamagata to experience life on a farm. During the trip she recalls her childhood, and rethinks her current lifestyle after meeting a local young man. The film features a grown woman as the protagonist, and deals with women's lives and views on love and marriage, changing family structures, and succession problems in rural areas as Japan transitions into the modernized world of the 1980s and 90s. The "present" of 1982 is depicted realistically: characters have collar bones and laugh lines, and the detailed backgrounds are the result of extensive location scouting. During

the flashbacks to the protagonist's memories of 1966, on the other hand, the drawings are faithful to the original, capitalizing on manga's patented use of negative space. The combination of these two different animation styles is what makes *Only Yesterday* so unique.

To create a nostalgic feel for Taeko's memories, the staff collected TV shows from the era like *NHK Amateur Singing Contest* and the puppet show *Pop-Up Gourd Island* and faithfully reproduced them as animation. They brought in television stars Miki Imai and Toshiro Yanagiba to voice the main characters for the part of the film that takes place in the present, and, as per the usual for Takahata films, recorded the dialogue first, then used the actors' expressions and movements as references for the animation.

STORY

Summer, 1982. Twenty-seven-year-old Taeko Okajima works in a Tokyo office, but is having doubts about her life choices, so she takes some time off and heads to her older sister's in-laws' in rural Yamagata. Born and raised in Tokyo, Taeko has dreamed of the countryside ever since she was a child, and now finally has the chance to go thanks to her sister's marriage.

For some reason, memories of fifth grade come rush-

ing back to Taeko during the ride: her first taste of pineapple, a scolding from her father, her first crush… At Yamagata Station, she's met by a young man named Toshio, and as Taeko enjoys the country life, helping out with the safflower harvest and weeding the rice paddies, her experience of Yamagata's natural beauty and her encounters with the people who live there push her to figure out who she really is at heart…

Release date: July 20, 1991
Running time: Approx. 119 minutes
© 1991 Hotaru Okamoto - Yuko Tone - Studio Ghibli - NH

Original Comic	Hotaru Okamoto Yuko Tone
Screenplay Written and Directed by	Isao Takahata
General Producer	Hayao Miyazaki
Producer	Toshio Suzuki
Music	Katz Hoshi
Character Design	Yoshifumi Kondo
Layout and Storyboards	Yoshiyuki Momose
Supervising Animators	Yoshifumi Kondo Katsuya Kondo Yoshiharu Sato
Art Director	Kazuo Oga
Color Design	Michiyo Yasuda
Theme song "Ai wa Hana, Kimi wa Sono Tane (Love Is a Flower and You Are Its Seed)" (From "The Rose") Performed by	Harumi Miyako
Production	Studio Ghibli
Production Committee	Tokuma Shoten Nippon Television Network Hakuhodo

Taeko	Miki Imai
Toshio	Toshiro Yanagiba
Taeko (Fifth-grader)	Yoko Honna
Mother	Michie Terada
Father	Masahiro Ito
Grandmother	Chie Kitagawa
Nanako	Yorie Yamashita
Yaeko	Yuki Minowa

The Original Manga

🟦 ***Only Yesterday* by Hotaru Okamoto, illustrated by Yuko Tone (Seirindo)**

Serialized in the weekly magazine *Myojo* from March 19 to September 10, 1987, the manga concerns only Taeko's memories of fifth grade; the character of 27-year-old Taeko was created expressly for the film.

TAEKO OKAJIMA

Twenty-seven years old and single, Taeko works in the office of a top-tier company in Tokyo. As she did last year, she goes to spend her vacation on her sister's in-laws' farm in Yamagata.

TOSHIO

A 25-year-old farmer Taeko meets in Yamagata. Also Taeko's brother-in-law's second cousin. Highly motivated, he just quit his corporate job and took up organic farming.

FIFTH-GRADE TAEKO

Ten years old, and a fifth grader at Kaishin Third Elementary School. The youngest of three sisters, she can be a little selfish. She's good at writing and bad at math.

MOTHER

A 42-year-old housewife. She defers to her husband while managing the Okajima household.

FATHER

A 43-year-old salaryman. Slightly stubborn, but he dotes on Taeko.

GRANDMOTHER

Usually quiet, but occasionally she surprises her family with her sharp words.

NANAKO

The eldest daughter of the Okajima family. At 18, she's a first-year art student and Beatles fan who will eventually marry Mitsuo, a man from Yamagata.

YAEKO

The middle Okajima daughter. A 16 year old genius and Takarazuka theater fan. She and Taeko are always butting heads.

NAOKO

A 13-year-old seventh-grader and Nanako's husband's niece. She looks up to Taeko.

COUNTRY GRANMA

Naoko's grandmother. She's pulling for Taeko to marry Toshio.

CHARACTER RELATIONSHIPS

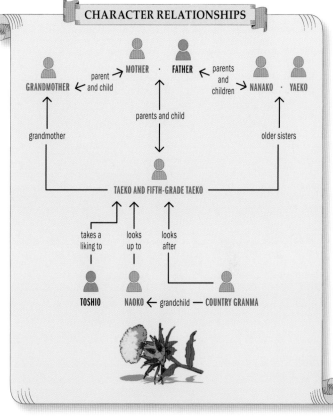

■ On her way to visit her sister's in-laws in Yamagata, memories of the fifth grade begin to come back to the 27-year-old Taeko.

■ In Yamagata, Taeko becomes close with her brother-in-law's second cousin Toshio.

■ Granny asks Taeko if she's going to marry Toshio, but Taeko boards the train back to Tokyo without being able to answer.

■ Encouraged by her fifth-grade self, Taeko decides to return to Yamagata.

TRIVIA

Director Isao Takahata wanted something that would combine organic farming with a picturesque crop. He became interested in safflowers, read widely on the subject, and sent his staff to interview Takao Suzuki, an authority on safflowers who lived in Yonezawa. In July of 1990, the height of safflower season, Takahata and his animation and art staff went to experience the safflower harvest for themselves.

■ Poster 2 focused on the "going on a journey" aspect of Taeko's experience.

■ Poster 1 shows the two Taekos holding hands.

■ North American poster.

POSTERS

Two posters were created for *Only Yesterday*, both of which used the memorable tagline "I'm going on a journey with myself."

BEHIND THE SCENES

Because Takahata had strong opinions about songs he wanted for certain scenes, a great many songs were used as-is. The music is very diverse, ranging from hits like 1964's "Tokyo Blues" to a performance by the Bulgarian State Female Vocal Choir, which appears during the part of the film set in the present day.

■ The first version was a 1/6-page ad that ran in the *Yomiuri Shimbun* on April 25, 1991, three months before the release and two days before advance tickets went on sale.

■ For the June 14 ad in the *Asahi Shimbun*, also at the 1/6-page size, stills featuring the fifth-grade Taeko were scattered around the central image.

■ The ad carried in the *Mainichi Shimbun* on July 5, about two weeks before the release, included the announcement of a commemorative gift.

■ The July 12 *Asahi Shimbun* ad included preview audiences' reactions.

NEWSPAPER ADS

All of the newspaper ads for *Only Yesterday* used the image from Poster 1.

■ Starting July 19, the day before the release, ads like this one from the *Asahi Shimbun* featured praise from famous people, including screenwriter and novelist Taichi Yamada and the comedy duo Ucchan Nanchan.

■ The 1/3-page color ad that ran in the Tokyo *Shimbun* on July 19 proclaimed *Only Yesterday* "the biggest movie of the summer" in a bid to raise expectations.

■ Starting with the August 2 edition of the *Yomiuri Shimbun*, ads consistently used a simplified version of the image from Poster 1.

■ The August 9 *Asahi Shimbun* ad emphasized audience numbers to show that the film was a massive hit.

PORCO ROSSO 1992

Porco Rosso was originally planned as an in-flight short for Japan Airlines. Having made a string of theatrical features starting with *Nausicaä of the Valley of the Wind*, Hayao Miyazaki wanted to create a lighthearted short film, partly to give his staff a break, and the idea came to him for an action film built around his passion for airplanes. As he worked on the story, based on a manga called *The Age of the Flying Boat* [Hikotei Jidai] that he had published in a hobby magazine, it grew and expanded into a feature film. The story is set in the Adriatic Sea during the late 1920s, just as the Great Depression is sweeping the world. The protagonist, Porco, is a bounty hunter who chases down the air pirates that rampage around the Adriatic. As he battles them and crosses swords with his rival Mr. Curtis, Porco embodies Miyazaki's masculine ideal and heroic

aesthetic. But why does he have the appearance of a pig? His old friend Madam Gina is the only one who knows. Their relationship has an air of sophistication straight out of an old foreign film, and indeed, *Porco Rosso* is more geared toward adults than the many Miyazaki films featuring child protagonists.

Although primarily a manly action adventure, the film also features memorable female characters like expert mechanic Fio and the other women who work at Master Piccolo's hangar. Many of the film's main staff were also women: *Porco Rosso* was the first major assignment for both supervising animator Megumi Kagawa and art director Katsu Hisamura, with Naoko Asari serving as recording director, a role she had performed on *Kiki's Delivery Service* and *Only Yesterday* as well.

Release date: July 18, 1992
Running time: Approx. 93 minutes
© 1992 Studio Ghibli - NN

Original Story, Screenplay Written and
Directed by ···················· Hayao Miyazaki
Producer ······················· Toshio Suzuki
Music ····························· Joe Hisaishi
Supervising Animators ········ Megumi Kagawa
Toshio Kawaguchi
Art Director ······················ Katsu Hisamura
Chief Color Design ·············· Michiyo Yasuda
Theme song "Sakurambo no Minoru Koro (Le Temps Des Cerises)" / Ending Theme Song "Toki ni wa mukashi no hanashi wo (Once in a While, Let's Talk About the Old Days)" Performed by ···· Tokiko Kato
Production ······················ Studio Ghibli
Production Committee ········ Tokuma Shoten
Japan Airlines
Nippon Television Network
Studio Ghibli

Porco Rosso ················· Shuichiro Moriyama
Madam Gina ················ Tokiko Kato
Master Piccolo ·············· Sanshi Katsura
Mamma Aiuto Boss ·········· Tsunehiko Kamijo
Fio Piccolo ··················· Akemi Okamura
Mr. Curtis ···················· Akio Otsuka

STORY

The film is set in the Adriatic Sea of the 1920s, during the tumultuous aftermath of World War I and the rise of fascism. Destitute aviators have turned to air piracy and are running amok, but there is one man they fear: the bounty hunter they call Porco Rosso, who flies the bright-red prototype fighter seaplane Savoia

S.21. Desperate to fight back, the air pirates hire an American pilot named Mr. Curtis as their bodyguard, and the two rivals begin their fateful duel over Madam Gina, the woman of the pilots' dreams, and Fio, the 17-year-old girl who fixes the battered Savoia S.21 after Curtis shoots it down.

The Original Manga

◆ **The Age of the Flying Boat, the basis for Porco Rosso by Hayao Miyazaki (Dainippon Kaiga)**

Originally serialized in *Model Graphics Monthly* from March to May of 1990, the story takes place in the ultimate hobby world, built on a wealth of military knowledge and imagination. (English title provisional)

CHARACTER RELATIONSHIPS

FIO ← grandchild — **MASTER PICCOLO**   **AIR PIRATES**   **MAMMA AIUTO**

looks up to   relies on   have it in for   adore

in love with   **PORCO ROSSO** ← love each other → **MADAM GINA**   hire

enemies   in love with

MR. CURTIS

CHARACTERS

PORCO ROSSO

Real name Marco Pagot. During WWI he was an ace pilot in the Italian Air Force, but after the war he left the military, and for unknown reasons cast a spell to turn himself into a pig.

MR. CURTIS

An ambitious man who becomes famous after shooting down Porco, he intends eventually to become President of the United States. He flies the Curtiss R3C-0, a navy-blue amphibious fighter.

MADAM GINA

Owner of the Hotel Adriano, where seaplane pilots gather to hear her sing. She and Porco created a flying club when they were young, and spent their salad days together.

FIO

A 17-year-old seaplane mechanic and Master Piccolo's granddaughter. Although young, her skills are second to none. Her optimism and energy change Porco.

MASTER PICCOLO

Head of the Piccolo Company, the seaplane repair facility in Milan that Porco frequents, and Fio's grandfather. Piccolo is the mechanic Porco most trusts.

MAMMA AIUTO

Air pirates who operate out of a camouflage flying boat called the *Dabohaze*. Constantly taking a thrashing from Porco, they end up joining forces with the Air Pirates Federation.

AIR PIRATES

An organization of seven air pirate groups based in the Adriatic. They bring Curtis over from the United States to take Porco down.

■ Curtis, the American pilot hired by the air pirates, shoots Porco down during a dogfight.

■ Gina is relieved when she gets a phone call from Porco after he is shot down.

■ Porco meets the mechanic Fio when he goes to Piccolo Co. to have his beloved plane repaired.

■ After finding out that Porco is still alive, Curtis challenges him to a second duel.

TRIVIA

The new engine installed on Porco's plane has "GHIBLI" written on it. When Miyazaki named the studio, he mistakenly pronounced it "jibli," but the correct pronunciation of the word is "gibli," with a hard 'g.' As a result, people in some countries pronounce the name of the studio with a hard 'g' as well.

POSTERS

Two posters were created for *Porco Rosso*. For the second, Hayao Miyazaki himself drew the rough sketch.

■ The original version of Poster 1 simply featured the black-and-white group photo, but eventually Porco was added to the foreground.

■ Korean poster.

■ Swedish poster.

■ In addition to the sophisticated mood conveyed by Porco and Gina, Poster 2 really gives a sense of the central role of seaplanes in the film.

BEHIND THE SCENES

Gina didn't appear in the original manga, but was added because the film felt lacking without a heroine on-screen until Fio's appearance later in the story. Originally, her bar was to be sparsely patronized because of the air pirates' rowdiness, and she would eventually close it and return to her own country. But as the story developed, the bar became an air pirate hangout instead, and the woman became Gina.

■ This June 17 1/3-page ad from the *Seikyo Shimbun* featured dialogue from the film in addition to the tagline.

NEWSPAPER ADS

Initially, the ads used the image from Poster 2, but after the film's release, some ads using stills from the film were created as well.

■ The ad from the May 2, 1992 edition of the *Asahi Shimbun*. Newspaper ads had started running about a week earlier, on April 24.

■ This full-page two-color ad ran in the Tokyo *Shimbun* on June 19, and used red text to make the title, tagline, and release date stand out.

■ The June 22 *Yomiuri Shimbun* featured a tie-in with Japan Airlines. The full-page two-color ad created a strong impression.

■ This boldly designed 1/3-page ad that debuted in the July 8 edition of the *Hochi Shimbun* ran across both pages of the spread, the righthand side featuring the title in huge characters.

■ This July 16 *Nikkan Gendai* full-page spread used the tagline "This summer, a pig will fly!" above the title to create a very striking ad.

■ On July 17, the day before the release, ads ran in the *Yomiuri Shimbun*, *Mainichi Shimbun*, *Tokyo Shimbun*, *Sankei Shimbun*, *Tokyo Times*, and *Yukan Fuji* in addition to this ad in the *Asahi Shimbun*, each with a different image.

■ Later ads like this one, which ran in the September 18 edition of the *Asahi Shimbun*, prominently featured Gina to create the mood of a foreign film or a grown-up love story.

■ After being attacked over the Sea of Decay, Nausicaä pilots a gunship with her feet and tells Gol, Muzu, and Gikkuri, "I'll save you. Trust me."

■ Early in the film, Nausicaä rides her Mehve to rescue Yupa from an Ohm.

Nausicaä of the Valley of the Wind

Wind-user Nausicaä rides the Mehve, an engine-assisted glider which she calls her "kite." Like the armed gunships and other machines that appear in the story, it incorporates the relics of an industrial civilization that died out a thousand years ago.

■ The Mehve uses an engine during take-off and acceleration, then glides on the wind.

GHIBLI DRAWS
FLIGHT

Flight features prominently in many Ghibli films, achieved through a wide variety of means, from magic to sci-fi machinery to old-fashioned prop planes. The sudden descent of a Tolmekian Corvette or the slow, ominous flight of a bomber as it turns the ground below into a sea of fire leaves an indelible impression. But the greatest pleasure of all comes in the sense of freedom and speed when Nausicaä or Kiki soars through the vast sky. It's impossible to talk about the appeal of Ghibli films without including flight in the conversation.

■ The Princess and Sutemaru hold hands as a flock of geese pass them in the air.

The Tale of The Princess Kaguya

Reluctant to return to the Moon, the princess is reunited with her childhood friend Sutemaru. They confess their feelings for each other and fly through the sky in joy. The mountains and flocks of birds seem to gently welcome them, but ultimately the power of the Moon tears them apart.

■ They see the peaceful valley spread out below them.

■ Howl takes Sophie's hands and floats up for a stroll through the sky to shake off his pursuers.

■ Howl sends Sophie in his place in attempt to skirt his former teacher Suliman's demands, but ends up having to help her escape in a flying kayak.

Howl's Moving Castle

Pursued by the Witch of the Waste's henchmen, Howl confounds them by flying up into the air with Sophie. Strictly speaking, it's more of a stroll through the sky, but this memorable scene reveals Howl's magical powers. The film also features military aircraft like bombers and flying kayaks.

The Wind Rises

As with *Porco Rosso,* Hayao Miyazaki drew on his love of airplanes for this film, which centers around real people and historical events. Jiro Horikoshi's childhood dreams of flying and the ideal plane he hopes to design are at the mercy of turbulent times.

On Your Mark

In a future city where most of humankind lives underground, two police officers rescue a girl with wings from a government facility and return her to the sky. The memorable scene in which the girl leaves the officers, spreading her wings and soaring through the sky with a smile, conveys a sense of hope for the future.

Kiki's Delivery Service

Kiki starts a delivery service using her ability to fly on a broomstick, but after she loses confidence her magic disappears and her broom breaks. The climactic scene, in which she borrows a scrub brush to rescue her friend Tombo, depicts the return of her magic *and* her personal growth.

Porco Rosso

Hayao Miyazaki, an airplane fanatic since his childhood, filled *Porco Rosso* with seaplanes and flying boats based both on real aircraft and on his original designs. The high-speed sea battle between Porco and his rival Mr. Curtis is quite a spectacle.

My Neighbor Totoro

Totoro rides a top through the night sky with Satsuki and Mei aboard. This dreamlike scene is enthralling for children and adults alike. The joy and exhilaration of watching Totoro's massive body soar lightly through the sky is what animation is all about.

Spirited Away

Haku, who treats Chihiro with kindness during her time at the bathhouse, turns out to be the spirit of the Kohaku River. With Chihiro's help, he remembers his real name, freeing him from Yubaba's control. Haku's identity and his relationship to Chihiro are revealed during this scene, in which they soar through the sky together.

Castle in the Sky

Pazu and the air pirates fly off to rescue Sheeta on flapters, aircraft that flap their wings like insects. Dola's line "You've got 40 seconds" has become famous. The pirates' airship *Tiger Moth* and the flying battleship *Goliath* are impressive as well, but it's Laputa itself that steals the show.

Only Yesterday

The dating scene from Taeko's fifth-grade memory includes a depiction of flight. After a casual conversation with Hirota, the boy from the next class who has a crush on her, Taeko is so overjoyed that she takes to the sky and swims through the air. This scene expressing the thrill of first love is truly memorable.

OCEAN WAVES — 1993

Ocean Waves is a mid-length TV movie based on a novel by Saeko Himuro, popular for her women's coming-of-age stories. The project was originally developed to give Ghibli's younger staff an opportunity to hone their skills. Katsuya Kondo, who drew the well-received illustrations for the novel during its serialization, acted as character designer and supervising animator for the film. Rounding out the staff were art director Naoya Tanaka and screenwriter Keiko Niwa (credited here as Kaori Nakamura), both of whom would go on to work on a number of other Ghibli films. *Ocean Waves* was directed by Tomomi Mochizuki, the first outside director to helm a Ghibli project. Known for his sensitive work on films like *Maison Ikkoku: The Final Chapter*, he elicited a vivid portrayal of the teenage characters' gamut of emotions.

Like the original novel, the film is set in a high school in Kochi, on the island of Shikoku, and revolves around strong-willed heroine Rikako Muto, a transfer student from Tokyo, protagonist Taku Morisaki, and his best friend Yutaka Matsuno. The film centers on the first half of the novel when the characters are still in high school, using the narrator's college years, which form the second half of the book, as a retrospective framing device. The film resonated with viewers who saw their own teenage experiences reflected in the relationship between the three main characters, not yet mature enough to constitute a love triangle.

Two of the voice actors who worked on the film, Sumi Shimamoto and Takeshi Watabe, were Kochi natives, and so doubled as dialect coaches to help evoke the local flavor of the setting. The combination of the characters' conversations in Tosa dialect and the local landscape recreated by the art department lent the film a heightened sense of realism. Along with *From Up on Poppy Hill*, *Ocean Waves* is one of the only Ghibli films with no element of fantasy.

Broadcast date: May 5, 1993
Running time: Approx. 72 minutes
© 1993 Saeko Himuro · Studio Ghibli · N

Original Story ···················· Saeko Himuro
Screenplay ························ Kaori Nakamura
Director ··························· Tomomi Mochizuki
Planning ·························· Toshio Suzuki
Seiji Okuda
Producer ·························· Nozomu Takahashi
Music ······························ Shigeru Nagata
Character Design and
Supervising Animator ········ Katsuya Kondo
Art Director ······················ Naoya Tanaka
Color Design ····················· Yumi Furuya
Theme Song "Umi ni Naretara (If I could Be the
Sea)" Performed by ··········· Yoko Sakamoto
Production ························· The Future Producers
of Studio Ghibli
Production Committee ········ Tokuma Shoten
Nippon Television Network
Studio Ghibli

Taku Morisaki ···················· Nobuo Tobita
Rikako Muto ······················ Yoko Sakamoto
Yutaka Matsuno ················· Toshihiko Seki

STORY

After graduating from a private high school in Kochi, Taku Morisaki has moved to Tokyo for college. He catches a momentary glimpse of a familiar figure standing on the opposite platform at Kichijoji Station before the person boards a train and disappears from sight. Could it have been Taku's high school classmate Rikako Muto? But hadn't Rikako gone to a local college in Shikoku…?

On his flight home for summer break, Taku recalls the summer of his second year of high school, when he first met Rikako, a beautiful transfer student who excelled at both academics and sports. Taku's best friend Matsuno was in love with her, but Taku kept his distance—until they got to know each other after he lent her money during a school trip. Jerked around at the whim of the self-centered and mercurial Rikako, Taku nevertheless found himself more and more drawn to her.

The Original Novel

◇ *Ocean Waves* by Saeko Himuro (Tokuma Shoten)

A coming-of-age novel serialized in *Animage* from February 1990 to January 1992.
The illustrations Katsuya Kondo drew based on Himuro's notes inspired the author herself. She wrote a sequel in 1995, *Ocean Waves II—Because there is love.*

TAKU MORISAKI

An honors student at a prestigious private school in Kochi, Taku is pure-hearted and rebellious. Even as he finds himself attracted to Rikako, he denies his own feelings.

RIKAKO MUTO

A transfer student who moves to her mother's hometown of Kochi in the summer of her junior year, following her parents' divorce. Academically and athletically gifted as well as gorgeous, the one thing she isn't good at is fitting in.

CHARACTER RELATIONSHIPS

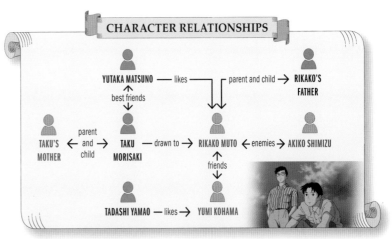

YUTAKA MATSUNO — likes · parent and child · RIKAKO'S FATHER

best friends

TAKU'S MOTHER · parent and child → TAKU MORISAKI — drawn to → RIKAKO MUTO ← enemies → AKIKO SHIMIZU

friends

TADASHI YAMAO — likes → YUMI KOHAMA

YUTAKA MATSUNO

Taku's best friend since middle school, he's had an unrequited crush on Rikako ever since she arrived. He worries about her because of how out of place she is.

YUMI KOHAMA

Rikako's only friend in Kochi. They become close after being seated next to each other on the first day of senior year, but everyone looks at them as a queen and her lady-in-waiting.

TADASHI YAMAO

A well-built guy who confesses at the class reunion that he had a crush on Yumi.

AKIKO SHIMIZU

A responsible, class president-type who the other girls look up to as a leader. She hates Rikako, but they run into each other in town after graduation and bury the hatchet.

RIKAKO'S FATHER

He stays in Tokyo after the divorce, living with a woman in the apartment he used to share with his family.

TAKU'S MOTHER

She tells Taku to be kind to Rikako out of sympathy toward her mother, who has returned to her hometown with her daughter in tow after her divorce.

■ The Japanese poster presented a fresh take, designed to look like part of a yearbook class photo.

■ Poster for the American theatrical release. The focus is squarely on the ocean, using completely different images from the Japanese version.

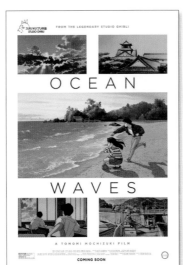

FROM THE LEGENDARY STUDIO GHIBLI

OCEAN
WAVES

A TOMOMI MOCHIZUKI FILM

COMING SOON

■ Rikako doesn't really try to fit in at all. Taku ends up wrapped around her finger after she asks to borrow money during a school trip.

■ Rikako gets Taku to go to Tokyo with her so she can live with her dad, but her hopes are dashed, and she breaks down crying.

TRIVIA

The main staff traveled to Kochi and gathered detailed information, dedicating themselves to an authentic depiction of the locale. For the view from Tenjin Bridge, which also appears in the illustrations from the original book, they erased all the tall buildings to make the view feel more expansive. This kind of creative license exemplifies the power of animation.

BEHIND THE SCENES

The most difficult part of the script to pin down was the last scene. Mochizuki was emphatic about creating "that situation where you think you saw someone but you just can't be sure." The characters were originally going to spot each other at the crossing in front of Shibuya Station, but after considering different possibilities, they decided on a train platform.

A story
of modern
tanuki
struggling to
survive the
destruction
of their
natural
habitat

POM POKO   1994

During the production of *Porco Rosso* (1992), Hayao Miyazaki decided that the next animal they should do a film about was the tanuki, a canine species unique to Japan and often referred to as the "raccoon dog." Thus was born *Pom Poko*. Isao Takahata, who directed the film, had long harbored an interest in stories and folktales concerning tanuki, and thought it was strange that there were no animated works about the creatures. He threw himself into his research, and created a tanuki film appropriate to the 1990s. The film centers around a community of tanuki who lose their homes after humans selfishly destroy their habitat in the name of residential development. Tanuki from across the land pull together and try to drive the humans out using shapeshifting skills handed down from generation to generation. The film is a slapstick fantasy portraying the tanuki as earnest but hapless, though the story is based on real events, including the construction of Tama New Town on the outskirts of Tokyo.

Animated animal protagonists are often anthropomorphized, but while some of the tanuki in this film stand on two legs or are particularly cartoonish, others are depicted realistically. The film is filled with show-stopping moments that reveal the myriad possibilities of animation, like Operation Specter, in which the tanuki demonstrate their shapeshifting abilities to the fullest. Another unique appeal is the casting of veteran comic actors and leading rakugo storytellers, including Shincho Kokontei as the narrator.

Release date: July 16, 1994
Running time: Approx. 119 minutes
© 1994 Hatake Jimusho - Studio Ghibli - NH

Original Story, Screenplay Written and
Directed by ···················· Isao Takahata
Planning ·························· Hayao Miyazaki
Producer ························· Toshio Suzuki
Music ···························· Koryu
                                Manto Watanobe
                                Yoko Ino
                                Masaru Goto
                                (Shang Shang Typhoon)
                                Ryojiro Furusawa
Layout Design ················· Yoshiyuki Momose
Character Design ·············· Shinji Otsuka
Supervising Animators ········ Shinji Otsuka
                                Megumi Kagawa
Art Director ···················· Kazuo Oga
Color Design ···················· Michiyo Yasuda
"Pom Poko" Love Song "Asia no Kono Machi
de (In This Asian City)" / Ending Theme Song
"Itsudemo Darekaga (Anytime, Somebody Will
Always)" Performed by ········ Shang Shang Typhoon
Production ······················ Studio Ghibli
Production Committee ·········· Tokuma Shoten
                                Nippon Television Network
                                Hakuhodo
                                Studio Ghibli

Narration ······················ Shincho Kokontei
Shokichi ························· Makoto Nonomura
Kiyo ···························· Yuriko Ishida
Seizaemon ······················ Norihei Miki
Oroku ··························· Nijiko Kiyokawa
Gonta ··························· Shigeru Izumiya
Gyobu ··························· Gannosuke Ashiya
Bunta ··························· Takehiro Murata
Ponkichi ························ Kobuhei Hayashiya
Ryutaro ························· Akira Fukuzawa
Otama ··························· Yorie Yamashita
Kincho the Sixth ··············· Beicho Katsura
Hage ··························· Bunshi Katsura
Tsurukame Osho ················ Kosan Yanagiya

STORY

A group of tanuki who have long lived a life of ease amid the lush nature of the Tama Hills find themselves threatened when humans start clearing the land for large-scale residential development. If things go on like this, the tanuki will run short of food, and maybe even lose their habitat altogether. All the local tanuki gather for a meeting, and decide to revive the shapeshifting skills of their forebears in order to challenge the humans and stop the development.

The young tanuki dedicate themselves to learning the art of shapeshifting from their elders, transform-ing into huge trees to block construction vehicles and threatening humans with spectral phenomena. But the humans have the advantage over the good-natured tanuki, and development continues to encroach into the hills. In desperation, the tanuki invite a trio of legendary elders from Shikoku, and plan their last stand in the form of Operation Specter.

■ The Tama Hills tanuki, whose food and habitat are disappearing because of human development, decide to call on legendary elders from Shikoku and Sado for backup. The messengers are selected via a heated battle of rock paper scissors.

■ The three elders finally arrive from Shikoku. What will their plan be...?

■ All the tanuki from the Tama Hills rally together to block the humans' development project.

■ The tanuki study to revive the lost art of shapeshifting.

■ Their hard work pays off, and they learn to take on human form.

■ The female tanuki also learn to shapeshift, including at least one who wants to transform into a man.

■ The Tama Hills tanuki and the Shikoku elders stage Operation Specter to force the humans to halt development, but things don't go the way they planned...

TRIVIA

As a sort of Easter egg, Takahata included Totoro, Kiki from *Kiki's Delivery Service*, and Porco's seaplane from *Porco Rosso* in Operation Specter, staged by the tanuki to force the humans' hand.

CHARACTERS

SHOKICHI

A young tanuki who lives in Kage Forest. Interested in humans since childhood, he's one of the quickest to master shapeshifting, but remains skeptical about the anti-human strategy.

KIYO

A beautiful tanuki from Mimikiri Mountain. She works with Shokichi to stage Operation Twin Stars in an attempt to drive out the humans, and they fall in love.

GONTA

A warrior from Taka Forest. Rough-and-tumble, but a skilled shapeshifter. Gonta truly hates humans, and is a hardliner in the anti-human operation.

OTAMA

Gonta's wife. Steady and devoted, she supports her hot-tempered husband.

TAMASABURO

A gentle tanuki who lives in Oni Forest. He journeys to Shikoku and brings back the three Shikoku elders to instruct the Tama tanuki in the art of shapeshifting.

KOHARU

The daughter of Kincho the Sixth. When Tamasaburo falls ill after reaching Shikoku, she nurses him back to health and they fall in love.

BUNTA

To save the endangered Tama tanuki, Bunta travels to Sado island, but the Sado elder is already dead and Bunta returns emptyhanded.

PONKICHI

Shokichi's childhood friend. An easygoing tanuki who's hopeless at shapeshifting.

SASUKE

Shokichi's friend. They study shapeshifting together.

HAYASHI

A tanuki from the mountains of Kanagawa, whose home is plagued by the illegal dumping of residual earth from construction.

RYUTARO

A shapeshifting fox from Horinouchi. He realizes the tanuki are behind Operation Specter, and suggests they survive by living as humans.

SEIZAEMON

An elder from Suzu Forest. He fought with Gonta and the other Taka Forest tanuki over feeding grounds, but at base is a smooth-talking opportunist.

OROKU

A female tanuki of indeterminate age, nicknamed "Fireball Oroku." Dependable and gutsy, she trains the younger tanuki in the art of shapeshifting.

GYOBU

603 years old and boss of the 808 tanuki of Shikoku. Said to have been an important player in the internal strife that beset the Matsuyama domain in 1732.

KINCHO THE SIXTH

58 years old and a sixth-generation descendant of the tanuki Kincho, who made his name during the Awa Tanuki Battle of the Tenpo era. He is one of the three Shikoku elders who orchestrate Operation Specter, along with Gyobu and Hage.

HAGE

Real name Tasaburo of Joganji, he is descended from the guardian spirits of the Heike clan. 999 years old, he is said to have witnessed the Battle of Yashima during the Genpei War with his own eyes.

TSURUKAME OSHO

A 105-year-old tanuki who makes his home at Manpukuji Temple on Mt. Bodaimochi. He unites the Tama tanuki.

PRESIDENT

He plots to use Operation Specter as publicity for Wonderland, the theme park he is building.

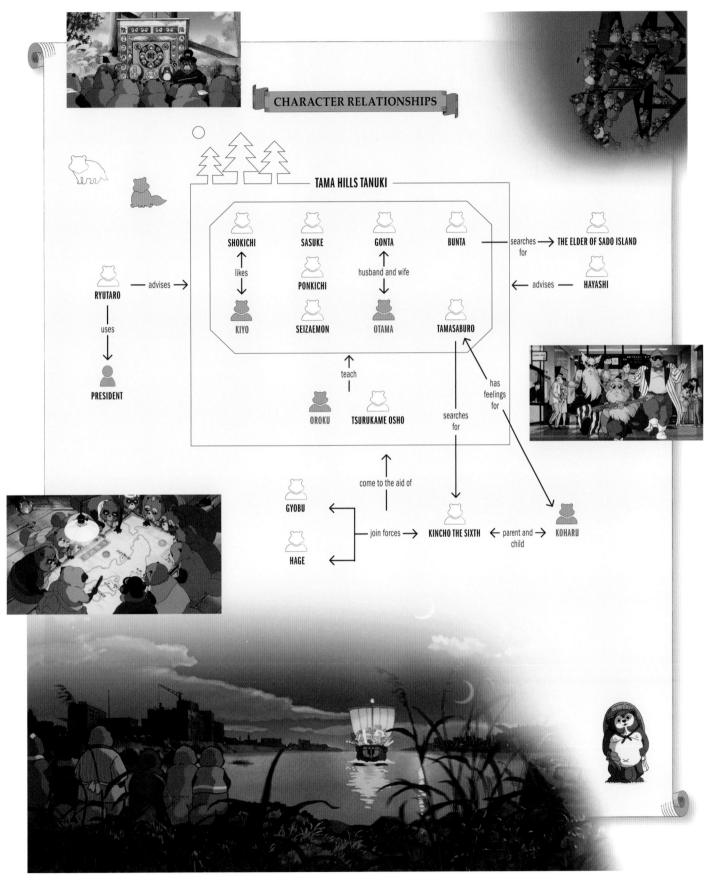

CHARACTER RELATIONSHIPS

TAMA HILLS TANUKI

SHOKICHI — likes — KIYO

SASUKE

PONKICHI

SEIZAEMON

GONTA — husband and wife — OTAMA

BUNTA

TAMASABURO

BUNTA — searches for → THE ELDER OF SADO ISLAND

HAYASHI — advises → (BUNTA)

RYUTARO — advises → (TAMA HILLS TANUKI)

RYUTARO — uses → PRESIDENT

OROKU

TSURUKAME OSHO — teach → (SEIZAEMON)

TAMASABURO — searches for → KINCHO THE SIXTH

TAMASABURO — has feelings for → KOHARU

GYOBU

HAGE

GYOBU / HAGE — join forces — KINCHO THE SIXTH

KINCHO THE SIXTH — come to the aid of → GYOBU / HAGE

KINCHO THE SIXTH — parent and child — KOHARU

59

POSTERS

There are two varieties of poster for *Pom Poko* with the tagline "The tanukis are doing their best, too": one with a realistic tanuki, and the other with cartoon-style tanuki.

■ Poster 1 features a realistic tanuki alone against a black background. The contrast between this and the colorful title, accompanied by the phrase "all-natural color manga film," arouses the interest of the viewer.

■ Poster 2 shows more cartoonish tanuki talking together in front of an animal mandala, giving a stronger sense of the world of the film and its humorous feel.

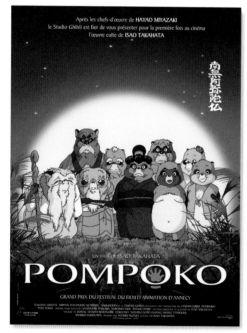

■ French poster.

■ Korean poster.

NEWSPAPER ADS

The newspaper ads for *Pom Poko* didn't use any of the images from the posters, opting instead for groups of the more cartoonish tanuki.

■ This ad ran in the *Yomiuri Shimbun* on June 20, 1994, about a month before the film's release. The main image shows tanuki standing in front of an animal mandala. This drawing appeared from time to time in later ads as well.

■ The 2/3-page ad in the June 30 edition of the Tokyo *Shimbun* also used the image of the group of tanuki standing in front of the mandala, but this time in full color.

■ The ad that ran in the *Yomiuri Shimbun* on July 15, the day before the release, featured Gonta leading the tanuki into battle, emphasizing the film's fun and excitement.

■ The ad that ran in the *Sankei Shimbun* on July 16, the day the film came out, featured the text "Opening today! The summer of tanuki starts here!" It was an attempt at an ad that focused on text instead of image.

■ This ad ran in the *Yomiuri Shimbun* on July 22, about a week after release. It showed the main characters exultant and ready to keep fighting, with copy that touted the film as a "massive hit! The tanuki's summer is going well!"

■ The August 5 *Yomiuri Shinbun* ad proclaimed *Pom Poko* "the no.1 hit of the summer," and highlighted that 1.38 million people had seen the film in its first three weeks.

■ Poster for Kodansha's twenty-one-magazine co-op previews, made to be a hanging train advertisement.

BEHIND THE SCENES

The slow, smooth pan across the packed bookshelves in the library when Oroku is lecturing the young tanuki represents Ghibli's first use of CG. Done at Takahata's insistence, the scene ended up taking almost a year to complete.

A youthful love story that encourages children to look to the future

WHISPER OF THE HEART   1995

Whisper of the Heart was the directorial debut of master animator Yoshifumi Kondo, a longtime collaborator of both Isao Takahata's and Hayao Miyazaki's. To help Kondo fulfill his goal of depicting the daily lives of adolescents, Miyazaki acted as general producer, in addition to writing the screenplay and creating the storyboards, based on Aoi Hiiragi's manga. Kondo vividly portrays the purity of first love and the nuances of life in middle school, as well as the daily experience of a family of four living in public housing. The film resonated with children of the same generation as the protagonist, and remains beloved by young fans to this day.

Unusually for Ghibli, *Whisper of the Heart* is not a fantasy film, though the scenes where the heroine Shizuku flies through the world of her own creation with Baron form a kind of story-within-a-story, visually bringing us into the novel Shizuku is writing. In order to create a smooth floating feeling and sense of three-dimensionality for this portion of the film, the animators used digital compositing to layer in backgrounds specially created by Naohisa Inoue, painter and author of *Iblard Monogatari*. Digital technology was introduced for the sound as well: *Whisper of the Heart* was the first Japanese animated film to use Dolby Stereo 5.1ch Digital Surround Sound. The song "Country Road," which appears throughout the film, was selected to suit Miyazaki's theme of what a "hometown" means to city-dwellers. The scene in the antique shop where Seiji, Shizuku, and Shiro sing was prescored, and the filmed performance was then used as a reference for the animation.

Release date: July 15, 1995
Running time: Approx. 111 minutes
© 1995 Aoi Hiiragi / Shueisha - Studio Ghibli - NH

Original Comic ···················· Aoi Hiiragi
General Producer, Screenplay and
Storyboards by ················· Hayao Miyazaki
Director ························· Yoshifumi Kondo
Producer ························· Toshio Suzuki
Music ··························· Yuji Nomi
Supervising Animator ·············· Kitaro Kosaka
Art Director ···················· Satoshi Kuroda
Character Color Design ·········· Michiyo Yasuda
"The Baron's Story"
Art Direction ··················· Naohisa Inoue
Theme song "Country Road"
Performed by ···················· Yoko Honna
Production ······················ Studio Ghibli
Production Committee ············· Tokuma Shoten
                                  Nippon Television Network
                                  Hakuhodo
                                  Studio Ghibli

Shizuku Tsukishima ··············· Yoko Honna
Seiji Amasawa ··················· Issei Takahashi
Yasuya Tsukishima ··············· Takashi Tachibana
Asako Tsukishima ················ Shigeru Muroi
Baron ··························· Shigeru Tsuyuguchi
Shiro Nishi ······················ Keiju Kobayashi
Shiho Tsukishima ················ Yorie Yamashita
Yuko Harada ···················· Maiko Kayama
Sugimura ······················· Yoshimi Nakajima

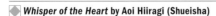

STORY

Shizuku Tsukishima is a middle-school bookworm, constantly borrowing books from the library. One day she sees the name Seiji Amasawa on a checkout card—and the same name begins to appear in every book she reads. Despite the fact that she knows nothing about him, this mysterious Seiji begins to loom large in her imagination.

One day, Shizuku meets a boy from her class who dreams of becoming a luthier—and who turns out to be the selfsame Seiji Amasawa. He plans to move to Italy to study violin-making once he graduates from middle school. Although Shizuku is attracted to Seiji, she feels frustrated with herself for not knowing what she wants to do or where her talents lie. To challenge herself, she starts writing a story about Baron, a statuette of a cat that Seiji's grandfather treasures.

The Original Manga

◆ *Whisper of the Heart* by Aoi Hiiragi (Shueisha)

A girls' manga serialized in *Ribbon* from August to November of 1989.
There are several differences between the manga and the film: Seiji's older brother Koji, who doesn't appear in the Ghibli film, has an important role in the original; Moon the cat has a twin named Luna; and Shizuku's age and Seiji's dream for the future are also different.

CHARACTERS

SHIZUKU TSUKISHIMA

An independent, 14-year-old bookworm who goes to Mukaihara Middle School. Although she's outgoing and active in public, at home she tends to clam up in response to her overachieving sister's nagging.

SEIJI AMASAWA

Shizuku's classmate at Mukaihara Middle. He wants to become a violin maker. Aware of Shizuku for some time now, he tries to read books she might borrow from the library in the hopes that she'll eventually notice him.

CHARACTER RELATIONSHIPS

SHIHO TSUKISHIMA — parents and child — ASAKO TSUKISHIMA — husband and wife → YASUYA TSUKISHIMA

MOON

older sister

parents and child

brings together

SHIZUKU TSUKISHIMA ← likes → SEIJI AMASAWA

likes   best friends   writes a story about   grandfather

SUGIMURA   BARON — owner — SHIRO NISHI

likes

YUKO HARADA

YASUYA TSUKISHIMA

Shizuku's father and a librarian at the local public library. His true passion is local history, however, which doesn't bring in any money. Having cut the cord early on, he doesn't interfere in his children's decisions.

ASAKO TSUKISHIMA

Shizuku's mother. An energetic woman who started graduate school once her kids were older, she struggles to balance housework with her studies.

SHIHO TSUKISHIMA

Shizuku's older sister. A beautiful, proactive college student, she helps her mother with the housework and is constantly telling Shizuku what to do. In truth, though, she's just worried about her little sister.

■ Shizuku follows after Moon, a cat she meets on the train on the way to the library.

■ Shizuku and Seiji are drawn to each other, and begin to confess their feelings on the school roof, when...

YUKO HARADA

Shizuku's classmate and best friend. Though she has a crush on Sugimura, she's too timid to tell him.

SUGIMURA

Shizuku's classmate and a member of the baseball team. He likes Shizuku.

SHIRO NISHI

Seiji's maternal grandfather. He fixes up and sells antique furniture and wind-up clocks at his store, the World Emporium. A cultured man, he enjoys playing modern jazz with his friends.

■ Shizuku accompanies Seiji's violin with her voice, and Seiji's grandfather joins in.

■ Shizuku goes on a journey to a strange land with Baron, the protagonist of a story she has begun writing.

MOON

The cat that brings Shizuku and Seiji together. Moon is what Seiji calls him, but he's no one's pet, instead wandering from house to house, where he has many different names.

BARON

A statuette of an aristocratic cat that Shiro acquired as a young man studying abroad in Germany. "Baron" is only a nickname, however, his full name being Baron Humbert von Gikkingen.

TRIVIA

When she goes to the library to do research for her story, Shizuku comes across a book that contains a picture of a man making a violin in prison. The print itself is the work of Hayao Miyazaki's younger son Keisuke, a printmaker and wood engraver.

POSTERS

Two posters were created for *Whisper of the Heart*, one showing our world and the other depicting a fantasy landscape.

■ Poster 2 features an image of Shizuku and Baron soaring through the sky of another world, taken from the story that Shizuku writes in the course of the film.

■ Poster 1 is based on a rough sketch by Hayao Miyazaki, with a rear view of the World Emporium in the background.

■ Korean poster.

■ The first ad, which ran in the *Seikyo Shimbun* on May 16, 1995, about two months before the release, combined the images from both posters to give an overall sense of the film. After that, only one image was used, depending on the publication.

■ A so-called "stick-out" ad, which gets its name from the fact that the tiny ad seems to jut out from the corner of an article. This one ran in the June 16 edition of *Sports Nippon*.

■ The 1/3-page ads in the June 23 *Yomiuri Shimbun* and *Asahi Shimbun* announced that Hayao Miyazaki's animated short film *On Your Mark* would be shown before *Whisper of the Heart*. They featured a big picture of Moon's face, with copy referring to him as a "strange cat."

NEWSPAPER ADS

In addition to the two poster images, ads featured a variety of motifs, from movie stills to photos of the line on opening day.

■ The ad that ran in the *Yomiuri Shimbun* on July 21 combined a photograph of the line outside the theater on opening day with a drawing of Shizuku's face.

■ This full-color full-page ad from the July 6 *Yomiuri Shimbun* was acclaimed for its design, and won the 52nd Yomiuri Film Ad Award.

BEHIND THE SCENES

The lines of the drawings in this film are thicker than usual because the animators used small frames intended for TV. The larger frames used for theatrical features require more detailed drawings, so they opted for the small frames to reduce the burden on first-time director Yoshifumi Kondo.

Hayao Miyazaki's first music video

ON YOUR MARK

1995

Shown with *Whisper of the Heart*, this short was originally made as a music video for CHAGE and ASKA's song "On Your Mark." It was also shown during performances on their 1995-1996 tour.

ASKA wanted to make an animated music video, and he wanted to work with the best, so, knowing it was a long shot from the start, the band contacted Studio Ghibli's producer Toshio Suzuki. At the time, Ghibli was ramping up to start production on *Princess Mononoke*, and Suzuki was aware that Hayao Miyazaki was having doubts about producing a feature-length film, so he agreed to take on the project in the hopes that Miyazaki's feelings might change if he worked on a short.

In the film, Miyazaki repeats key scenes but leads each one to different endings, adroitly expressing the many possibilities the future holds.

Release date: July 15, 1995
Running time: 6 minutes 48 seconds
Animation © 1995 Studio Ghibli
Music © 1994 YAMAHA MUSIC PUBLISHING, Inc. & Rockdom Artists Inc.

Original Story, Screenplay Written and
Directed by ····················· Hayao Miyazaki
Producer ·························· Toshio Suzuki
Song "On Your Mark"
Performed by ················ CHAGE and ASKA
Supervising Animator ··········· Masashi Ando
Art Director ···················· Yoji Takeshige
Color Design ···················· Michiyo Yasuda
Production ······················· Studio Ghibli
Production ······················· Real Cast Inc.
*Shown with *Whisper of the Heart*

STORY

In the future, people have been forced underground by radioactive contamination and disease. Armed police officers storm a tower with a flashing neon sign which reads "Saint Nova's Church," seizing control from the religious organization headquartered there. Two of the officers rescue a winged girl from deep within the building, but the authorities take custody of her as an experimental subject.

Unable to put her out of their minds, the two officers put together a plan to rescue the winged girl and return her to the sky.

■ This June 30, 1995 ad in *Sports Nippon* was the only newspaper advertisement for *On Your Mark* alone. It emphasized that the short was a Hayao Miyazaki film.

■ Two officers who resemble CHAGE and ASKA rescue the winged girl from the authorities.

■ Having managed to elude their pursuers, the officers speed through the contaminated zone with the frightened girl.

■ Freed by the two officers, the girl smiles as she flies away into the sky.

A profound, majestic historical fantasy depicting the clash between gods and humans, nature and civilization

PRINCESS MONONOKE 1997

Though Hayao Miyazaki set *Princess Mononoke* in the Japan of the Muromachi era (14th-16th centuries), it is neither a hack-and-slash action film nor a sweeping military epic. Rather, this original fantasy depicts the struggle between nature, where the gods dwell, and human civilization, which destroys nature to live.

Princess Mononoke is no simple adventure movie depicting a battle between clearly delineated forces of good and evil. The story is challenging, and contains brutal imagery not usually seen in Ghibli films. Despite the tough subject matter, the film caused a huge sensation, breaking all Japanese records for domestic and foreign films alike, with a box office of ¥19.3 billion and a theatrical audience of 14.2 million. The moving relationship between the protagonist Ashitaka, who tries to break the cycle of hate, and San, a girl raised by wolves; the charm of the spirits who live in the forest and the unique, complicated supporting cast of characters including Lady Eboshi and the monk Jiko; and the compelling exploration of the coexistence of humans and nature, a theme still resonant in the 21st century, captured the hearts of a multi-generational audience.

Princess Mononoke was also the first Miyazaki film to make use of digital technology. CG was used throughout the film to depict things like the life-giving Deer God and the transformations of the spirits, and the "ink and paint" process, where color is added to the massive numbers of cels, was accomplished using digital paint.

Release date: July 12, 1997
Running time: Approx. 133 minutes
© 1997 Studio Ghibli - ND

Original Story, Screenplay Written and Directed by ·············· Hayao Miyazaki
Producer ·························· Toshio Suzuki
Music ······························ Joe Hisaishi
Supervising Animators ········ Masashi Ando
Kitaro Kosaka
Yoshifumi Kondo
Art Directors ·················· Nizo Yamamoto
Naoya Tanaka
Yoji Takeshige
Satoshi Kuroda
Kazuo Oga
Color Design ·················· Michiyo Yasuda
Theme Song "Mononoke-Hime (Princess Mononoke)" Performed by ···· Yoshikazu Mera
Production ······················ Studio Ghibli
Production Committee ········ Tokuma Shoten
Nippon Television Network
Dentsu
Studio Ghibli

Ashitaka ························ Yoji Matsuda
San ······························· Yuriko Ishida
Lady Eboshi ···················· Yuko Tanaka
Jiko ······························· Kaoru Kobayashi
Koroku ·························· Masahiko Nishimura
Gonza ·························· Tsunehiko Kamijo
Toki ······························· Sumi Shimamoto
Wolf ······························· Tetsu Watanabe
Demon god ···················· Makoto Sato
Ushikai ·························· Akira Nagoya
Moro ······························· Akihiro Miwa
Oracle ·························· Mitsuko Mori
Okkoto ·························· Hisaya Morishige

STORY

A demon god covered in black, snake-like tentacles attacks an Emishi village hidden in the far northern reaches. Ashitaka is forced to slay it to save his village, but it curses him before it dies. The village oracle advises him to go west, whence the demon god came, and Ashitaka sets off in search of a way to lift the curse.

After several days' journey, he arrives in a western land covered by the sprawling wood of the Deer God. The great beasts who live there just as they have since ancient times are locked in a battle with the humans, who seek to clear the forest in pursuit of wealth and comfort. There Ashitaka meets San, the titular "Princess Mononoke," a girl raised by wolves to hate the humans who defile the forest.

■ San, who was raised by wolves, resolves to fight alongside the boar god Okkoto and his clan against the humans.

■ Ashitaka sets out on a journey to break the demon god's curse...

■ San comes after Lady Eboshi, the head of Iron Town.

■ San saves Ashitaka after he's badly injured while breaking up her battle with Lady Eboshi.

■ San charges into battle against the humans alongside Okkoto and his troops.

■ Lady Eboshi succeeds in taking the head of the Deer God.

■ San and Ashitaka enter the withering forest to return the Deer God's head.

TRIVIA

The kodama, one of Studio Ghibli's most popular creations, came out of Miyazaki pondering how to embody the spiritual significance of the forest. Inspiration struck when he peered down the length of a fluorescent tube, suggesting the shape and color of what would grow to become the kodama.

CHARACTERS

ASHITAKA

A young man whose people, the Emishi, took refuge in the far north after being defeated in battle by the Yamato court. Supposed to become chief, he instead leaves the village after being cursed.

SAN

A young woman raised by wolves in the Deer God's forest. She hates the humans who encroach on the woods, and repeatedly attacks Iron Town wearing an eerie clay mask.

LADY EBOSHI

A calm, collected woman who leads the group producing iron at the feet of the mountains. She uses a hand cannon to fight the beasts in her attempt to clear the forest and claim it for the humans.

MORO

A 300-year-old wolf god who raises San as her daughter. Able to speak the humans' tongue and possessed of mighty powers, she despises Lady Eboshi and seeks to kill her.

ORACLE

The wise woman of the Emishi. She divines the future by lining up stones and pieces of wood.

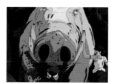

OKKOTO

A 500-year-old boar god, eldest of the boars of Chinzai (Kyushu) and an old acquaintance of Moro's. He leads the other boars in a major offensive against the humans.

JIKO

Operating on the orders of a mysterious organization called the Shishoren, Jiko is after the Deer God's head. He meets Ashitaka during his travels and tells him about the Deer God's forest.

KOROKU

A cattleman who lives in Iron Town and uses his oxen to haul iron and rice. Ashitaka saves him when he's attacked by Moro and falls over a cliff.

GONZA

Lady Eboshi's loyal henchman, and leader of both the cattlemen and the Iron Town guard.

TOKI

Koroku's wife and informal leader of the women who work the bellows in Iron Town. Strong-willed enough to argue down Gonza on occasion.

NAGO

A boar god who was badly wounded by Lady Eboshi's gunners. Transformed into a rampaging demon by his pain and hatred of humankind, he attacks the Emishi village.

DEER GOD

An animal god that gives and takes life from living things. He dies and is reborn with the cycles of the moon. The humans are after his head, which is said to grant immortality.

NIGHTWALKER

The Deer God's nighttime form. A huge, transparent creature with a unique pattern on his body, he roams the forest at night emitting a pale light.

KODAMA

Transparent spirits with pale green bodies who live in the lush forest. The rattling sound they make with their heads is said to summon the Deer God.

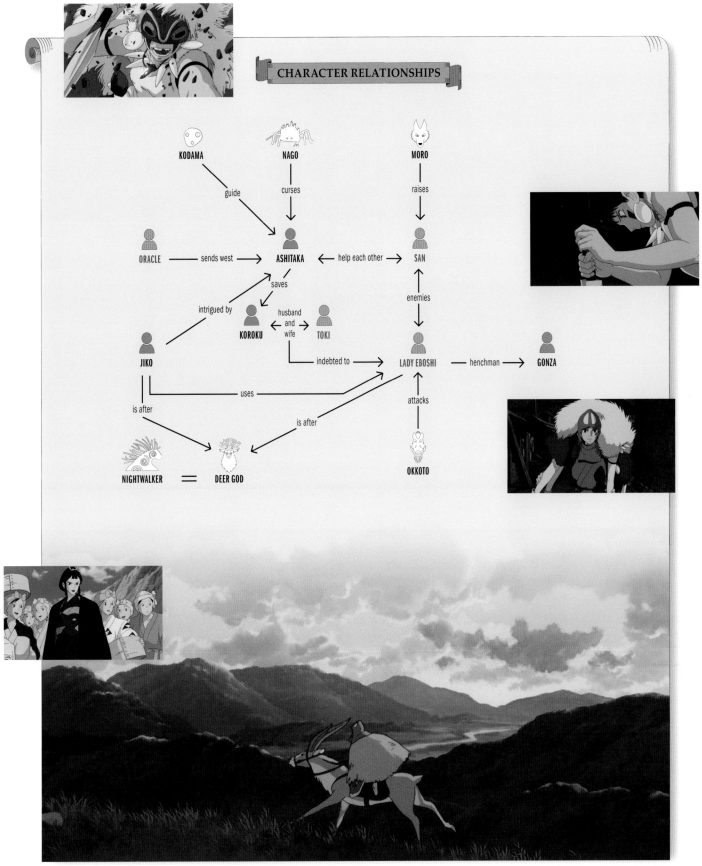

CHARACTER RELATIONSHIPS

KODAMA

NAGO

MORO

ORACLE —sends west→ ASHITAKA ←help each other→ SAN

KODAMA —guide→ ASHITAKA

NAGO —curses→ ASHITAKA

MORO —raises→ SAN

saves

intrigued by

KOROKU ←husband and wife→ TOKI

JIKO —indebted to→ LADY EBOSHI —henchman→ GONZA

SAN ←enemies→ LADY EBOSHI

uses

is after

attacks

is after

NIGHTWALKER = DEER GOD

OKKOTO

POSTERS

Two posters were created for *Princess Mononoke*, one featuring Ashitaka and the other San.

■ Version 1 poster with Ashitaka riding Yakul.

■ Version 2 poster with San and Moro. The blood around San's mouth conveys the film's eerie feel.

NEWSPAPER ADS

In addition to the poster images, the ads used stills from the movie, including a close-up of San's face in profile.

■ This high-impact color ad ran in the *Asahi Shimbun* on July 3, 1997.

■ The June 20 *Asahi Shimbun* ad centered on the profile of warrior heroine San.

■ These tiny ads counting down to the release, which ran in the *Asahi Shimbun* from July 5-10, won in the film ad category at the 1997 Asahi Advertising Awards.

■ Korean poster.

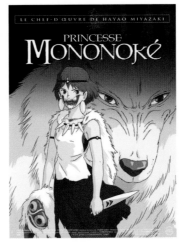

■ French poster.

■ Italian poster.

■ Swedish poster.

■ Norwegian poster.

BEHIND THE SCENES

Five art directors worked on this film in order to fully express its important theme of the conflict between nature and civilization. Miyazaki asked the art department to portray a vision of a natural world that would be just as well off without humankind. The Deer God's forest was based on the island of Yakushima, and the Emishi village where Ashitaka lived was based on Shirakami-sanchi in the northeastern part of Honshu.

■ The ad that ran on June 25 in the *Yomiuri Shimbun* was a tie-in with the Tokuma Group. The top half used stills to introduce the film, while the bottom half announced the release of an image album, soundtrack album, and related books under the title "Here they come! *Princess Mononoke* music & books!"

■ This June 25 ad from the *Yomiuri Shimbun*, which used more or less the same design as the original May 7 *Sankei Shimbun* ad, won a Yomiuri Film Advertisement Award.

■ This *Sports Nippon* ad from July 11, the day before the release, squeezed a lot of information into a small space. Centered mainly around the announcement of the film's release the next day and an on-stage speech before the screening, the only characters it featured were the kodama.

A combination of hand-drawn animation and digital technology brings the fun of the four-panel comic strip to the big screen

MY NEIGHBORS THE YAMADAS 1999

My Neighbors the Yamadas is a film adaptation of the comic strip of the same name (later changed to *Nono-chan*) by Hisaichi Ishii, which began serialization in the *Asahi Shimbun* morning edition in 1991. Isao Takahata had long been dissatisfied with the traditional animation process of layering character cels on top of background drawings with a very different feel. He wanted to make a film that would give viewers a taste of the true joy of animation, and thought he might be able to do it with computers. As he started work on the film, Takahata experimented with a variety of methods, ultimately deciding to use digital techniques to draw the characters and backgrounds as if they were part of the same picture, and then make these move. To accomplish this, both the characters and backgrounds were rendered as simple line drawings.

To best take advantage of comic strip pacing, brief "manga sections" were connected by "bobsled sections": the former are short vignettes of daily life, while the latter, in which the Yamadas travel around in various vehicles, are dynamic showpieces created with the power of CG. Both sections have a hand-drawn watercolor feel, surrounded by the characteristic negative space of manga. Even the backgrounds were painted in soft watercolors rather than the usual poster colors. These elements were then processed by computer, yielding a moving image that made it seem as if the original comic had come to life. *My Neighbors the Yamadas* is infused with the same experimental spirit Isao Takahata showed in carefully reproducing the manga style of *Only Yesterday* (1991).

Release date: July 17, 1999
Running time: Approx. 104 minutes
© 1999 Hisaichi Ishii - Hatake Jimusho - Studio Ghibli - NHD

Original Comic Strip ·········· Hisaichi Ishii
Screenplay Written and
Directed by ····················· Isao Takahata
Producer ························· Toshio Suzuki
Music ···························· Akiko Yano
Storyboard and Layout Design ·· Osamu Tanabe
                                 Yoshiyuki Momose
Supervising Animator ·········· Kenichi Konishi
Art Directors ··················· Naoya Tanaka
                                 Yoji Takeshige
Color Design ···················· Michiyo Yasuda
Theme Song "Hitoribocchi Wa Yameta (QUIT BEING
ALONE)" Performed by ········· Akiko Yano
Production ······················ Studio Ghibli
Production Committee ········· Tokuma Shoten
                                 Studio Ghibli
                                 Nippon Television Network
                                 Hakuhodo
                                 Walt Disney Japan

Matsuko ························· Yukiji Asaoka
Takashi ························· Toru Masuoka
Shige ··························· Masako Araki
Noboru ·························· Hayato Isohata
Nonoko ·························· Naomi Uno
Miss Fujiwara ·················· Akiko Yano
Neighbor Lady ················· Tamao Nakamura
Mrs. Kikuchi ··················· Chocho Miyako
Haiku Poems Read by ········· Kosanji Yanagiya

STORY

Matsuko, Takashi, Noboru, Nonoko, and Shige. Oh, and don't forget Pochi the pooch! This is everyday life for a family of five idlers (plus one dog) living in a regular house in a regular Japanese suburb.

The daughter gets lost in a department store, but blithely thinks it's the other four members of her family who are lost; the son bombs a test and finally gets it together to start studying; the parents engage in a heated battle over who gets to control the remote; Grandma is talkative and energetic; and the family dog coolly observes the proceedings. No matter what happens, *que sera, sera*—it'll all work out somehow for the Yamadas.

The Original Strip

◆ *My Neighbors the Yamadas* by Hisaichi Ishii (Asahi Shimbunsha), 6 volumes

A four-panel comic strip with a satiric touch, which debuted on October 10, 1991 in the *Asahi Shimbun* (the title became *Nono-chan* starting April 1, 1997), depicting the daily life of the Yamadas, a family of layabouts. It's the *Asahi Shimbun*'s longest-running comic, with new strips still published every day.

CHARACTERS

MATSUKO

A full-time housewife around 42 or 43, who speaks with a Kansai accent. She's incredibly lazy and is always racking her brains to figure out how to make dinner as easy as possible on herself.

SHIGE

Matsuko's mother, 70ish. Extremely energetic, she participates in all kinds of things like ballet and volunteer trash pick-up. Also speaks with a Kansai accent, and is very strict with the youngsters.

NONOKO

The daughter of the Yamada household. A third-grader with a huge mouth and a loud voice who eats like a horse. Not much good at studying, she's nevertheless a steady girl who worries about her older brother.

NOBORU

The Yamadas' elder child, in his second year of middle school. Dead average when it comes to test scores and completely unremarkable at anything, he plays on the school baseball team.

TAKASHI

A salaryman in the 43-45 range who's section chief of the Miscellaneous Affairs Department for a company in a city in the boonies. Though he's apparently from Kansai, he speaks standard Japanese. Something of a do-it-yourselfer in his spare time.

POCHI

The Yamadas' pet and watchdog. Ever po-faced, he never barks or comes when called. Nor does he give paw or wag his tail. He does bite sometimes, though.

MAMI

Noboru's classmate. Her younger brother is in Nonoko's class.

MISS FUJIWARA

Nonoko's teacher. In her late twenties, her mother sets her up on numerous dates, but they all go badly. Somewhat disorganized, her teaching policy is "Don't overdo it."

CHARACTER RELATIONSHIPS

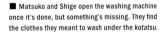

■ On the way back from the department store, they realize Nonoko's not in the car!

■ Takashi is watching a baseball game when Matsuko walks in, and the battle for control of the remote begins.

■ Matsuko and Shige open the washing machine once it's done, but something's missing. They find the clothes they meant to wash under the *kotatsu*.

■ The light in the entryway burns out and Matsuko doesn't have any more bulbs, so she takes the one from Noboru's desk lamp while he snoozes.

TRIVIA

The last scene, in which all the characters from the film sing "Que Sera, Sera," is particularly memorable. Most of the voices actually belong to Studio Ghibli employees, though! About forty volunteers gathered at Hayao Miyazaki's art studio, and the recording was later combined with the actors' voices.

■ Poster 1 features a bush warbler and plum blossoms more prominently than the Yamadas themselves. The design is modeled on a *hanafuda* playing card, and plays thematically on the warbler's cry of "ho-ho-ke-kyo," which was part of the Japanese title for the film.

POSTERS

Two comical posters were made for *My Neighbors the Yamadas*, in keeping with the original comic strip's tone.

■ The poster for a screening of Isao Takahata's films held in Korea in June 2006. *My Neighbors the Yamadas* didn't receive a general release in Korea, and was only screened there as part of events like these.

■ Poster 2 also plays on the bush warbler's song, and features an enlargement of a matchbook-sized drawing by Hisaichi Ishii, artist and writer of the original comic strip.

■ This full-page ad from the May 28, 1999 edition of the *Asahi Shimbun* used Poster 2 more or less unaltered.

NEWSPAPER ADS

The newspaper campaign started off with humorous drawings before transitioning to ads focused on the theme of family.

■ Starting with this film, advertising copy began to tout Isao Takahata as "one of Japan's leading directors." This 1/2-page ad from the May 31 *Nihon Keizai Shimbun* is one such example.

■ The June 18 *Asahi Shimbun* ad featured one of Miss Fujiwara's lines from the movie, and centered on her motto of "Don't overdo it," blown up from the film's storyboards.

■ Like the June 18 ad, this ad from the June 29 *Asahi Shimbun* prominently featured the motto "Don't overdo it" as an apt expression of the film's vibe.

■ The 1/2-page ad that ran in the *Yomiuri Shimbun* on June 30 used a scene of the Yamadas flying through the sky as the main image.

■ The July 9 *Mainichi Shimbun* ad used the same image as the ad from June 30, of the five Yamadas beaming as they float through the sky.

BEHIND THE SCENES

My Neighbors the Yamadas largely takes place around a low table called a *chabudai*, which gets converted into a heated *kotatsu* in the winter. Accordingly, the Ghibli office was outfitted with a woven rush mat and *chabudai* to use as a reference for gestures and poses. Production manager Osamu Tanabe referred to it daily, but it also became a nice break spot for the staff, who found it a "quintessentially Japanese" way to relax.

■ The trees bend aside, opening a path for the Cat Bus.

■ The Cat Bus races across the fields at full speed.

My Neighbor Totoro

The Cat Bus races in search of the lost Mei, with Satsuki inside. In addition to its whirlwind speed, the Cat Bus has other amazing abilities: eyes that become headlights, and the ability to leap into the sky and run across electrical wires. And then there's the enjoyment of seeing the trees bend out of the way so the Cat Bus can pass.

Castle in the Sky

Sheeta and Pazu run along the light rail tracks, pursued by both the military and Dola's clan of air pirates, all of whom are after the Levitation Crystal. Dodging gunfire from armored trains, they use the Crystal to escape by the skin of their teeth. This chase scene is a high point of the first half of the film.

GHIBLI DRAWS SPEED

Lively, dynamic movement is one of the attractions of a Ghibli film. Watching the characters race across the screen in various ways is exhilarating—Satsuki desperately running around looking for her little sister, or Seiji and Shizuku racing along on a bicycle after having glimpsed their futures. These depictions of speed also reflect the characters' emotions in the moment.

Kiki's Delivery Service

Tombo races along on his propeller bike with Kiki in tow, hoping to see the dirigible that made an emergency landing. During the closing credits, Tombo flies alongside Kiki in a pedal-powered aircraft. His knack for invention is a talent on par with Kiki's magic or Ursula's artistic skill.

Whisper of the Heart

Just before daybreak, Seiji's bike races through the hills with Shizuku on the back. Her desire for them to grow together is expressed in the scene where she gets off during an uphill climb and pushes the bike from behind. Here the bike is a prop to show the deepening of their relationship.

From Up on Poppy Hill

On her way down to the shopping district, Umi hitches a ride with the passing Shun, and they speed down the long, winding roads of Poppy Hill together on his bicycle. The animators used CG to draw the varied movements and create the depth of field and sense of the landscape rushing by.

The Cat Returns

The "cat raft" is one of the stranger conveyances ever dreamed up by Studio Ghibli. Haru, a high school student chosen to wed the prince of cats, is swept away by a horde of cats while discussing her situation with Baron, who follows the raft through a wormhole to the Cat Kingdom.

■ The cats carry Haru along like a raft.

■ The cat raft goes through a wormhole to the Cat Kingdom.

■ Ponyo runs with a school of fish.

Ponyo on the Cliff by the Sea

Fish-child Ponyo runs atop the giant school of fish her sisters have become, on her way to the human world where her favorite person, Sosuke, lives. She seems delighted when she finds Sosuke's car, but Ponyo's escape upsets the balance and causes a storm.

■ Lisa races through the storm in her car.

■ The princess sheds her twelve-layered kimono as she runs away down the road.

■ The princess's startling expression evinces rage, sorrow, and even madness.

My Neighbors the Yamadas

The scene where the Yamada patriarch Takashi tries and fails to tell off a biker gang features his generation's favorite superhero, the motorcycle-riding Moonlight Mask.

The Tale of The Princess Kaguya

On the night of the party held to celebrate her naming, Princess Kaguya hears guests gossiping about her. She flees the mansion in anger and despair at their mockery, racing down the main road of the capital and out into the grasslands and bamboo forests, with the moon as the only witness.

■ The intensity as the princess runs is expressed in the rush of the landscape going by.

■ Noboru and Nonoko run after Matsuko and Shige, who were kidnapped by ruffians.

■ In his imagination, Takashi becomes Moonlight Mask and rides to Matsuko and Shige's rescue.

In Hayao Miyazaki's fantasy gift to the girls of today, a strange land waits on the other side of a tunnel

SPIRITED AWAY   2001

Spirited Away was Hayao Miyazaki's first feature film in the four years since *Princess Mononoke* had become such a phenomenon. Every summer, Miyazaki spent time at a mountain cabin with his family and five young girls who were friends of theirs. As these girls grew into their early teens, he decided he wanted to make a film they could truly enjoy.

The heroine Chihiro is a somewhat listless ten-year-old who wanders into an alternate world. There, the witch Yubaba names her Sen and gives her a job at her bathhouse for gods. Through her experiences there, Sen (Chihiro) unconsciously acquires the strength to live. The film also features beings who represent microcosms of modern Japan, including No Face, whose unfettered appetites make him grow and run out of control, and the Stink Spirit, whose true form is completely obscured by the trash and sludge covering him. The setting is loaded with Miyazaki's signature brand of satire, the film's appeal embodied in the silent, forlorn No Face, who became especially popular. The emotional connection between Haku and Sen, and supporting characters like bathhouse worker Lin, boiler room superintendent Kamaji, and the soot sprites make *Spirited Away* an unforgettable delight.

The film was a massive hit, running for over a year and raking in a total of ¥30.8 billion at the box office, leading some to call it a "national anime." The 2020 rerelease also attracted a huge audience, and reestablished the film's popularity. The film was highly acclaimed overseas as well, winning many awards including the Academy Award for Best Animated Feature and the Golden Bear at the Berlin International Film Festival.

Release date: July 20, 2001
Running time: Approx. 125 minutes
© 2001 Studio Ghibli - NDDTM

Original Story, Screenplay Written and
Directed by ························· Hayao Miyazaki
Producer ··························· Toshio Suzuki
Music ······························ Joe Hisaishi
Supervising Animators ··········· Masashi Ando
                                   Kitaro Kosaka
                                   Megumi Kagawa
Art Director ······················ Yoji Takeshige
Color Design ····················· Michiyo Yasuda
Director of Digital Imaging ······· Atsushi Okui
Theme Song "Itsumo Nando-demo (Always with me)"
Performed by ····················· Youmi Kimura
Production ························· Studio Ghibli
Production Committee ············· Tokuma Shoten
                                   Studio Ghibli
                                   Nippon Television Network
                                   Dentsu
                                   Walt Disney Japan
                                   Tohokushinsha Film
                                   Mitsubishi

Chihiro ·························· Rumi Hiiragi
Haku ····························· Miyu Irino
Yubaba / Zeniba ················· Mari Natsuki
Chihiro's Father ················· Takashi Naito
Chihiro's Mother ················· Yasuko Sawaguchi
Frog-man ························· Tatsuya Gashuin
Boh ······························ Ryunosuke Kamiki
Lin ······························ Yumi Tamai
Frog-foreman ····················· Yo Oizumi
River-god ························ Koba Hayashi
Frog-headmaster ················· Tsunehiko Kamijo
Frog-manager ····················· Takehiko Ono
Kamaji ··························· Bunta Sugawara

STORY

Ten-year-old Chihiro wanders into a strange town with her parents, who are tempted by the delicious smells from a food stall…but after eating the food set out there, they transform into pigs. A boy who calls himself Haku comes to the terrified Chihiro's aid, and she ends up working at a bathhouse called the "Yuya," run by the witch Yubaba, where the myriad gods and spirits come to relax and refresh themselves.

Yubaba takes away Chihiro's name, and she starts working under the name "Sen." Desperate to rescue her parents who have been turned into pigs, Sen scrubs the great hall on her hands and knees, cleans the bathrooms, tends to the gods who visit the bathhouse… and as she does so, the power to live that has lain dormant inside her gradually awakens.

■ Chihiro rides the train to Zeniba's place to save Haku, accompanied by No Face and the transformed Boh and Yu-Bird.

■ As she rides on his back through the sky, Chihiro recalls the name of Haku's river.

■ No Face attempts to entice Chihiro with money, but she refuses.

■ After she finishes work, Chihiro eats her meal while looking out at the water below the bathhouse.

■ When Haku tells her that her precious Boh is missing, Yubaba bears down on him with a terrifying expression.

■ The scenery outside the train on the way to Zeniba's is vast and beautiful. The tracks back have disappeared.

■ Zeniba gives Chihiro and her companions a warm welcome.

TRIVIA

On March 26, 2001, Hayao Miyazaki held a production briefing for *Spirited Away* at the Edo-Tokyo Open Air Architectural Museum, an outdoor facility featuring relocated homes and shops built during the 16th-20th centuries. He did so because the museum, which he loves, had been a model for the film's setting: he used its so-called "billboard architecture" as a reference for the townscape around the bathhouse.

CHARACTERS

CHIHIRO

A perfectly average, if somewhat soft, 10-year-old girl. She wanders into a strange town, and finds within herself an unexpected strength and ability to adapt.

HAKU

A boy of about 12 who helps Chihiro when she wanders into the strange city, and continues to encourage her. As Yubaba's apprentice, he handles the accounts at the Yuya and studies magic with her.

CHIHIRO'S FATHER

An optimistic 38-year-old man with an unfounded confidence that he can make things work out.

CHIHIRO'S MOTHER

Pragmatic and strong-willed, at 35 she's every inch her husband's equal.

YUBABA

A witch with an immense head who runs the Yuya. Age unknown. Greedy, critical, and blunt, she gains control over people by taking away their names.

ZENIBA

Yubaba's older twin, though the two don't get along. She lives a quiet life in a house in Swamp Bottom.

KAMAJI

A six-armed old man who manages the boiler room in the basement of the Yuya. With the help of the Soot Sprites he boils the water and prepares the medicinal baths.

FROG-MAN

An employee of the Yuya who has the appearance of a frog.

FROG-HEADMASTER

A giant frog in charge of all the frogmen at the Yuya. He throws his weight around with his subordinates, but is totally subservient to Yubaba.

FROG-MANAGER

He assists the Frog-headmaster in handling the frogs.

BOH

Yubaba's son, literally a giant baby. Spoiled by his doting mother, he matures through his adventure with Chihiro.

LIN

A curt but kindhearted girl of about 14 who takes Chihiro under her wing at the Yuya.

FROG-FOREMAN

A giant frog who works at the attendant's booth. He manages the tags for the medicinal baths, and determines the type of bath each customer receives according to their status.

RADISH SPIRIT

A daikon radish spirit who wears a red loincloth and a red sake cup on his head.

STINK SPIRIT

His sludge-like body reeks, but he is in fact the spirit of a river polluted by humans' discarded trash. With Chihiro's help, he regains his true form: the body of a white snake with an old-man mask for a face.

NO FACE

A mysterious and melancholy man who wanders into the world of the Yuya from somewhere else, he has no self and can only speak in the borrowed voices of those he has swallowed.

KASHIRA

A trio of heads who live in Yubaba's room. They bounce around, saying, "Hey, hey."

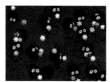

SOOT SPRITES

Kamaji's assistants who deliver coal to the boiler. Their favorite food is the sugar candy *konpeito*.

YU-BIRD

A guardian bird with a face exactly like Yubaba's.

HAKU (DRAGON)

Haku's other form, a white dragon named Nigihayami Kohakunushi, and the very river spirit who saved Chihiro when she almost drowned as a child.

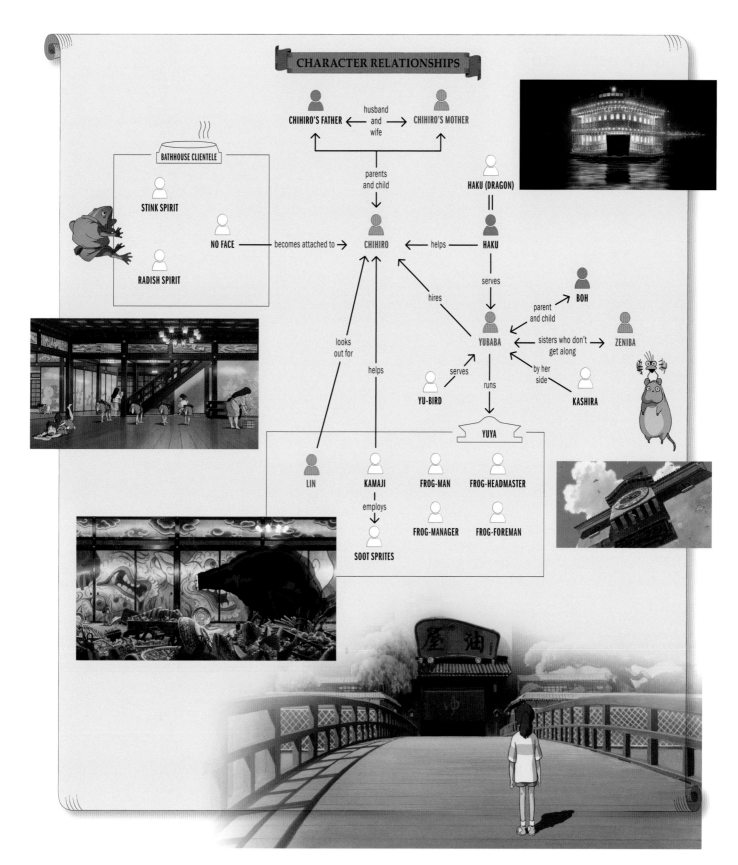

CHARACTER RELATIONSHIPS

BATHHOUSE CLIENTELE

STINK SPIRIT

RADISH SPIRIT

NO FACE — becomes attached to → CHIHIRO

CHIHIRO'S FATHER ← husband and wife → CHIHIRO'S MOTHER

parents and child

CHIHIRO ← helps — HAKU

HAKU (DRAGON) = HAKU

HAKU serves YUBABA

YUBABA — parent and child → BOH

YUBABA ← sisters who don't get along → ZENIBA

hires

YU-BIRD — serves → YUBABA

KASHIRA — by her side → YUBABA

YUBABA runs YUYA

looks out for

helps

LIN

KAMAJI employs → SOOT SPRITES

FROG-MAN

FROG-HEADMASTER

FROG-MANAGER

FROG-FOREMAN

YUYA

POSTERS

Three posters were created for the Japanese market, and with each successive poster, Chihiro's expression changed, demonstrating her awakening and her burgeoning will to live.

■ In Poster 2, Chihiro has had to begin working to survive, and there's a quiet strength in her eyes and posture.

■ Chihiro's expression in Poster 3 gives the sense that she has awakened to her own inner strength.

■ Poster 1. With her sulky expression, Chihiro looks like a typical 10-year-old.

NEWSPAPER ADS

The film was released on July 20, 2001 and ran in major theaters through April of the following year. Because of its long run, they were able to liven things up with a variety of ads featuring supporting characters and referring to current events.

■ The full-page ad that ran in the *Asahi Shimbun* on June 26, 2001 had a relatively simple design, featuring the image from Poster 2.

■ This full-page ad from the July 13 *Yomiuri Shimbun* won top prize in the Yomiuri Film Ad Awards.

■ Starting July 16, four days before the film's release, stick-out ads with different images and taglines ran each day in the *Sankei Shimbun*. They're shown here leading up to the release from left to right.

■ This full-color 1/2-page ad ran in the *Asahi Shimbun* on July 19, the day before the release. When Miyazaki saw the entire completed film, he said, "This is No Face's film." The ad uses a still from a scene between No Face and Chihiro.

■ Poster for the Korean release.

■ Alternate Korean poster.

■ The imagery used for the Brazilian poster was completely different from anything used in Japan.

■ The Australian poster was also very different from the Japanese posters.

■ The UK poster shows Chihiro and the Yuya against a black background.

■ Italian poster.

■ German poster.

■ The Russian poster used a different background than the Japanese poster.

■ The American poster also used a different background.

■ The background for the Chinese poster was different as well.

■ The Hong Kong poster was based on the Japanese version of Poster 2.

■ The 1/3-page ad that ran in the *Yomiuri Shimbun* on July 27, one week after the release, referred to the July 29 election with the tagline "A big hit, with an approval rating of 1,000%! This summer, let's go to the movies *and* the polls." The ad puns on Sen's name, written with the character for "1,000."

■ The 1/6-page ad that ran in the *Asahi Shimbun* on October 12 featured a previously unused picture of Chihiro's face, and the tagline "Ichiro, congrats on winning the batting title."

■ Chihiro doesn't appear in this 1/6-page ad from the January 1, 2002 *Asahi Shimbun*. Instead, No Face is front and center, with the tagline "Still hitting it big on New Year's Day."

■ The 1/4-page ad in the September 14 *Mainichi Shimbun* emphasized the theme of the "strength to live."

■ This 1/4-page ad from the October 5 *Asahi Shimbun* included a message of support for Ichiro Suzuki, as well as announcing the opening of the Ghibli Museum.

BEHIND THE SCENES

Originally, the story called for Zeniba to appear only after Yubaba's defeat; Chihiro, unable to resist her on her own, would take her down with Haku's help and reclaim her name and rescue her parents. This plotline would have made the film an unwieldy three hours plus, however, so the current storyline was adopted instead, with No Face getting more screen time.

Baron from Whisper of the Heart returns for this cat-filled fantasy

THE CAT RETURNS — 2002

The Cat Returns is based on an original manga by Aoi Hiiragi, author of *Whisper of the Heart,* created at Hayao Miyazaki's request. While not a direct sequel, it purports to be written by Shizuku Tsukishima, the protagonist of *Whisper of the Heart,* and features the return of Baron. The story itself is a fantastical adventure depicting Baron and his colleagues from the Cat Bureau's attempt to save Haru, a high school student who has been kidnapped and taken to the Cat Kingdom. The Cat Kingdom, ruled by the Cat King, is a peaceful, cheery land, and late riser Haru takes a shine to it, starting to think it might not be so bad to stay. But the Cat Kingdom turns out to be a place for people who have no control over their own time. The depictions of Haru slowly turning into a cat and of the tyrannical Cat King present an ironic take on humanity's tendency to be influenced by others, while the film itself is jammed with exciting showstoppers, like Haru's action-packed rescue. The way she matures after returning safely to her own world is also not to be missed.

Many staff from outside Studio Ghibli worked on the film, including animator Hiroyuki Morita, who directed, Reiko Yoshida, who wrote the screenplay, and Satoko Morikawa, who was in charge of character design and layouts. At the head of a similarly diverse cast, Tetsuro Tanba gives an idiosyncratic and commanding performance as the Cat King who takes a shine to Haru. Yoko Honna, who voiced Shizuku in *Whisper of the Heart,* also makes an appearance as Haru's classmate. Due to its shorter-than-average runtime, *The Cat Returns* was shown with *the GHIBLIES episode 2,* a collection of shorts.

Release date: July 20, 2002
Running time: Approx. 75 minutes
© 2002 Nekonote-Do - Studio Ghibli - NDHMT

Original Graphic Novel	Aoi Hiiragi
Screenplay	Reiko Yoshida
Director	Hiroyuki Morita
Project Concept	Hayao Miyazaki
General Producers	Toshio Suzuki
	Nozomu Takahashi
Music	Yuji Nomi
Character Design and Layout Design	Satoko Morikawa
Supervising Animators	Ei Inoue
	Kazutaka Ozaki
Art Director	Naoya Tanaka
Color Design	Osamu Mikasa
Theme Song "Kaze ni Naru (Like the Breeze)" Performed by	Ayano Tsuji
Production	Studio Ghibli
Production Committee	Tokuma Shoten
	Studio Ghibli
	Nippon Television Network
	Walt Disney Japan
	Hakuhodo
	Mitsubishi
	Toho

Haru	Chizuru Ikewaki
Baron	Yoshihiko Hakamada
Yuki	Aki Maeda
Lune	Takayuki Yamada
Hiromi	Hitomi Sato
Natori	Kenta Satoi
Natoru	Mari Hamada
Muta	Tetsu Watanabe
Toto	Yosuke Saito
Haru's Mother	Kumiko Okae
Cat King	Tetsuro Tanba

STORY

Seventeen-year-old Haru is a thoroughly average teenage girl. One day on her way home from school, she saves a cat from being hit by a truck, and the cat promptly stands up on its hind legs and thanks her in a human voice. He is Prince Lune, heir to the Cat Kingdom, and thus Haru earns the Cat King's gratitude—but the repayment of his debt comes in the form of a string of annoying gifts like foxtails, catnip, and mice. To top it all off, the Cat King invites Haru to his kingdom to become Lune's bride. Unsure of what to do, Haru follows the advice of a mysterious voice and seeks aid at the Cat Bureau—but a horde of cats arrives at the Bureau and whisks Haru off to the Cat Kingdom.

The Original Manga

Baron: The Cat Returns by Aoi Hiiragi (Tokuma Shoten)

A spin-off of *Whisper of the Heart* featuring the Baron, Moon, and the World Emporium. Aoi Hiiragi wrote this manga at Hayao Miyazaki's request, and it was published in May 2002. The conceit is that it's "a story written by Shizuku Tsukishima," and it's extremely popular with *Whisper of the Heart* fans.

CHARACTERS

HARU

An average, somewhat indecisive 17-year-old girl who lives with her mother. She has a crush on her classmate Machida, but lacks the initiative to do anything about it.

BARON

The calm, collected proprietor of the Cat Bureau. His real name is Baron Humbert von Gikkingen. A cat statuette by day, he comes to life when the sun sets.

MUTA

A comrade of Baron's who spends his time wandering around the city. Legend has it that in the days when he was known as Renaldo Moon, he ate up all the fish in the Cat Kingdom.

TOTO

A crow of Baron's acquaintance. He usually takes the form of a stone statue in the square outside the Cat Bureau, but comes to life when the sun sets just as Baron does.

CAT KING

King of the Cat Kingdom and Lune's father. Self-centered, he always has to have his way. He's a Persian, with a cat's-eye—the mark of the ruler—set upon his brow.

HARU'S MOTHER

Works at home making patchwork quilts. She's a strong woman who raised Haru on her own.

LUNE

The prince of the Cat Kingdom. Unlike his father, Lune is a gentleman. He goes to the land of the humans to get a present for Yuki, and there Haru saves him from being run over by a truck.

YUKI

A white cat who serves at the Cat King's castle, and Lune's sweetheart. She used to live in the human world, where Haru once gave her a cookie. It's Yuki who leads Haru to the Cat Bureau.

NATORI

First secretary to the Cat King, he serves the spoiled monarch without hesitation. Natori is a Siamese-Angora mix.

NATORU

Second secretary to the Cat King. Compared to the always-calm Natori, she's frivolous and a little glib. Natoru is a Scottish Fold, with the breed's characteristic drooping ears.

CHARACTER RELATIONSHIPS

■ A strange guest visits Haru's house the night after she saves the life of Lune, the Cat Prince.

■ Prince Lune's father, the Cat King himself, visits Haru's house and invites her to the Cat Kingdom.

■ At a loss as to how to respond to the Cat King's invitation, Haru hears a mysterious voice that leads her to the Cat Bureau...

■ Haru has begun turning into a cat in the Cat Kingdom, when Baron appears...

TRIVIA

In the original manga, the Cat Kingdom is depicted as a closed-off world filled with light. In the film, however, Morita and art director Naoya Tanaka transformed it into a languid, balmy land centered around the castle, with a rainbow of light pouring down from the sky. It's this that makes Haru consider staying in the Cat Kingdom for good.

■ Poster 1 shows Muta outside the Cat Bureau.

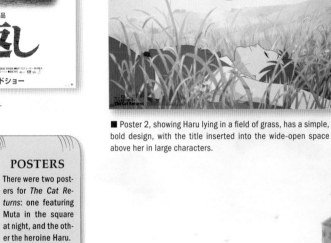

■ Poster 2, showing Haru lying in a field of grass, has a simple, bold design, with the title inserted into the wide-open space above her in large characters.

POSTERS

There were two posters for *The Cat Returns*: one featuring Muta in the square at night, and the other the heroine Haru.

■ Italian poster.

■ Korean poster.

■ UK poster.

■ The first ad announcing the double feature of *The Cat Returns* and *the GHIBLIES episode 2* was a stick-out ad in the June 14, 2002 edition of *Sports Nippon*.

■ The June 21 full-page ad that ran in the *Asahi Shimbun* used the image from Poster 1 in full color to create more impact.

■ A 1/6-page ad that ran in the *Seikyo Shimbun* on June 20.

NEWSPAPER ADS

Newspaper ads started running 25 days before the film's release. Virtually all of them used the image from Poster 2.

■ This poster for the Kodansha thirty-magazine co-op previews was designed as a hanging ad for trains.

BEHIND THE SCENES

This film started out as a project for a theme park, meant to rival Lotte World, an extremely popular Korean tourist attraction. An advertising agency asked Studio Ghibli to create an exclusive video for the park featuring a cat mascot, which eventually led to *The Cat Returns*.

An omnibus comedy featuring cartoon versions of actual Ghibli employees and collaborators

the GHIBLIES episode 2 — 2002

the GHIBLIES episode 2 is a collection of shorts depicting the daily life of the employees of fictional company "Studio Ghibli" (pronounced with a hard 'G,' unlike the real studio). An expanded sequel to the TV special the GHIBLIES that aired on NTV in 2000, it was released as part of a double feature with The Cat Returns. The characters, including Nonaka-kun and Yukari-san, derive from caricatures producer Toshio Suzuki doodled of Ghibli employees and collaborators. He himself appears as Toshi-chan, though in his case the character was designed by Hisaichi Ishii, the creator of the My Neighbors the Yamadas comic strip. the GHIBLIES episode 2 boasts a dazzling lineup of voice actors perfect for a live-action comedy, including Kaoru Kobayashi as Toshi-chan and Masahiko Nishimura as the protagonist Nonaka-kun.

The film is comprised of six episodes: Hot Curry, First Love, Afternoon, Dance, Beauty and the Nonaka, and Epilogue. Each with a unique feel, from the surreal slapstick of Hot Curry, where the characters take up an extra-hot curry eating challenge, to Nonaka-kun's heartwarming memories in First Love and the music video aesthetic of Dance, in which Yukari-san dances her heart out to relieve stress. Yoshiyuki Momose, writer and director of both the GHIBLIES and the GHIBLIES episode 2, is a crucial staff member who also worked with Isao Takahata on Grave of the Fireflies, Only Yesterday, and The Tale of The Princess Kaguya. He was in charge of CG for Miyazaki's Princess Mononoke as well, and utilized those skills to create this film's unique and appealing visuals.

STORY

Six episodes from the daily life of the Ghiblies, regular people who work at a fictional animation studio. Hot Curry tackles the constant quandary of where to eat lunch when you've worked at the same company for years. In search of a new experience, Nonaka-kun, Oku-chan, and Yukari-san head to a super-spicy curry place they've heard about, and do their best in the face of the overwhelming heat. In Beauty and the Nonaka, Nonaka-kun gets flustered when a beautiful woman falls asleep on his shoulder during the train ride home. Unable to push her off, he misses his stop and has to take a taxi home from the end of the line, since that was the last train. Kind and gentle Nonaka-kun's first love, we discover, was his elementary school classmate Ai-chan.

Release date: July 20, 2002
Running time: Approx. 25 minutes
© 2002 TS - Studio Ghibli - NDHMT

Original Characters Created by · Toshio Suzuki
Special Character Creation ··· Hisaichi Ishii
Screenplay Written and
Directed by ···················· Yoshiyuki Momose
General Producers ············ Toshio Suzuki
                                     Nozomu Takahashi
Music ···························· Manto Watanobe
Art Director ····················· Noboru Yoshida
Color Design ···················· Michiyo Yasuda
Song "No Woman, No Cry"
Performed by ··················· Tina
Production ······················ Studio Ghibli
Production Committee ········ Tokuma Shoten
                                     Studio Ghibli
                                     Nippon Television Network
                                     Walt Disney Japan
                                     Hakuhodo
                                     Mitsubishi
                                     Toho

Nonaka-kun ····················· Masahiko Nishimura
Yukari-san ······················ Kyoka Suzuki
Oku-chan ························· Arata Furuta
Toku-san ························· Satoru Saito
Hotaru-chan ····················· Tomoe Shinohara
Yone-chan ······················· Koji Imada
Toshi-chan ······················ Kaoru Kobayashi
                          *Shown with The Cat Returns

NONAKA-KUN

Section chief of the studio's copyright office. Single, 38 years old. He's always flustered thanks to his timid nature, but to everyone else he just appears to be doing things at his own pace.

YUKARI-SAN

An energetic career woman who heads the publishing department. Her age is a secret. Though a celebrated beauty, she's competitive and lacks attention to detail.

OKU-CHAN

The 42-year-old head of the studio's production department. He eats a lot and often falls asleep during meetings thanks to a full belly.

TOKU-SAN

58-year-old head of advertising. His dad jokes annoy everyone around him, but he doesn't notice.

HOTARU-CHAN

A 24-year-old animator. Adored by her colleagues both inside and outside the company, she's vigorous and outgoing, but also something of an airhead.

YONE-CHAN

The studio's 27-year-old PR person. Originally from Kansai, he used to be an industrial spy for a rival company, but he's since given that up.

TOSHI-CHAN

Proprietor of "Toshi-chan," a curry shop known for being cheap, as well as for its super-spicy challenge. He's an expert at roping people into his way of doing things. Originally from Nagoya, he's a big Chunichi Dragons fan.

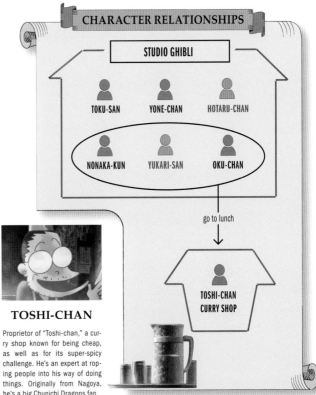

STUDIO GHIBLI

TOKU-SAN YONE-CHAN HOTARU-CHAN

NONAKA-KUN YUKARI-SAN OKU-CHAN

go to lunch

TOSHI-CHAN CURRY SHOP

■ the GHIBLIES episode 2 poster.

■ Nonaka-kun and Oku-chan talk about going to lunch early. Yukari-san comes along, and the three of them head to the curry shop.

■ Nonaka-kun, Oku-chan, and Yukari-san dance like crazy, with the color themes of red, blue, and yellow.

■ Toshi-chan, the owner, tells them the menu is on the wall. The three of them turn to look, and Yukari-san takes up the gauntlet.

■ Nonaka-kun's vague memories of first love. One is of a class photo, which was also used for the poster.

The CG in the GHIBLIES episode 2 is made to look like watercolors or colored pencil, but in fact it's mostly 3DCG, including the opening sequence when the Totoro logo turns around to become what appears to be a line drawing of Nonaka-kun.

Momose wanted the background and characters in each segment to feel seamless. *Hot Curry* uses an oil painting style to mirror the heavy, rich feel of the food, while for *Dance*, the art department created an over-the-top world based on imageboards drawn by the key animators.

The strange tale of the love between a handsome wizard and a very old woman

HOWL'S MOVING CASTLE   2004

Hayao Miyazaki followed up his unprecedented 2001 hit *Spirited Away* with this, his ninth feature, based on the 1986 novel by the British fantasy writer Diana Wynne Jones. Drawn to the moving castle and the idea of a heroine being turned into a 90-year-old woman, Miyazaki thought it would make a good film. The project originally proceeded with another director in place, but ran into problems and finally stalled. Ultimately, Miyazaki himself decided to direct.

He started by designing the moving castle, arguably the story's true protagonist, creating a unique building that was neither fully machine nor monster. The setting was modeled on the Alsace region of France, which Miyazaki had visited, and

the art deparment staff went location scouting there, bringing the feel of the old buildings and a uniquely European mood and light to the backgrounds.

The story centers around the romance between the heroine Sophie and the wizard Howl, but it's also something of a domestic drama, as the fire demon Calcifer, the scarecrow Turnip, and even the Witch of the Waste who curses Sophie become her found family. Another of the film's main attractions is the stunning array of voice actors, each more compelling than the last: Chieko Baisho voices Sophie from girlhood to old crone, Takuya Kimura plays Howl, who resists the King's order to aid in the war effort, and Haruko Kato plays the king's sorceress Suliman.

STORY

Howl, a wizard who lives in a massive moving castle and is rumored to eat the hearts of beautiful girls, rescues 18-year-old milliner Sophie when a soldier hits on her during a military parade through her town. But because of her interaction with Howl, Sophie is transformed into a 90-year-old woman by the Witch of the Waste, who is forever stalking the

wizard.

Sophie leaves home and takes up residence in Howl's castle as his housekeeper. As she spends her days living with the young boy Markl and fire demon Calcifer, she discovers that Howl is really a timid, kind youth, and she begins to fall in love with him. But as the war intensifies, danger closes in…

Release date: November 20, 2004
Running time: Approx. 119 minutes
© 2004 Studio Ghibli - NDDMT

From the Novel by	Diana Wynne Jones
Screenplay Written and Directed by	Hayao Miyazaki
Producer	Toshio Suzuki
Music	Joe Hisaishi
Supervising Animators	Akihiko Yamashita
	Takeshi Inamura
	Kitaro Kosaka
Art Directors	Yoji Takeshige
	Noboru Yoshida
Color Design	Michiyo Yasuda
Director of Digital Imaging	Atsushi Okui
Theme Song "Sekai no Yakusoku (The Universal Promise)" Performed by	Chieko Baisho
Production	Studio Ghibli
Production Committee	Tokuma Shoten
	Studio Ghibli
	Nippon Television Network
	Dentsu
	Walt Disney Japan
	Mitsubishi
	Toho

Sophie	Chieko Baisho
Howl	Takuya Kimura
Witch of the Waste	Akihiro Miwa
Calcifer	Tatsuya Gashuin
Markl	Ryunosuke Kamiki
Turnip	Yo Oizumi
King	Akio Otsuka
Heen	Daijiro Harada
Suliman	Haruko Kato

The Original Novel

◆ *Howl's Moving Castle* by Diana Wynne Jones, 1986
◇ Japanese edition translated by Junko Nishimura (Tokuma Shoten)

A popular series by the author of *Charmed Life*, for which she won the Guardian children's fiction prize. The characters are more complex in the novel, and the story is more of a rollercoaster ride. Howl and Sophie also appear in two later books.

CHARACTERS

SOPHIE

Eldest daughter of the owners of Hatter's Hat Shop, where she took over after her father's death. Transformed into a 90-year-old woman by the Witch of the Waste, she takes up residence in Howl's castle.

HOWL

Wizard and master of a gigantic moving castle, he goes by many names, including Jenkins and Pendragon. A lovely youth with great powers, he nevertheless idles away his days.

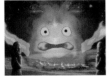

WITCH OF THE WASTE

A witch forever on Howl's tail. Once the king's royal sorceress, she lives secretly in the wastelands after being chased out of the court fifty years ago.

CALCIFER

A fire demon who lives in the fireplace at Howl's castle and keeps the massive structure moving. Bound by his contract with Howl, he can't leave the hearth, but he thirsts for freedom.

MARKL

Howl's orphaned apprentice. He takes on the appearance of an old man to deal with guests who visit the castle.

TURNIP

A scarecrow with a turnip for a head. He follows Sophie after she saves him in the wastelands.

HEEN

An old dog named for his bark, which sounds like a sneeze. He is Suliman's familiar, but becomes attached to Sophie for some reason.

SULIMAN

A sorceress who serves the royal family of Kingsbury. Howl's former master, she possesses great magic and is the true power behind the throne.

CHARACTER RELATIONSHIPS

■ Howl rescues 18-year-old Sophie from a sticky situation during a military parade through her town.

■ Because of her interaction with Howl, Sophie is turned into a 90-year-old woman by the Witch of the Waste.

■ Transformed into an old woman, Sophie travels to the wastelands to find Howl's castle.

■ Sophie joins the castle household as Howl's housekeeper.

TRIVIA

Miyazaki was intrigued by the moving castle of the book's title, but struggled with the castle's design. He went to consult producer Toshio Suzuki, and as they talked, he drew in the cannons, roofs, and chimneys which would adorn the finished product in the film. He wavered between using chicken's feet or the feet of medieval foot soldiers, but ultimately opted for the former.

この城が動く。

■ Poster 1. Alongside the dramatic image of the moving castle, which looks like it might pop right out of the poster, the straightforward tagline "This castle moves" builds a sense of anticipation.

ふたりが暮らした。

■ Poster 2. Based on an idea of producer Toshio Suzuki's, there's something unexpected about this image, which foregrounds Sophie as an old woman.

未来で待ってて。私、きっと行くから。

■ Poster 3 features Howl as a boy and Sophie as she appears in the last half of the movie, accompanied by a dramatic line from the film.

ふたりが暮らした。

■ The campaign for Howl's used an abundance of color, starting with this full-page ad that ran in the Asahi Shimbun, Yomiuri Shimbun, and Mainichi Shimbun on October 22, 2004.

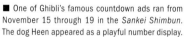

■ One of Ghibli's famous countdown ads ran from November 15 through 19 in the Sankei Shimbun. The dog Heen appeared as a playful number display.

■ As the release date approached, ads like this one from the November 19 Asahi Shimbun began to feature a young, handsome Howl with the aged Sophie.

■ UK poster.

■ Alternate UK poster.

■ Russian poster.

■ North American poster.

■ Polish poster.

■ Taiwanese poster.

■ German poster.

■ Hong Kong poster.

■ Mexican poster.

■ Italian poster.

■ Australian poster.

■ Portuguese poster.

■ Swedish poster.

■ Sophie's cheerful smile in this December 21 *Yomiuri Shimbun* full-page color ad makes a lasting impression. The message "Shows have been sold out every day and every night—thank you!" was added in producer Toshio Suzuki's own handwriting.

■ The February 4, 2005 ad that ran in the *Asahi Shimbun* was created with Valentine's Day in mind. Ads targeted at other seasonal events, including Girls' Day, followed during the film's long run.

■ This February 18 *Asahi Shimbun* ad celebrated the fact that director Hayao Miyazaki had received the Golden Lion for Lifetime Achievement at the Venice Film Festival, and included a message of gratitude to audiences around the world.

■ This ad from the April 15 edition of the *Asahi Shimbun* announced that the venues would change, but the film would continue its run. It used a still from the credits of the castle flying off into the sky, with the clever tagline "It's moving day!"

BEHIND THE SCENES

In the scene where Sophie and the Witch of the Waste ascend the long staircase in the royal palace, Sophie was originally intended to stop and hold out her hand to the Witch. After this scene was assigned to master animator Shinji Otsuka, however, Miyazaki doubled its length and left the details up to him. The result is the memorable scene where the two compete as they desperately struggle up the stairs.

93

■ Ashitaka tries to stop the demon god from reaching the village.

■ San storms Iron Town to avenge the wounded Moro.

Princess Mononoke

A film depicting the battle between the spirit guardians of the forest and the humans who clear the land and defile nature, with San and Lady Eboshi respectively representing the two sides. Cursed after he slays the demon god, Ashitaka learns that hate and resentment only serve to destroy, and he tries to stop the battle between the two.

■ Ashitaka spots the demon god from the watchtower.

■ The showdown between San and Lady Eboshi.

■ Fleeing from an air raid, Seita and Setsuko take shelter near the mouth of the river.

■ The demon god curses Ashitaka's right arm.

■ Ashitaka gets between them.

■ The still-burning town after it has been leveled in an air raid.

GHIBLI DRAWS
BATTLE

Ghibli protagonists fight all manner of things, engaging in fierce battles to protect people and save the world. Some Ghibli films even turn an eye to the historical tragedies of real wars. Action scenes that are purely about the joy of animation and characters' internal conflicts both constitute "battles" as well. The dramatic emotion and excitement these different kinds of battle create are part of what makes Ghibli films so much fun to watch time and time again.

■ Seita is reunited with his mother, who is on the verge of death.

Grave of the Fireflies

The air attack on Kobe during World War II shatters a brother and sister's happiness, dramatically altering their fates. Images of Seita and Setsuko's gravely injured mother and the town engulfed in the raging flames of incendiary bombs make the horrors of war intensely real.

■ Nausicaä goes into a frenzy when she hears of her father's death.

■ The Giant Warriors lay waste to an entire city.

■ Yupa takes the Tolmekian soldiers by surprise.

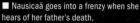

Nausicaä of the Valley of the Wind

Under Kushana's command, the Tolmekian army is trying to revive the Giant Warriors and reignite the flames of war. The film depicts Nausicaä and her allies' attempt to stop them, and is filled with show-stopping sequences of Nausicaä and master swordsman Lord Yupa in action.

■ Yupa stops Nausicaä's frenzy using his own body as a shield.

■ The Giant Warrior attacks the Ohm on Kushana's orders.

■ Yupa uses his two-sword style to save others.

■ A giant skeleton borrowed from a woodblock print by Utagawa Kuniyoshi.

■ The children are delighted by a miniature Raijin, god of thunder.

■ Operation Specter passes behind two men drinking at a food stall.

Pom Poko

The tanuki finally stand up and fight back against the humans who have stolen their habitat, using their shapeshifting abilities to frighten them away—just the kind of plan the easygoing tanuki would hatch. After vigorous training they stage Operation Specter, but a theme park owner claims it was a PR stunt, snatching away their hard-won victory.

■ A giant Fukusuke doll bows to the crowd.

■ Walking bridge girders make their way across the tennis courts.

■ Tiny Awa Odori dancers also put in an appearance.

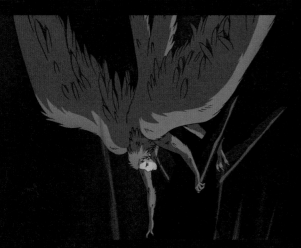
■ Howl protects Sophie by grabbing onto a bomb and turning it into a dud.

■ A bomber attacks Sophie's town.

Howl's Moving Castle

The powerful sorceress Suliman leads Sophie's country into war. The king orders Howl, Suliman's former apprentice, to aid the war effort, but Howl continually evades the king's men and demonstrates his intentions by interfering with combat.

■ Air pirates surround Porco on all sides.

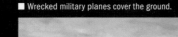
■ Wrecked military planes cover the ground.

■ Porco and Curtis's decisive battle draws a big crowd.

Porco Rosso

There's bad blood between bounty hunter Porco and the air pirates—they're always at each other's throats, but because they're a good-natured bunch at heart, kind to women and children, the fights never get too serious. Even Porco and Curtis's final duel for the honor of Fio, Master Piccolo's granddaughter, comes down to simple fisticuffs in the end.

The Wind Rises

Jiro's effort to create the ideal aircraft gets swallowed up by the war, resulting in a sea of wrecked planes. Most of the soldiers who went off to fight didn't return, and the film expresses the hollow futility of war without ever showing the battles themselves. Encouraged by the words of his late wife Nahoko, Jiro lives on to shape the post-war history of the airplane.

■ Jiro and company watch as a formation of fighters flies off to battle.

For his first film, Goro Miyazaki adapts the fantasy classic that influenced his father

TALES FROM EARTHSEA
2006

Tales from Earthsea is an adaptation of Ursula K. Le Guin's classic fantasy series, which has continued to enjoy an international readership since the publication of its first volume in 1968. Hayao Miyazaki ranks them among his favorite books, and acknowledges their huge influence on his work, from *Nausicaä of the Valley of the Wind* to the graphic novel *Shuna's Journey*. He had contacted the author about a film adaptation only to be turned down, but the project finally got off the ground after the author, having since become a Ghibli fan, in turn contacted the studio in 2003 to sound out Hayao Miyazaki about adapting the *Earthsea* books. Goro Miyazaki, Hayao's eldest son, was involved in the exploratory side of the project from the start, and was ultimately chosen as director.

Goro had served as head of Ghibli Museum, Mita-ka since its opening, but had never made an animated film or even drawn storyboards. He had been studying his father's work in his own way, however, and stunned Ghibli's staff by turning out highly polished storyboards right off the bat.

The film tells the story of Prince Arren, who wanders aimlessly until he meets Archmage Sparrowhawk (Ged) and a girl named Therru. Through his battle with the evil warlock Lord Cob, Prince Arren matures and finds his path. *The Farthest Shore*, the third book in the *Earthsea* series, forms the core of the film, with additional characters and backgrounds brought in from Hayao Miyazaki's *Shuna's Journey*. As such, it is a sort of Miyazaki father-son collaboration through the medium of Le Guin's novels.

Release date: July 29, 2006
Running time: Approx. 115 minutes
© 2006 Studio Ghibli - NDHDMT

Based on the "Earthsea" Series by	Ursula K. Le Guin
Inspired by "Shuna's Journey" by	Hayao Miyazaki
Screenplay	Goro Miyazaki
	Keiko Niwa
Director	Goro Miyazaki
Producer	Toshio Suzuki
Music	Tamiya Terashima
Directing Animator	Akihiko Yamashita
Supervising Animator	Takeshi Inamura
Art Director	Yoji Takeshige
Color Design	Michiyo Yasuda
Director of Digital Imaging	Atsushi Okui
Theme Song "Toki no Uta (Song of Time)" / Image Song "Therru no Uta (Therru's Song)" Performed by	Aoi Teshima
Production	Studio Ghibli
Production Committee	Studio Ghibli
	Nippon Television Network
	Dentsu
	Hakuhodo DY Media Partners
	Walt Disney Japan
	Mitsubishi
	Toho

Arren	Junichi Okada
Therru	Aoi Teshima
Cob	Yuko Tanaka
Hare	Teruyuki Kagawa
Tenar	Jun Fubuki
Hazia Pusher	Takashi Naito
Shop Lady	Mitsuko Baisho
Queen	Yui Natsukawa
King	Kaoru Kobayashi
Sparrowhawk (Ged)	Bunta Sugawara

STORY

The film takes place in Earthsea, also known as the Archipelago World, a vast ocean dotted with islands. Humans have settled in the east, and in the west live dragons, who don't meddle in human affairs—until they suddenly begin to appear where they never had before. As if in response, crops start to wither and livestock die across the land. The balance of the world is crumbling.

A powerful sorcerer named Ged sets out to discover the source of this calamity, and in the course of his journey meets Prince Arren of Enlad. Arren is haunted by the darkness in his heart and lives in fear of the mysterious "shadow" that stalks him. As they travel together, Ged discovers that behind the collapse is Lord Cob, a warlock whom he once defeated in battle. In fear of his own mortality, Cob is upsetting the balance with his attempts to acquire eternal life.

The Original Novels

◆ **The Earthsea Cycle** by Ursula K. Le Guin, 1968-2001, 5 volumes + short stories
◇ Japanese edition translated by Masako Shimizu (Iwanami Shoten)

An epic fantasy series set in a world where magic is real, written by "the Queen of Science Fiction," Ursula K. Le Guin. It has influenced many writers and directors, including Hayao Miyazaki, and is one of the world's three great works of fantasy along with *The Lord of the Rings* and *The Chronicles of Narnia*. Another book that had a huge impact on the film was Hayao Miyazaki's *Shuna's Journey* (Tokuma Shoten), a full-color graphic novel based on the Tibetan folk tale "The Prince who Became a Dog." *Shuna's Journey* shows the profound philosophical influence of Le Guin's *Earthsea Cycle*, as do *Nausicaä of the Valley of the Wind* and *Princess Mononoke*.

CHARACTERS

ARREN

The prince of Enlad. Though he wanted for nothing during his life in the castle of his worthy parents, he leaves his country after killing his father the king. In the course of his subsequent travels, he meets Ged.

THERRU

A girl with a burn scar on her face. She was abused and abandoned by her parents, and now lives with Tenar, the only person she trusts.

SPARROWHAWK (GED)

Known as the Archmage, he is the most powerful sorcerer in Earthsea. Discovering that the world's balance is collapsing, he leaves on a journey to find the cause.

COB

So afraid of death that he has lost his grasp on the meaning of life, Cob opens the door between life and death in an attempt to gain immortality. He hates Sparrowhawk because of something that happened in the past.

HAZIA PUSHER

Recommends the narcotic Hazia to Arren, who lives in fear of a "shadow." Regular use of Hazia impairs both body and mind, eventually leading to death.

SHOP LADY

The owner of a shop that sells only imitation fabrics. Formerly a fortune teller, she has lost the ability to believe in magic because of the balance's collapse.

HARE

A slaver and the leader of Cob's minions. He is a coward who nevertheless behaves outrageously, hiding behind Cob's power.

TENAR

Ged's old friend. As a girl she served as shrine maiden at the Tombs of Atuan until Ged rescued her. Widowed, she now lives alone with Therru.

QUEEN

Queen of Enlad and Arren's mother. She is strict with him, knowing that he will take the throne someday.

KING

Enlad's king and Arren's father. Renowned for his wisdom, he thinks only of his people and dedicates himself day and night to affairs of state.

CHARACTER RELATIONSHIPS

■ Surrounded by a wolf pack in the desert, Arren tries to harness his rage and fight, but...

■ Helped out of a tight spot by Ged, Arren decides to travel with the mage for a while.

■ In Hort Town, Arren comes upon Therru in Hare's clutches.

■ Fleeing in terror from his own shadow, Arren loses consciousness and is saved by the warlock Cob...

TRIVIA

Injured and in the depths of despair, Arren regains his strength after he meets Ged and goes to help out on Tenar's farm. Goro Miyazaki added this scene to the film based on his own experience as director of the Ghibli Museum: through his work with the young staff there, he realized that people forget their worries when they labor under the sun.

■ Poster 2 is based on Hayao Miyazaki's rough sketch of Hort Town, where the film is set.

POSTERS

There were two posters made for the film, each with its own tagline designed to suit the image.

■ Poster 1. The drawing is based on a rough sketch Goro Miyazaki made from his impression of the original novels.

NEWSPAPER ADS

In addition to the poster images, a number of different ads were created featuring the protagonists Arren and Therru.

■ Full-page color ads ran in the July 7, 2006 editions of the *Mainichi Shimbun*, *Nikkei Shimbun*, *Sankei Shimbun*, and Tokyo *Shimbun*.

■ Early ads, like this one from the July 21 *Yomiuri Shimbun*, showed Arren and Therru with contrasting expressions.

■ On July 28, the day before the release, color ads ran in many papers, including the *Sankei Shimbun*, *Nikkei Shimbun*, Tokyo *Shimbun*, *Evening Fuji*, and *Nikkan Gendai*.

■ Italian poster.

■ North American poster.

■ Korean poster.

■ Alternate Hong Kong poster.

■ Hong Kong poster.

■ French poster.

■ UK poster.

■ This ad, which ran on August 11 in the *Asahi Shimbun* and *Yomiuri Shimbun*, featured a message of thanks from producer Toshio Suzuki to director Goro Miyazaki.

■ The warlock Cob, who lusts after eternal life, dominates this ad that ran in the September 1 editions of the *Asahi Shimbun* and *Yomiuri Shimbun*.

■ This August 25 *Asahi Shimbun* ad memorably included a message to the film's cast in Toshio Suzuki's own handwriting.

BEHIND THE SCENES

Goro Miyazaki referred back to Sakutaro Hagiwara's poem "Heart" when he was writing the lyrics for "Therru's Song"—all the characters who appear in the film are lonely or isolated, and the poem expresses this same feeling. The director's firm belief that to live is to share things with other people is embedded in the finished lyric.

In this aquatic fantasy, a fish named Ponyo falls in love with a human and brings about a miracle

PONYO ON THE CLIFF BY THE SEA   2008

Ponyo on the Cliff by the Sea was Hayao Miyazaki's 10th theatrical animated feature, and the first with an original story since 2001's *Spirited Away*. While on a Ghibli company retreat in a town on the Seto Inland Sea, Miyazaki was taken with his lodgings on a cliff overlooking the water and started kicking around ideas for his new film. During his stay there, he immersed himself in Natsume Soseki's novel *The Gate*, which inspired the film's title and the protagonist's name. He added various elements to create a modest love story between Ponyo, a fish child, and a human boy named Sosuke.

Miyazaki had two aims with this film: to create a viscerally entertaining film for all ages, including very young children; and to showcase the joy of traditional hand-drawn animation at a time when CG was becoming the norm. In addition to focusing on Sosuke and his nursery-school classmates, Miyazaki wrote scenes for each of the characters to shine, from Sosuke's mother Lisa to the energetic old ladies from the adult day care center. The film is striking in its focus on female characters, including Ponyo's mother, the mystical Gran Mamare.

Ghibli films are known for their detailed, realistic backgrounds, but with *Ponyo*, Miyazaki opted for a simple, colorful style reminiscent of picture books. This harmonizes with the hand-drawn characters and gentle movements, and part of the film's fun lies in this return to animation's origins.

 STORY

Five-year-old Sosuke lives in a house on a cliff in a small seaside town. One day he encounters a red fish girl, whom he names Ponyo and dotes on tenderly. Ponyo, who was raised in the sea by her father Fujimoto, had decided she wanted to see the outside world and rode to the surface on a jellyfish. Sosuke and Ponyo fall in love, but Fujimoto takes Ponyo back to the sea.

In her desire to see Sosuke again, she uses "The Water of Life," a dangerous, powerful liquid Fujimoto created by refining sea water, to transform into a human girl. Reunited with Sosuke, they both rejoice. But some Water of Life leaks out into the ocean, causing a massive storm and sending the town sinking into the sea…

Release date: July 19, 2008
Running time: Approx. 101 minutes
© 2008 Studio Ghibli - NDHDMT

Original Story, Screenplay Written and
Directed by ················· Hayao Miyazaki
Producer ····················· Toshio Suzuki
Executive Producer ··········· Koji Hoshino
Music ······················· Joe Hisaishi
Animation ···················· Katsuya Kondo
Backgrounds ·················· Noboru Yoshida
Color Design ················· Michiyo Yasuda
Imaging ······················ Atsushi Okui
Theme Song "Umi no Okasan (Mother Sea)"
Performed by ················· Masako Hayashi
"Gake no Ue no Ponyo (Ponyo on the Cliff by the Sea)"
Performed by ··········· FUJIOKA FUJIMAKI &
                        Nozomi Ohashi
Production ··················· Studio Ghibli
Production Committee ········· Studio Ghibli
                        Nippon Television Network
                        Dentsu
                        Hakuhodo DY Media Partners
                        Walt Disney Japan
                        Mitsubishi
                        Toho

Lisa ························· Tomoko Yamaguchi
Koichi ······················ Kazushige Nagashima
Gran Mamare ················· Yuki Amami
Fujimoto ···················· George Tokoro
Ponyo ······················· Yuria Nara
Sosuke ······················ Hiroki Doi
Young Woman ················· Rumi Hiiragi
Ponyo's Sisters ············· Akiko Yano
Toki ························· Kazuko Yoshiyuki
Yoshie ······················ Tomoko Naraoka

CHARACTERS

PONYO

An extremely curious fish girl who rebels against her restrictive father and runs away. Ponyo is the name Sosuke gives her, but her real one is Brunhilde. Her favorite food is ham.

SOSUKE

An intelligent, sincere boy of five who lives in a house on a cliff overlooking the sea. He takes a shine to Ponyo, who he meets on the beach, and swears to protect her.

LISA

Sosuke's mother. Because her husband is away at sea so often, she largely takes care of the house and her son on her own, while also working at Sunflower House, an adult day care center.

KOICHI

Sosuke's father and the captain of the *Koganei-Maru*, a coastal freighter. An old-fashioned seafarer, he's rarely home because of his job, but he loves his family deeply.

GRAN MAMARE

Ponyo's mother. A majestic presence like Mother Ocean herself, she has watched over the creatures of the sea since ancient times. She can change her size at will.

FUJIMOTO

Ponyo's father. He was once a human being, but disgusted with his race's pollution of the oceans, he chose to abandon life on shore and live with the creatures of the sea.

PONYO'S SISTERS

Fish girls raised by Fujimoto. They move in schools, and always support their beloved older sister Ponyo.

TOKI

An old woman who spends time at Sunflower House. Cynical and rude to Sosuke, she is in fact kind at heart and just doesn't know how to express her affection.

YOSHIE

One of the old ladies who come to Sunflower House. As her plump appearance suggests, Yoshie is easygoing and always looks forward to Sosuke's visits.

KAYO

Another old woman who comes to Sunflower House.

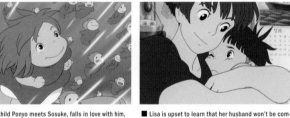

CHARACTER RELATIONSHIPS

SUNFLOWER HOUSE

GRAN MAMARE — husband and wife → FUJIMOTO

TOKI   YOSHIE   KAYO

parents and children — rooting for — good friends

PONYO'S SISTERS ← siblings → PONYO ← love each other → SOSUKE — takes care of

saves

parents and child

LISA ← husband and wife → KOICHI

■ Fish child Ponyo meets Sosuke, falls in love with him, and escapes from the sea.

■ Lisa is upset to learn that her husband won't be coming home again today, but she cheers up with Sosuke's encouragement.

■ Gran Mamare comes up with a solution when she learns that Ponyo has gone to be with the humans...

■ Ponyo decides to remain a human on shore with Sosuke...

TRIVIA

Toki is modeled on Hayao Miyazaki's own mother. Though it was ultimately shortened, the scene at the end of the film in which Toki and the other old ladies frolic in a place resembling heaven was much longer in the storyboards, perhaps because the director was imagining his mother in the afterlife.

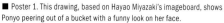

■ Poster 1. This drawing, based on Hayao Miyazaki's imageboard, shows Ponyo peering out of a bucket with a funny look on her face.

■ Poster 2. It was producer Toshio Suzuki's idea to use the scene where Ponyo and Sosuke meet.

■ This full-page color ad that ran in the *Asahi Shimbun* and *Yomiuri Shimbun* on June 20, 2008, used the image from Poster 2 with the tagline "It's great to be alive!"

■ The now-customary Ghibli countdown ads began on July 15 in the *Sankei Shimbun*.

■ On July 18, the day before the release, an ad with Ponyo running atop a school of fish was carried in the *Nihon Keizai Shimbun* and other papers.

■ French poster.

■ Alternate French poster.

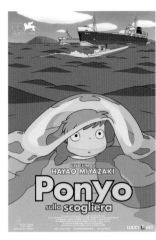

■ Italian poster.

■ Korean poster.

■ Australian poster.

■ Alternate Spanish poster.

■ Spanish poster.

■ Taiwanese poster.

■ North American poster.

■ Singaporean poster.

■ The copy for this 1/3-page ad from the August 15 *Yomiuri Shimbun* paired a line from the movie with a message thanking audiences for the "super-full houses."

■ The ad that ran in the *Asahi Shimbun* and *Yomiuri Shimbun* on August 29, as summer vacation drew to a close, used underwater creatures to create a summery feeling.

■ This ad announcing an extended theatrical run appeared in the *Asahi Shimbun* and *Yomiuri Shimbun* on October 3, and featured a dynamic still from the film.

■ This ad designed especially for the Christmas season ran in the *Asahi Shimbun* and *Yomiuri Shimbun* on December 19.

■ This December 26 *Asahi Shimbun* ad featured a joyful Ponyo, and announced that Nozomi Ohashi and FUJIOKA FUJIMAKI, who performed the theme song, would appear in NHK's annual New Year's Eve singing contest.

BEHIND THE SCENES

In February of 2006, Miyazaki went on a research trip to England, where he saw John Everett Millais's painting *Ophelia*. He was stunned to discover that what he and his colleagues were trying to do "had already been accomplished in oils 140-plus years ago." This was his impetus to change course on the film from a "highly precise maturity to simplicity."

Ghibli animator Hiromasa Yonebayashi makes his directorial debut with this film about a world of tiny people living under the floor

ARRIETTY

2010

Release date: July 17, 2010
Running time: Approx. 94 minutes
© 2010 Studio Ghibli - NDHDMTW

After *Whisper of the Heart*'s Yoshifumi Kondo in 1995 and *Tales from Earthsea*'s Goro Miyazaki in 2006, Hiromasa Yonebayashi was the third new director to emerge from Studio Ghibli, which he had joined in 1996. His work on *Ponyo on the Cliff by the Sea*—in particular the scene where Ponyo made for land atop a school of fish—stunned Hayao Miyazaki, and it was this exceptional display of the animator's craft that led to his selection as director for *Arrietty*.

The Borrowers, the book on which the film is based, is a 1952 children's fantasy by British author Mary Norton. Miyazaki read the novel during his days at Toei Animation and had even considered adapting the book with Isao Takahata. Forty-odd years later, the film became reality as a Studio Ghibli project, with Miyazaki and Keiko Niwa co-writing the screenplay. They made some changes, including moving the setting to Japan, but the Borrowers' names remained the same. And for the first time ever, Ghibli asked a foreign musician, Cécile Corbel, to sing the theme song because they felt it best fit the film's mood.

Although the story is a fantasy, part of the film's success lies in the realistic depiction of the Borrowers' everyday life, as they cleverly put to use the small items they "borrow" from the humans. Two peoples and two worlds that were never supposed to meet come together for a brief time when Arrietty and the human boy Sho connect in something resembling first love before parting once more. The ending, both a separation and a journey's beginning, leaves viewers with the combination of Arrietty's hope, as she matures into an adult, and a lingering sadness for the fate of the Borrowers, who are being driven to extinction by the humans.

Based on "The Borrowers" by	Mary Norton
Screenplay	Hayao Miyazaki
	Keiko Niwa
Director	Hiromasa Yonebayashi
Planning	Hayao Miyazaki
Producer	Toshio Suzuki
Executive Producer	Koji Hoshino
Music	Cécile Corbel
Supervising Animators	Megumi Kagawa
	Akihiko Yamashita
Art Directors	Yoji Takeshige
	Noboru Yoshida
Color Design	Naomi Mori
Director of Digital Imaging	Atsushi Okui
Theme Song "Arrietty's Song"	
Performed by	Cécile Corbel
Production	Studio Ghibli
Production Committee	Studio Ghibli
	Nippon Television Network
	Dentsu
	Hakuhodo DY Media Partners
	Walt Disney Japan
	Mitsubishi
	Toho
	Wild Bunch

Arrietty	Mirai Shida
Sho	Ryunosuke Kamiki
Homily	Shinobu Otake
Sadako	Keiko Takeshita
Spiller	Tatsuya Fujiwara
Pod	Tomokazu Miura
Haru	Kirin Kiki

STORY

Arrietty, a young Borrower, lives with her mother and father under the floor of an old mansion. The Borrowers' code is "Never be seen by humans," so Arrietty and her family "borrow" what they need to live without revealing their presence to the occupants.

One day, a boy named Sho comes to the house to convalesce. That evening he sees Arrietty, who has gone out with her father for her first "borrowing." To top it all off, Arrietty drops the sugar cube she "borrowed" from the kitchen. Little by little, Arrietty and Sho start to become closer, but this puts Arrietty and her entire family in danger.

The Original Books

◈ *The Borrowers* series by Mary Norton, 1952-1983, 5 volumes
◇ Japanese edition volumes 1-4 translated by Yokichi Hayashi, volume 5 translated by Yoko Inokuma (Iwanami Shoten)

Pioneering British children's writer Mary Norton broke new ground in the fantasy genre with these adventures about "little people without magical powers," which won her the Carnegie Prize. There are also a number of live-action adaptations of the series, including one by the BBC.

CHARACTERS

ARRIETTY

A 14-year-old Borrower who lives under the floor of an old mansion with her parents. Cheerful and energetic, she also has a reckless streak.

SHO

A 12-year-old boy. He goes to the house where his mother was raised to rest up before surgery for a congenital heart condition, and there he encounters Arrietty.

HOMILY

Arrietty's mother, who manages the household. She's always worried about free-spirited Arrietty and her husband Pod, who goes out to do the dangerous work of "borrowing."

SADAKO

Sho's mild-mannered great aunt and the owner of the old mansion. Her late father told her about seeing little people in the house.

SPILLER

A 12-year-old Borrower who lives a rugged life outside the house. He uses a bow to hunt.

POD

Arrietty's father. To obtain the essentials, he goes above the floor and "borrows" things from the humans who live there. He made things like his family's furniture and dishes himself.

HARU

A live-in housekeeper who's been at Sadako's for many years. Intensely curious, she thinks Sho is acting strangely, and discovers the Borrowers' home.

NIYA

The mansion's cat, who knows the Borrowers live under the floor. He gets attached to Sho.

CHARACTER RELATIONSHIPS

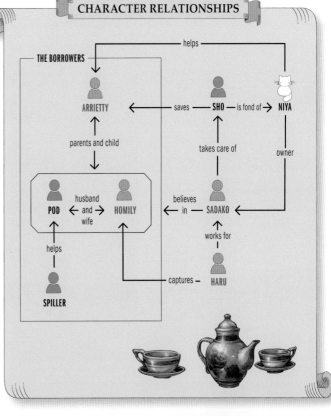

■ Borrower Arrietty loves to gather flowers and leaves from the garden of the old mansion where she lives.

■ Arrietty is enjoying tea with her mother and father as usual in their home under the floor, when...

■ Arrietty shows herself to Sho, breaking the Borrowers' code.

■ Arrietty and her family decide to leave the mansion with Spiller's help.

TRIVIA

Director Hiromasa Yonebayashi hates bugs, which is why the bugs in the film seem like characters, rather than being realistic. Arrietty's friends the crickets, in particular, are drawn very sympathetically.

POSTERS

There was only one poster for *Arrietty*, but for the first time Ghibli also created a banner for theaters as part of the publicity campaign.

■ Theatrical poster. Arrietty's red clothing contrasts vividly with the green of the leaves around her, and the dew drops add an extra touch of beauty to the scene.

BANNER

■ This massive banner created for theaters, which depicts the landscape around the mansion, was about 6 feet tall and almost 35 feet long.

NEWSPAPER ADS

Early ads used the image from the poster. After the film's release, ads featuring Arrietty with a variety of expressions were created.

■ This full-page color ad ran in the *Asahi Shimbun* on June 11, 2010, and featured the art from the poster.

■ This July 23 ad that ran in the *Asahi Shimbun* and *Yomiuri Shimbun* continued to use a still of Arrietty with her ponytail, which had debuted the day before the release.

■ The *Asahi Shimbun* and *Yomiuri Shimbun* ran this ad on August 6, which included a photo of Cécile Corbel, who sang the theme song.

106

■ Korean poster.

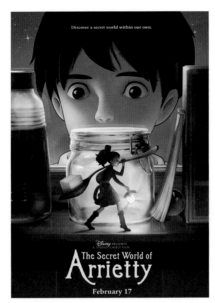

■ North American poster.

■ Italian poster.

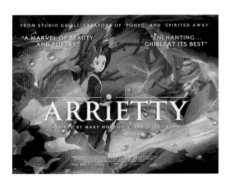

■ UK poster.

■ Taiwanese poster.

■ The August 13 ad that ran in papers including the *Asahi Shimbun* and *Yomiuri Shimbun* evoked the summer through seasonal phrases and a reference to the Obon holiday.

■ Later ads, like this one from August 27, featured stills from memorable scenes.

■ This 1/3-page ad that ran in the *Asahi Shimbun* and *Yomiuri Shimbun* on September 17 boldly centered on Arrietty's retreating figure. Other ads featured Yonebayashi's imageboards.

BEHIND THE SCENES

One of the details Atsushi Okui, director of digital imaging for almost all Ghibli films since *Porco Rosso*, took special care with when it came to backgrounds for *Arrietty* was camera blur. If a camera were to zoom in on Arrietty in the garden, the background would inevitably get blurry, so Okui intentionally created such an effect for the film.

107

Bright, optimistic days unfold for high school students in the 1960s

FROM UP ON POPPY HILL 2011

For his second feature, Goro Miyazaki moved away from the fantasy of *Tales from Earthsea* (2006) to create a completely down-to-earth coming-of-age story. The original manga (illustrated by Chizuru Takahashi and written by Tetsuro Sayama) was set around 1980, but Hayao Miyazaki, who co-wrote the screenplay with Keiko Niwa, changed the year to 1963, during Japan's period of rapid economic growth, and gave the story a specific setting in Yokohama. During this era Japan made a remarkable post-war recovery and became a true mass-consumer society, but the impact and memories of the war that had ended eighteen years previously still lingered, and Hayao Miyazaki wanted to set the story against this backdrop.

The Pacific and Korean wars have left an indelible mark on Umi's and Shun's parents. The teenagers are attracted to each other, but the truth of their origins complicates things. Instead of gravely emphasizing the part of the story that Shun himself says is "like a cheesy melodrama," however, the film focuses on the growth of a group of young people centered around Umi and Shun. In that sense, it's a positive, openhearted coming-of-age film. The portrayal of 1960s school life is a joy to watch, overflowing with now-unusual details like people riding two-to-a-bike, mimeograph printing, student meeting choruses, and the niceties of distance between boys and girls during the major cleaning scenes. For some this all feels nostalgic, while for the current generation it feels excitingly fresh.

STORY

The story is set in Yokohama in 1963. Japan has recovered from the war and is enjoying a period of rapid economic growth as it looks forward to next year's Tokyo Olympics. Second-year high school student Umi Matsuzaki lives in Coquelicot Manor, a boarding house on top of a hill. Every morning, she raises signal flags praying for a safe voyage in memory of her father, who died at sea when she was little. Shun Kazama, a third-year at the same school, raises answering flags in response.

Meanwhile, the "Latin Quarter," a historic building used by the cultural clubs at school, is set to be demolished. Shun, a member of the literature club, creates a weekly school paper and wages an opposition campaign. As Umi helps him cut stencils for the mimeograph, they begin to fall for each other, but…

Release date: July 16, 2011
Running time: Approx. 91 minutes
© 2011 Chizuru Takahashi - Tetsuro Sayama - Studio Ghibli - NDHDMT

Original Graphic Novel	Chizuru Takahashi Tetsuro Sayama
Screenplay	Hayao Miyazaki Keiko Niwa
Director	Goro Miyazaki
Planning	Hayao Miyazaki
Producer	Toshio Suzuki
Executive Producer	Koji Hoshino
Music	Satoshi Takebe
Character Design	Katsuya Kondo
Art Directors	Noboru Yoshida Kamon Oba Yohei Takamatsu Takashi Omori
Director of Digital Imaging	Atsushi Okui
Theme Song "Sayonara no Natsu – Kokurikozaka kara – (Summer of Farewells – From Up On Poppy Hill –)"	
Performance	Aoi Teshima
Song "Ue wo Muite Aruko"	
Performance	Kyu Sakamoto
Production	Studio Ghibli
Production Committee	Studio Ghibli Nippon Television Network Dentsu Hakuhodo DY Media Partners Walt Disney Japan Mitsubishi Toho
Umi Matsuzaki	Masami Nagasawa
Shun Kazama	Junichi Okada
Hana Matsuzaki	Keiko Takeshita
Miki Hokuto	Yuriko Ishida
Sachiko Hirokoji	Rumi Hiiragi
Ryoko Matsuzaki	Jun Fubuki
Yoshio Onodera	Takashi Naito
Shiro Mizunuma	Shunsuke Kazama
Akio Kazama	Nao Omori
Chairman Tokumaru	Teruyuki Kagawa
Sora Matsuzaki	Haruka Shiraishi
Riku Matsuzaki	Tsubasa Kobayashi
Yuichiro Sawamura	Junichi Okada
Saori Makimura	Yuko Masuoka

The Original Manga

◆ *From Up on Poppy Hill* illustrated by Chizuru Takahashi, written by Tetsuro Sayama (Kodansha) 2 volumes (Kadokawa Shoten)

Serialized in *Nakayoshi* from January to August 1980. While the art and script were similar to that of other popular girls' manga of the time, this coming-of-age story was a little more mature than *Nakayoshi*'s readers were used to. The Ghibli film took the framework of the manga and dramatically altered the setting and plot.

UMI MATSUZAKI

A girl in her second year of high school at Konan Academy. Very responsible, she takes care of her little brother and sister in addition to managing the Coquelicot Manor boarding house. Her nickname is Mer, French for "ocean" (which is also what Umi means in Japanese).

SHUN KAZAMA

A third-year at Konan Academy. He's head of the literature club and opposes the demolition of the "Latin Quarter," the old building where the school clubs meet.

CHARACTER RELATIONSHIPS

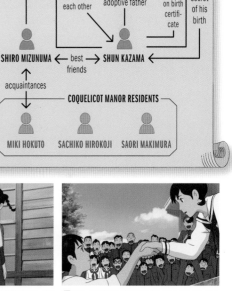

MATSUZAKI FAMILY

HANA ← parent and child → RYOKO

grandmother

RIKU — SORA — UMI — parents and children

husband and wife

FRIENDS

YOSHIO ONODERA

HIROSHI TACHIBANA

YUICHIRO SAWAMURA

AKIO KAZAMA

makes a direct appeal against demolishing the clubhouse

attracted to each other

adoptive father

birth father

tells him the secret of his birth

father on birth certificate

SHIRO MIZUNUMA ← best friends → SHUN KAZAMA

CHAIRMAN TOKUMARU — acquaintances

runs the boarding house →

COQUELICOT MANOR RESIDENTS

MIKI HOKUTO — SACHIKO HIROKOJI — SAORI MAKIMURA

HANA MATSUZAKI

Umi's grandmother. As head of the household, she watches over her grandchildren, and worries about Umi, who still raises signal flags in memory of her father.

SORA MATSUZAKI

Umi's little sister. Sora is a first-year at Konan Academy with a penchant for fashion. She has a crush on Shun, and accompanies Umi to visit the Latin Quarter's editorial department.

RIKU MATSUZAKI

Umi's little brother, in his second year of middle school. As the only boy at Coquelicot Manor, everyone dotes on him. He's good friends with Sachiko.

MIKI HOKUTO

One of the lodgers at Coquelicot Manor. A 25-year-old medical resident and Konan Academy alum, she's a big-sister type and Umi depends on her.

SACHIKO HIROKOJI

Another of the Coquelicot Manor lodgers. Though poor, she's dedicated to studying art, and often paints late into the night.

SAORI MAKIMURA

A lodger at Coquelicot Manor who works at the consulate in Yokohama. Trend-conscious, she and Sora often talk about fashion and boys.

■ Every morning Umi Matsuzaki raises signal flags praying for a safe voyage in memory of her father, but little does she realize an older boy at school is raising flags in reply...

■ One day Umi meets Shun Kazama, the boy who has been raising the reply flags, and they fall for each other.

RYOKO MATSUZAKI

Umi's mother. An assistant professor of English and American literature, currently studying abroad in the US. Nothing if not decisive, she eloped with Umi's father.

YUICHIRO SAWAMURA

Umi's father. After taking responsibility for his friend's son Shun and registering himself as the father on the boy's birth certificate, he died in the line of duty while serving as captain of a tank landing ship during the Korean War.

YOSHIO ONODERA

A sailor who was in the same grade as Umi's father and Shun's birth father, who died young, in their days at the nautical college.

■ It starts to look like Umi and Shun might actually be siblings.

■ Together they go to see Onodera, who knows the truth about their pasts.

TRIVIA

SHIRO MIZUNUMA

A third-year at Konan Academy, Shiro is a brilliant student who serves as class president. He joins Shun in protesting the demolition of the Latin Quarter.

AKIO KAZAMA

A tugboat captain and Shun's adoptive father. Though curt, he loves his family very much.

CHAIRMAN TOKUMARU

Entrepreneur, head of the Tokumaru Foundation, and chairman of Konan Academy. Hard at work across a range of businesses, he also wants to create opportunities for young people to grow.

The character of Chairman Tokumaru came out of Hayao Miyazaki's desire to pay homage to Yasuyoshi Tokuma, the founder of Tokuma Shoten, who died in 2000. Tokuma contributed to the creation of Studio Ghibli and supported Hayao Miyazaki on the road to success, in addition to serving as Chairman of Zushi Kaisei Academy. The character in the film is meant as an expression of Miyazaki's gratitude to Tokuma, and as a memorial.

■ Poster 2 was created during the film's run, and shows a reunion between the heroine Umi and her late father.

POSTERS

There were two posters for *From Up on Poppy Hill*, both of which used the title of Kyu Sakamoto's hit song, which appears in the movie, as a tagline.

■ Poster 1 used a preliminary illustration by Hayao Miyazaki, who developed the film and co-wrote the screenplay. There was also a version that included only the title, without mentioning the cast or release date.

NEWSPAPER ADS

Initially, the ads used the image from Poster 1, but after the film's release, they focused on characters, most often Umi.

■ The newspaper campaign kicked off with full-page color ads in the June 24, 2011, editions of the *Asahi Shimbun* and *Yomiuri Shimbun*. The copy focused on director Goro Miyazaki's name to draw in viewers.

■ Ads like this 1/3-page one from the July 22 *Asahi Shimbun* and *Yomiuri Shimbun* used a still of a hopeful-looking Umi to match the tagline.

■ The ad that ran in the *Asahi Shimbun* and *Yomiuri Shimbun* on July 29 used a rough sketch by Katsuya Kondo, the character designer. A line from Miyazaki's development notes was used as copy.

■ French poster.

■ Italian poster.

■ Hong Kong poster.

■ UK poster.

■ Taiwanese poster.

■ Swedish poster.

■ North American poster.

■ The ad in the August 12 *Yomiuri Shimbun* and *Asahi Shimbun* pulled together stills of many of the characters from the film.

■ The September 9 ad that ran in the *Asahi Shimbun* and *Yomiuri Shimbun* used a still of Shun jumping onto the cargo ship to show how cool he is.

■ This ad, which ran in the *Asahi Shimbun* and *Yomiuri Shimbun* on September 2, announced the extended run of the film in producer Toshio Suzuki's own calligraphy.

■ The ads that ran on September 16 and September 22 each emphasized that it was a three-day weekend (there were two that month). There was also a three-day weekend ad featuring Chairman Tokumaru, which ran on October 7.

BEHIND THE SCENES

The Tohoku earthquake and tsunami occurred on March 11, 2011. This was during the final push to finish the film, with rolling blackouts instituted after the Fukushima Daiichi nuclear disaster. Faced with the question of whether work should continue, Hayao Miyazaki decided they couldn't abandon the studio. He stressed how important it was to struggle on at such a time, and encouraged by his words, the staff worked on the film in shifts.

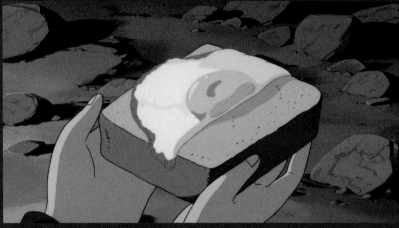

Pazu's breakfast of a fried egg on bread. He and Sheeta split one fried egg between them.

■ The two tell each other their life stories as they eat.

Castle in the Sky

While he and Sheeta are hiding in an abandoned mine after escaping from their pursuers, Pazu brings out the fried egg on bread he made for breakfast. The way the egg looks sliding into their mouths when they take a bite will make you want your own! Their dessert of green apples and candy comes from Pazu's bag as well.

Only Yesterday

After her father buys a pineapple from an expensive store in Ginza, we get to see the young Taeko try it for the first time—but only after they've left it out on display for a while, because no one knows how to eat it! At the time, melons and even bananas were similarly exotic items.

GHIBLI DRAWS
EATING

More than almost anything, people love to talk about the food scenes in Ghibli films. Fans call these "Ghibli meals," and some even try to figure out the recipes, though many of them don't require anything more than bread, cheese, eggs, and a frying pan. Rather than painstaking, expensive, or lavish, they're simple and easy—approachable, not unlike the characters themselves. Depictions of food and eating are crucial elements that often relate to the film's worldview or historical background.

■ The widow sees Setsuko and Seita as freeloaders, discriminating against them even during meals.

■ Setsuko looks intently at the candy solution.

■ The siblings start living in an abandoned bomb shelter near a pond.

Grave of the Fireflies

The war drags on, and people struggle as food becomes scarce. Food provides the strength to live, and without it Seita and Setsuko are driven to the brink. Sweets were precious at that time, and the scene in which they put water into a candy tin to dissolve the remnants is heartrending.

Spirited Away

The bathhouse meals are made to welcome the gods who come there to relax and refresh themselves; humans like Chihiro's parents who eat the food without permission are turned into animals. For Chihiro, simple foods like the rice balls Haku gives her or the bean buns she eats with Lin become the greatest treats imaginable.

■ The kitchen is in a frenzy preparing dishes for No Face.

■ Haku's enchanted rice balls restore the eater's energy.

■ Chihiro eats a bean bun given to her by Lin. In her right hand, she clutches the magical emetic dumpling she received from the River-god.

■ The soup Tenar makes to welcome Sparrowhawk.

■ Dinner at Tenar's.

■ A lunch of black bread and cheese.

Tales from Earthsea

Even in a fantasy set in another world, the residents live normal lives. At Tenar's house, where Arren and Sparrowhawk begin living, they're served warm soup, or milk and oatmeal for breakfast. The bread and cheese they eat while out working the land looks delicious as well.

■ Instant ramen with ham, egg, and green onion.

■ Markl is engrossed with his first decent breakfast in a while.

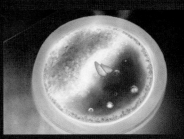

■ 10x spicy curry that looks like lava.

■ Sosuke is happy to see Ponyo enjoying her food.

■ Howl adroitly cracks the eggs and throws the shells into the fire.

■ The Ghiblies trio tries to down the super-spicy curry.

Ponyo on the Cliff by the Sea

Sosuke's mother Lisa makes instant ramen and hot milk with honey for Sosuke and Ponyo. All the ramen requires is hot water, but she tops it with Ponyo's favorite: ham. Ponyo is adorable as she falls asleep while she's eating.

Howl's Moving Castle

Howl skillfully makes bacon and eggs in front of the aged Sophie, who has become his live-in housekeeper. The way Markl scarfs down his meal makes clear just how good it tastes! The eggshells Howl cracks with one hand become Calcifer's food (and fuel).

the GHIBLIES episode 2

The first episode, *Hot Curry*, features a 10x spicy curry that hurts just to look at. The three Studio Ghibli employees face off with the proud owner-chef of the restaurant they go to for lunch, and Yukari wins ¥1,000 for polishing off her curry...but the heat propels her into outer space, and sends her spinning around the globe.

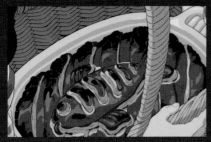

The Red Turtle

The sea turtle transforms itself into a woman and feeds the man clams. He becomes ashamed of hurting the turtle, and gradually falls for the woman. The couple have a child, and the three live together on the island, the story continuing until the man eventually dies.

Kiki's Delivery Service

The kindly Madame hires Kiki to deliver a herring and pumpkin pie to her granddaughter. Kiki helps her bake the pie in an old-fashioned wood-fired oven and struggles through the rain to make the delivery, but the granddaughter isn't exactly thrilled. To top it all off, Kiki catches a cold for her trouble.

When Marnie Was There

The fruits and vegetables in Ghibli films look real right down to their texture. The juicy tomatoes Anna picks from the Oiwas' vegetable garden are a perfect example, and their dazzle continues into the cooking scene, where it represents Anna's slowly changing emotions.

Arrietty

The Borrowers cook using ingredients they've borrowed from the humans' table: tea, cheese, bread...more or less the same things the humans eat. But Borrowers who live in the wild, like Spiller, hunt bugs and small animals for food.

The Wind Rises

Honjo remarks on what a strange thing Jiro has bought: Siberia, a uniquely Japanese sweet consisting of a red bean filling sandwiched between pieces of sponge cake. Pouring tea through a strainer was an everyday sight in Japanese households before teabags became prevalent.

From Up on Poppy Hill

While Umi is at the butcher's, Shun buys croquettes for them to eat together. Eating something you've just bought on the way home from school is a privilege born of the hearty appetite of youth, and an everyday thing for high school students. This casual scene, not a date or anything special, hints at the puppy love to come.

Combining fiction and historical fact, Hayao Miyazaki weaves a new world around a real protagonist

THE WIND RISES

2013

The Wind Rises follows Jiro Horikoshi, real-life designer of the Imperial Japanese Navy's fighter plane known as the "Zero," through the turbulent years of the Great Kanto Earthquake, the Great Depression, and World War II. Like *Porco Rosso*, it expands on a manga Miyazaki had serialized in a model magazine, combining this with Tatsuo Hori's romantic novel *The Wind Has Risen*. The setting and story are faithful to historical fact, but the film is packed with dreams and flights of fancy, like Jiro's encounter with a formation of strange flying objects or his conversation with Caproni, the Italian aircraft designer he admires. As a result, it creates a unique mood, not like Miyazaki's past fantasy films or the average biopic, but a mixture of the two.

The story of Jiro and heroine Nahoko falling in love, marrying, and being separated once more by Nahoko's death is unusual for a Ghibli film, as are unexpected audio choices like the intentional use of mono. Not to mention the fact that most of the sound effects, including aircraft engines, spinning propellers, and the roar of the great earthquake, were created by processing human voices. Likewise, unconventional casting choices contributed to creating a fresh appeal: film director Hideaki Anno played Jiro, and Stephen Alpert, former head of Ghibli's international division, voiced and provided the character model for Castorp, the mysterious figure who appears along with an excerpt from Thomas Mann's *The Magic Mountain*.

Release date: July 20, 2013
Running time: Approx. 126 minutes
© 2013 Studio Ghibli - NDHDMTK

Original Story, Screenplay Written
and Directed by ·············· Hayao Miyazaki
Producer ····················· Toshio Suzuki
Production ···················· Koji Hoshino
Music ························· Joe Hisaishi
Supervising Animator ·········· Kitaro Kosaka
Art Director ·················· Yoji Takeshige
Color Design ················· Michiyo Yasuda
Director of Digital Imaging ···· Atsushi Okui
Theme Song "Hikoki Gumo"
Performed by ················· Yumi Arai
Production ···················· Studio Ghibli
Production Committee ········· Studio Ghibli
Nippon Television Network
Dentsu
Hakuhodo DY Media Partners
Walt Disney Japan
Mitsubishi
Toho
KDDI

STORY

From economic depression and poverty to disease and a massive earthquake, the 1920s was a difficult time in Japan. Against this turbulent backdrop, Jiro Horikoshi pursues his dream of creating beautiful airplanes, following in the footsteps of his hero, the great Italian aircraft designer Caproni.

After graduating from college, Jiro is hired to design airplanes for Mitsubishi Internal Combus-

tion. At the age of thirty, he goes for some R&R at a resort hotel in Karuizawa, where he runs into Nahoko, a girl he met ten years earlier during the Great Kanto Earthquake. They fall in love and get engaged, but Nahoko is ill with tuberculosis. Though she never recovers, they marry and try to live their remaining days together to the fullest.

Jiro Horikoshi ·············· Hideaki Anno
Nahoko Satomi ·············· Miori Takimoto
Honjo ····················· Hidetoshi Nishijima
Kurokawa ·················· Masahiko Nishimura
Castorp ··················· Stephen Alpert
Satomi ···················· Morio Kazama
Jiro's Mother ·············· Keiko Takeshita
Kayo Horikoshi ············· Mirai Shida
Hattori ··················· Jun Kunimura
Mrs. Kurokawa ············· Shinobu Otake
Caproni ··················· Mansai Nomura

The Original Manga

The Wind Rises—Hayao Miyazaki's Daydream Comeback by Hayao Miyazaki (Dai Nippon Kaiga)

A nine-part manga serialized in the hobby magazine *Model Graphix* (Dai Nippon Kaiga) from April 2009 to January 2010. Dai Nippon Kaiga published the paperback version in 2015, after the film's release. (English title provisional)

CHARACTERS

JIRO HORIKOSHI

Obsessed with airplanes since childhood, he had to give up his dream of becoming a pilot due to his poor vision. Instead, Jiro sets his sights on designing aircraft, and goes to work for the design department at Mitsubishi Internal Combustion.

NAHOKO SATOMI

A beautiful, intelligent woman who was on the same steam train as Jiro, a college student at the time, during the Great Kanto Earthquake. They fall completely out of touch, but are fatefully reunited in Karuizawa.

CAPRONI

An Italian airplane design genius whom Jiro admires, modeled on a historical figure. He designs innovative airplanes, and provides guidance to Jiro in his dreams.

HONJO

Jiro's best friend. Educated at Tokyo Imperial University, Faculty of Engineering, Department of Aeronautics, he goes to work at Mitsubishi Internal Combustion alongside Jiro. He designs airplanes as well, and he and Jiro have a friendly rivalry.

KUROKAWA

Jiro's supervisor at Mitsubishi Internal Combustion. A strict boss, he nevertheless acknowledges Jiro's talent and helps him both at work and in his personal life. When Jiro and Nahoko are looking for a new home, he rents them his guest house.

MRS. KUROKAWA

Kurokawa's wife. She supports her husband, and welcomes Jiro and Nahoko.

SATOMI

Nahoko's father. He lost his wife to tuberculosis two years earlier, and is worried about Nahoko's health.

HATTORI

Chief of the design section at Mitsubishi Internal Combustion, where Jiro works. He and Kurokawa are counting on young Jiro and Honjo.

JIRO'S MOTHER

An elegant, graceful woman who kindly watches over Jiro.

KAYO HORIKOSHI

Jiro's sister, seven years his junior. A tomboy, she looks up to Jiro from a very young age, and calls him Big Big Brother. Highly independent as an adult, she becomes a doctor.

CASTORP

A mysterious German man Jiro meets at the hotel in Karuizawa. Very knowledgeable about international affairs, he is worried about where Japan and Germany are headed.

CHARACTER RELATIONSHIPS

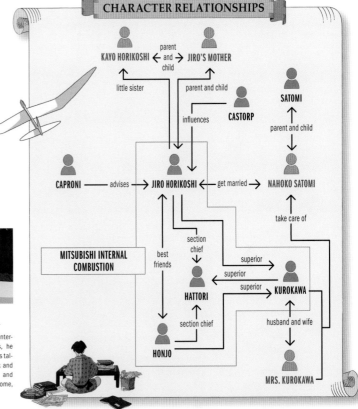

KAYO HORIKOSHI ← parent and child → JIRO'S MOTHER

little sister — parent and child

SATOMI

influences — CASTORP

parent and child

CAPRONI — advises → JIRO HORIKOSHI ← get married → NAHOKO SATOMI

MITSUBISHI INTERNAL COMBUSTION

best friends — section chief

take care of

superior

HATTORI ← superior → KUROKAWA

section chief

HONJO

husband and wife

MRS. KUROKAWA

■ As a boy, Jiro meets Italian airplane designer Caproni in a dream, and Caproni gives him advice.

■ Jiro, now thirty, falls in love with Nahoko at the Karuizawa hotel where he goes for some R&R, and decides to marry her.

■ Though ill with tuberculosis, Nahoko goes ahead with the wedding, and she and Jiro move into the Kurokawas' guest house.

■ Jiro becomes enthralled with building airplanes, just as he was with his childhood dream of flying an airplane he built himself.

TRIVIA

Caproni, the aircraft designer who appears in Jiro's dream, designed a surveillance plane for the Italian military called the Ca.309, nicknamed the Ghibli (with a hard 'G'). Hayao Miyazaki named his studio after Caproni's plane, which gives a sense of his great admiration for the designer.

POSTERS

The two posters for *The Wind Rises* both expressed the filmmakers' admiration with the tagline "To Jiro Horikoshi and Tatsuo Hori, with respect. We must live."

■ Poster 1 was centered on the heroine, Nahoko.

■ Poster 2 focused on Jiro, and made it apparent that aircraft were a major theme of the film.

■ Norwegian poster.

■ Swedish poster.

■ Hong Kong poster.

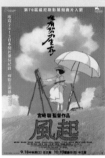

■ Taiwanese poster.

NEWSPAPER ADS

There were a wide range of ads for *The Wind Rises*, starting with the image from Poster 2 and then bringing in the grown-up love story, the unique characters, and a boy with big dreams.

■ The full-page color ad published in the *Asahi Shimbun* and *Yomiuri Shimbun* on June 28, 2013, about a month before the film's release, included the entire text of director Hayao Miyazaki's proposal for the film. This ad ran again on July 18 in the *Sankei Shimbun*.

■ This ad, published in the *Asahi Shimbun* on August 2, about two weeks after the release, used a still of a happy Jiro and Nahoko with the hopeful tagline "Life is beautiful, isn't it."

■ The August 9 ad that ran in the *Asahi Shimbun* and *Yomiuri Shimbun* featured Caproni and Castorp, and really foregrounded the fun.

■ Studio Ghibli's trademark countdown ads started running in the *Sankei Shimbun* on July 16, four days before the release. They pushed the appeal of Caproni, Honjo, Kurokawa, Nahoko, and Jiro to drum up anticipation.

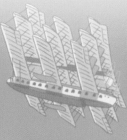

■ Italian poster.

■ Spanish poster.

■ Israeli poster.

■ Polish poster.

■ UK poster.

■ Korean poster.

■ Australian poster.

■ The August 16 ad in the *Asahi Shimbun* and *Yomiuri Shimbun* showed Jiro as a young man, and announced that "over five million people have seen the film!" as well as the film's entry into the Venice International Film Festival.

■ The October 25 ad that ran in *Asahi Shimbun* and *Yomiuri Shimbun* featured this eye-catching image of Nahoko in her wedding kimono.

■ This ad featuring a close-up of Jiro's face appeared frequently between August 23 and September 27. Here we see the one that ran in the *Asahi Shimbun* and *Yomiuri Shimbun* on September 13.

■ This entertaining ad, which ran in the *Asahi Shimbun* and *Yomiuri Shimbun* on November 1, featured a photo of director Hayao Miyazaki and producer Toshio Suzuki with Jiro, Nahoko, and Caproni.

BEHIND THE SCENES

Because *The Wind Rises* is based on real people and events and set mostly in the Japan of almost a hundred years ago, the production team held classes to refresh the animators on drawing Japanese-style clothing of the period. The art department also took a company drawing trip to Uchiko in Ehime Prefecture, known for its old streets and houses.

Director Isao Takahata's ambitious masterpiece revives a classic tale for the modern age

THE TALE OF THE PRINCESS KAGUYA 2013

This epic adaptation of *The Tale of the Bamboo Cutter*, Japan's oldest story, took eight years to complete. Back in his Toei days, Takahata had written a proposal in response to the company's call for ideas for an animated version of the tale. In it, he asked himself why Princess Kaguya had come down to Earth from the moon, and came up with a premise that would make for a great film. Half a century later, he revisited his proposal and got started on making it a reality.

The story largely centers around scenes from the original tale, such as the noblemen's attempts to win Princess Kaguya's hand, but the film also adds new material, like the rich depiction of her girlhood in the mountains. Though everyone in Japan knows the story, Takahata's version is loaded with new treasures, from the tragic love between Kaguya and Sutemaru to comedic supporting characters like Me no Warawa.

Takahata continued to develop the techniques he had used for his previous film, *My Neighbors the Yamadas* (1999), in pursuit of a visual style different from that of traditional animation, which is composed of cels layered over backgrounds. In *The Tale of The Princess Kaguya*, characters whose outlines appear sketched by pencil move as one with simplified backgrounds resembling ink and wash. To help realize his visual ideal, Takahata brought together an outstanding staff including animator Osamu Tanabe, whom he had worked with on *My Neighbors the Yamadas*, and Kazuo Oga, who returned as art director for the first time in 16 years.

Sadly, Isao Takahata passed away five years after the film's release, making *The Tale of The Princess Kaguya* his last film.

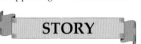
STORY

Once upon a time, there lived an old bamboo cutter called Okina and his wife, Ona. Okina gathered bamboo in the mountains to be made into baskets and such, and one day, while he was about his work, he found a girl inside a glowing stalk of bamboo. The couple saw the girl as a gift from the gods, and raised her lovingly, calling her "Princess." The girl grew at an astonishing rate, and in less than a year had become a beautiful young woman.

Okina decided the girl belonged in the capital, where she could be raised as a noblewoman. There she became famous for her beauty, and came to be called Princess Kaguya, the "shining princess." Many noble suitors sought her hand, but Kaguya gave them impossible tasks to perform and refused their proposals. In truth, Princess Kaguya was an inhabitant of the moon come down to Earth.

Release date: November 23, 2013
Running time: Approx. 137 minutes
© 2013 Hatake Jimusho - Studio Ghibli - NDHDMTK

Based on the Japanese Folktale	"The Tale of the Bamboo Cutter"
Original Concept	Isao Takahata
Screenplay	Isao Takahata Riko Sakaguchi
Director	Isao Takahata
Planning	Toshio Suzuki
Producer	Yoshiaki Nishimura
Production	Koji Hoshino
Music	Joe Hisaishi
Character Design Directing Animator	Osamu Tanabe
Supervising Animator	Kenichi Konishi
Art Director	Kazuo Oga
Color Setting	Yukiko Kakita
Director of Digital Imaging	Keisuke Nakamura
Theme Song "Inochi no Kioku (When I Remember This Life)" Performed by	Kazumi Nikaido
Songs "Warabe Uta (Nursery Rhyme)" / "Tennyo no Uta (Song of the Heavenly Maiden)"	
Production	Studio Ghibli
Production Committee	Studio Ghibli Nippon Television Network Dentsu Hakuhodo DY Media Partners Walt Disney Japan Mitsubishi Toho KDDI
Princess Kaguya	Aki Asakura
Sutemaru	Kengo Kora
Okina	Takeo Chii
Ona (Bamboo cutter's wife), Narrator	Nobuko Miyamoto
Lady Sagami	Atsuko Takahata
Me no Warawa	Tomoko Tabata
Inbe no Akita	Shinosuke Tatekawa
Prince Ishitsukuri	Takaya Kamikawa
Lord Minister of the Right Abe	Hikaru Ijuin
Great Counselor Otomo	Ryudo Uzaki
The Mikado	Shichinosuke Nakamura
Prince Kuramochi	Isao Hashizume
Okina	Yuji Miyake
Kita no Kata	Yukiji Asaoka
Old Charcoal Burner	Tatsuya Nakadai

The Original Tale

◆ **The Tale of the Bamboo Cutter**, author and date unknown

Set down during the early Heian Period (794-1185), this ancient work is described as "the father of all tales" in *The Tale of Genji*. It can also be considered Japan's oldest sci-fi/fantasy story. Writers like Yasunari Kawabata, Seiko Tanabe, Shin'ichi Hoshi, Kaori Ekuni, and Tomihiko Morimi have all published their own unique versions in modern Japanese.

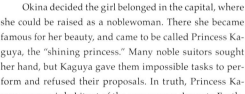

PRINCESS KAGUYA

Born from a stalk of bamboo, she's nicknamed "Bamboo Shoot" by the other children in the mountain village where she is raised because she grows so quickly. She becomes a beautiful young woman and goes to live in the capital.

SUTEMARU

Princess Kaguya's childhood friend. Eldest of the village children, he's like a big brother to them. Princess Kaguya calls him "Big Brother Sutemaru."

OKINA

Along with his wife, he raises Princess Kaguya from the time she is a baby, and loves her like his own. He believes she'll be happiest marrying a nobleman in the capital.

ONA

Okina's wife. A kind woman who understands Princess Kaguya, and cares about her feelings.

LADY SAGAMI

A tutor from the imperial court who Okina hires to educate Princess Kaguya. She teaches her everything a noblewoman needs to know, from playing the koto to calligraphy and etiquette.

ME NO WARAWA

A girl who waits on Princess Kaguya when she lives in the capital.

INBE NO AKITA

An educated old man who, at Okina's request, provides the princess with her new name when she comes of age. Moved by the girl's beauty, he names her "Princess Kaguya," with an epithet that means "graceful as the supple bamboo."

PRINCE KURAMOCHI, PRINCE ISHITSUKURI, LORD MINISTER OF THE RIGHT ABE, GREAT COUNSELOR OTOMO, MIDDLE COUNSELOR ISONOKAMI

Princess Kaguya's suitors, all of whom are noblemen of high rank. The Princess assigns them each the impossible task of bringing her a mythical treasure.

THE MIKADO

The most powerful man in the land. He hears rumor of Princess Kaguya, and summons her to the palace, convinced that she must want to be by his side.

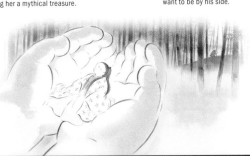

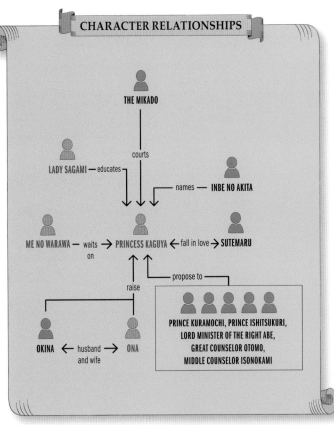

THE MIKADO

LADY SAGAMI — educates

courts

names — INBE NO AKITA

ME NO WARAWA — waits on → PRINCESS KAGUYA ← fall in love → SUTEMARU

propose to

raise

OKINA ← husband and wife → ONA

PRINCE KURAMOCHI, PRINCE ISHITSUKURI, LORD MINISTER OF THE RIGHT ABE, GREAT COUNSELOR OTOMO, MIDDLE COUNSELOR ISONOKAMI

■ Once she gets old enough, Princess Kaguya falls for her childhood friend Sutemaru.

■ They move to the capital because Okina wants his daughter to become a princess, and initially she's delighted by the beautiful clothes and grand house, but...

■ As she learns the necessary etiquette to become a noblewoman, Kaguya begins to feel trapped by life in the capital.

■ Having silently begged to return to the moon, Princess Kaguya has no choice but to accept when the emissaries from the moon come to reclaim her.

The sequence where Princess Kaguya and Sutemaru fly through the sky together was one of the most important for Takahata. To properly express the beauty of the Earth during the scene where they pass in front of the moon, he showed very little of the sky before this point in the film.

POSTERS

Three different posters were created for *The Tale of The Princess Kaguya*, all of them featuring the princess herself.

■ In a complete turnabout from the happily sleeping princess of the first poster, Poster 2 presents her as a pitiful figure lying in the snow, giving a sense of the film's overall mood.

■ Because the release date kept changing as production fell behind schedule, there are three different versions of Poster 1, each with a different date.

■ Poster 3 uses a joyful image of the princess under a blossoming cherry tree.

NEWSPAPER ADS

The campaign largely used joyful images of the princess, like the one from Poster 3.

■ The full-page color ad that ran on November 1, 2013, in the *Asahi Shimbun* and *Yomiuri Shimbun* was the first for the film, and used the image from Poster 3 in all its glory.

■ On November 22, the day before the release, black and white ads ran in papers including the *Mainichi Shimbun*, Tokyo *Shimbun*, *Sankei Shimbun*, *Nihon Keizai Shimbun*, and *Jomo Shimbun*.

■ On November 29, a series of color ads began running in the *Asahi Shimbun* and *Yomiuri Shimbun*. There were several versions, but all used taglines that ended with the words, "A princess!"

■ Italian poster.

■ Taiwanese poster.

■ North American poster.

■ Hong Kong poster.

■ Spanish poster.

■ Brazilian poster.

■ One of the "A princess!" series, which ran in the *Asahi Shimbun* and *Yomiuri Shimbun* on December 27. In addition to this New Year's version, there were ads referencing Christmas, end-of-the-year parties, and the first shrine visit of the new year.

■ The ad that ran in the *Asahi Shimbun* and *Yomiuri Shimbun* on January 10, 2014, was a collaboration with a popular variety show.

■ Ads announcing the film's Japan Academy Film Prize for Animation of the Year were published in both the *Asahi Shimbun* and *Yomiuri Shimbun* on January 17.

■ The ad from the January 31 editions of the *Asahi Shimbun* and *Yomiuri Shimbun* was created to accompany "Movie Day," the 1st of every month, when movie tickets were discounted.

BEHIND THE SCENES

Me No Warawa, the lady-in-waiting who serves the princess in the capital, was originally supposed to be depicted as an adolescent girl the same age as her mistress, but Takahata decided he wanted to turn her bangs, eyes, and mouth into straight lines. He was enormously entertained by this character, and she ended up appearing in more scenes than initially intended.

THE MUSIC FOR GHIBLI FILMS STARTED WITH THE IMAGE ALBUM FOR *NAUSICAÄ OF THE VALLEY OF THE WIND*

TAKUTO KAKU (FILM AND MUSIC CRITIC)

THE IMAGE ALBUM IS A FIRST DRAFT FOR THE SOUNDTRACK

Ghibli films are embellished with unique music, and many of them shine all the brighter thanks precisely to that music. Ten or more composers work on the score for each film, not including whoever's in charge of the theme song. It's fruitless to try and find a common methodology or style, but tracing the creation of each score does provide some sense of overall identity.

A search for the origins of the Ghibli musical universe leads us to the *Nausicaä of the Valley of the Wind Image Album: Tori no Hito* [Bird Person]..., released on November 25, 1983, by Tokuma Japan (now Tokuma Japan Communications) and based on Hayao Miyazaki's manga. The history of Ghibli's music really begins with Isao Takahata, impressed by this album, inviting Joe Hisaishi to take charge of the music for the film adaptation, with Miyazaki's blessing.

Takahata was the one who suggested Joe Hisaishi compose the image album in the first place. Tokuma Music Industries (the forerunner to Tokuma Japan) recommended Hisaishi, who had just completed his solo album *INFORMATION* (released by Tokuma on October 25, 1982), to score the film, but he was still an up-and-coming musician and it was unclear whether he was really the right person for the job. Takahata did some digging into Hisaishi's career on his own, and saw the composer's potential once they met in person, but the image album represented a kind of final confirmation for Takahata. The soundtrack to the film makes abundantly clear just how satisfied he was.

Takahata brought Hisaishi back to put together the image album for the follow-up, *Castle in the Sky*, the difference this time being that Hisaishi was working on the album with the understanding that he would score the film as well. For Hisaishi, it meant he had finally won Takahata and Miyazaki's trust, but it also established the approach they would take to the music for subsequent Ghibli films: using the image album as a kind of first draft for the soundtrack.

With the next image album, for *My Neighbor Totoro,* they took the inventive step of writing original children's songs. For Miyazaki, who loved folk songs and popular music, the "song" was the most familiar musical form, and viewed in light of his later films this was perhaps a natural development. In contrast to the previous two films, where Takahata had handled the music production side of things, on *Totoro*, Miyazaki worked directly with

Hisaishi for the first time. Having discovered how much fun it could be to work on the music together, Miyazaki thereafter took Hisaishi as his "lawfully wedded musical wife."

By contrast, Isao Takahata, the "matchmaker" who brought Miyazaki and Hisaishi together, invited different musical partners to participate in each film. For *Grave of the Fireflies,* he called in the contemporary classical composer Michio Mamiya, whom he had worked with on *The Little Norse Prince Valiant*; for *Only Yesterday,* it was Katz Hoshi, whom he knew from *Downtown Story*; for *Pom Poko,* the band Shang Shang Typhoon; and for *My Neighbors the Yamadas,* he entrusted the musical development to pop singer Akiko Yano. Each of these films is inscribed with a unique sound, and while it may appear to be meticulously filling in the gaps, in fact what we're hearing is musical freedom, liberation...and what could be more thrilling? One could ascribe this to a constant drive to seek out new forms of expression, but that right there is the consistent guiding principle across all of Ghibli's music.

GHIBLI MUSIC'S "THIRD MAN": PRODUCER TOSHIO SUZUKI

So what about the films directed by other people?

Miyazaki has developed and produced several films to foster Ghibli's younger talent, and we can see the influence of his unique authorial approach reflected for instance in Yuji Nomi, who wrote the music for *Whisper of the Heart* and *The Cat Returns*. Using John Denver's "Take Me Home, Country Roads" as the theme song for *Whisper of the Heart* was itself Miyazaki's idea. Then there's Michael Dudok de Wit's *The Red Turtle,* for which Takahata acted as artistic producer. Ultimately the director decided to bring in a new composer, but even that was apparently on Takahata's advice. As with their own directorial work, both Miyazaki and Takahata's leadership styles reflect their own unique personalities.

For films by the next generation of directors, which Takahata and Miyazaki weren't involved in or from which they distanced themselves, another crucial Ghibli figure played the role of "guardian": producer Toshio Suzuki, the "third man" after Takahata and Miyazaki.

Suzuki can spearhead the selection of composers or theme song performers under a variety of circumstances, and it's not unusual for his recommendations to stem from material pro-

vided by an enthusiastic music industry. Aoi Teshima's performances for *Tales from Earthsea* and *From Up on Poppy Hill,* Cécile Corbel's for *Arrietty,* and Satoshi Takebe's score for *From Up on Poppy Hill* are excellent examples. Suzuki pushed to hire Takebe partly because he saw a documentary in which Takebe appeared. It goes without saying that these musicians added another dimension of sound to Ghibli's films.

If there's a difference between Takahata and Miyazaki on the one hand and Suzuki on the other, it's that Suzuki is more attuned to music's potential for publicity. His strategic use of "Therru's Song" in the previews for *Tales from Earthsea* is probably still a vivid memory for many Japanese filmgoers. Asking Yumi Matsutoya (Yumi Arai) for permission to use "Hikoki Gumo (Vapor Trails)" in *The Wind Rises* during a public event was another masterstroke.

Over the years, Suzuki has assisted both Takahata and Miyazaki with the music for their own films as well. For Miyazaki in particular, who doesn't have Takahata's "musical vocabulary," he's taken on something like the role of music producer. Hisaishi himself has said that when he was struggling to write the children's songs for *My Neighbor Totoro,* Suzuki made the ingenious suggestion that he should try singing a song for the image album as a change of pace. Less well known is the fact that Suzuki suggested he use the scores from *Braveheart* (composed by James Horner) and *Ryan's Daughter* (composed by Maurice Jarre) as musical references for *Princess Mononoke* and *Howl's Moving Castle* respectively. As a longtime devotee of David Lean's *Ryan's Daughter,* Suzuki was a passionate Jarre fan, and his taste may go some way toward unlocking the mystery of Ghibli's musical appeal.

JOE HISAISHI FINDS FREEDOM

Over the course of thirty years, Joe Hisaishi has scored more Ghibli films than any other composer, and one of the unique pleasures of Ghibli's oeuvre lies in the fact that we can watch his approach change over time. Hisaishi originally composed for small ensembles and electronic instruments but came to prefer large orchestras, and now regularly conducts classical concerts. The tones and devices he uses in his orchestrations have also changed over the years. For example, though *Princess Mononoke* and *Spirited Away* were only four years apart, the scores feel so different that it's hard to believe they were composed by the same person. How fascinating, how thrilling! At the same time, work-

ing with a humane, compassionate creator like Hayao Miyazaki has meant a continuous effort to create songs and melodies that go to the heart of the story. The recognition and approbation he has received for this work may well strike a contradictory note for Hisaishi, who started out as a composer of sophisticated, experimental minimalist music. The goal is to generate emotion but not drown in it. Seeing the struggle between these diametrically opposed aspects of Hisaishi's music bear fruit is yet another pleasure of Ghibli films.

For Hisaishi, reuniting with Takahata to work on the music for *The Tale of The Princess Kaguya* almost thirty years after *Nausicaä of the Valley of the Wind* and *Castle in the Sky* was a major event. Takahata ran into various difficulties in selecting a composer for the film, and Hisaishi's participation wasn't settled until the production was already at a critical stage. The timing overlapped with Hisaishi's work on *The Wind Rises,* and normally he would never have been able to take on another project, but composing music for a Takahata film was his longstanding dream. Takahata's admiration for his score to the recent live-action film *Villain* also played a significant part. Composing the score for *Villain,* which completely eschewed explanations and sensational effects, was a dream job for Hisaishi, with his roots in minimalist music, and it probably felt like Takahata was discovering him afresh. The two men have a similar way of coming up with ideas in the first place, with newfound freedom lying at the end of exhaustive discussion. Thinking about Takahata and Hisaishi coming full circle over the course of thirty years can only enhance the pleasure of listening to Ghibli's music.

The history of Studio Ghibli isn't over, of course. Hayao Miyazaki is hard at work on the feature film *Kimitachi wa Do Ikiruka* (*The Boy and the Heron*) and we can only wonder what sonic delights it will contain.

I still can't take my ears off of Ghibli's films.

WHEN MARNIE WAS THERE   2014

Hiromasa Yonebayashi, who made his directorial debut with *Arrietty* in 2010, wanted to make another Ghibli film for children. The result was *When Marnie Was There*, the story of Anna, a closed-off middle-schooler who learns the truth about her family through her encounter with a mysterious girl named Marnie. Occupying a space somewhere between dream and reality, this heartfelt film traces Anna's inner turmoil as she begins opening up to the people around her. It also marks Ghibli's first film with two female leads.

When Marnie Was There is based on a 1967 children's book by British author Joan G. Robinson, with some changes, like giving Anna an enthusiasm for drawing and moving the story from England to Japan.

They chose Hokkaido for the setting because the mansion on the salt marsh where the two girls meet and the other Western-style buildings in the surrounding seaside town wouldn't seem out of place there. Yohei Taneda, active in Hollywood and China as well as Japan and who had worked on films like *Swallowtail Butterfly* and *Kill Bill: Vol 1*, was chosen as art director. He helped create beautiful backdrops by introducing the use of three-dimensional models to check how the finished scenes would look, a method widely used in live-action filmmaking. It's extremely rare in animation to have a live-action art director participate so fully in the production, from location scouting and set design to the final check of all backgrounds for the movie.

STORY

Anna is twelve. Her parents died in a car accident when she was little, and she went to live with her grandmother, but she too died shortly thereafter. After leading a lonely life in an orphanage until the age of five, Anna now lives with her foster parents, but finds it hard to let herself accept their kindness.

Because of her asthma, she leaves the urban confines of Sapporo to spend the summer in the fresh seaside air of her relatives' village. In an old, supposedly abandoned mansion called the Marsh House, she meets a mysterious girl named Marnie and the two quickly become friends. Anna, who's used to shutting other people out, begins to open up to the beautiful, kind girl...but who is Marnie, really?

Release date: July 19, 2014
Running time: Approx. 103 minutes
© 2014 Studio Ghibli - NDHDMTK

Based on the Novel by	Joan G. Robinson
Screenplay	Keiko Niwa
	Masashi Ando
	Hiromasa Yonebayashi
Directed by	Hiromasa Yonebayashi
Executive Producer	Toshio Suzuki
Producer	Yoshiaki Nishimura
Production	Koji Hoshino
Music	Takatsugu Muramatsu
Supervising Animator	Masashi Ando
Production Designer	Yohei Taneda
Director of Digital Imaging	Atsushi Okui
Theme Song "Fine on the Outside"	
Performed by	Priscilla Ahn
Production	Studio Ghibli
Production Committee	Studio Ghibli
	Nippon Television Network
	Dentsu
	Hakuhodo DY Media Partners
	Walt Disney Japan
	Mitsubishi
	Toho
	KDDI

Anna	Sara Takatsuki
Marnie	Kasumi Arimura
Yoriko	Nanako Matsushima
Kiyomasa Oiwa	Susumu Terajima
Setsu Oiwa	Toshie Negishi
Old Lady	Ryoko Moriyama
Sayaka	Hana Sugisaki
Nan	Kazuko Yoshiyuki
Hisako	Hitomi Kuroki
Toichi	Ken Yasuda
	(TEAM NACS)

The Original Book

When Marnie Was There by Joan G. Robinson, 1967
◇ Japanese edition translated by Masako Matsuno (Iwanami Shoten), 2 volumes

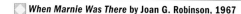

Considered by many to be the finest British children's book. The novel follows Anna's emotional trajectory over a single summer as she breaks free from loneliness through her friendship with her "secret friend Marnie." The Ghibli film boldly reverses the first and second halves of the plot.

ANNA

A closed-off 12-year-old, she leaves her foster parents for the summer and goes to the shore to stay with the Oi-was for her asthma.

MARNIE

A mysterious girl Anna meets at the Marsh House.

YORIKO

Anna's foster mother. Anna calls her "Auntie."

KIYOMASA OIWA

Setsu's husband, who Anna stays with for the summer.

SETSU OIWA

Yoriko's relative who Anna goes to stay with. Her children are grown, and she now lives alone with her husband.

OLD LADY

An old woman who lived at the Marsh House. She has a deep connection with Marnie and Anna.

SAYAKA

A girl who moves from Tokyo to the Marsh House. She and Anna become friends.

NAN

A servant at the Marsh House. She comes down hard on Mar-nie.

HISAKO

A woman by the shore drawing the Marsh House.

TOICHI

A taciturn old man who gives Anna a ride in his boat.

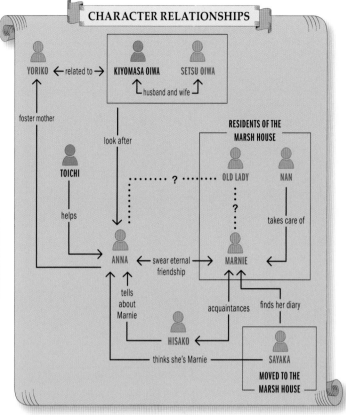

YORIKO ← related to → KIYOMASA OIWA   SETSU OIWA
← husband and wife →

foster mother

look after

TOICHI

helps

RESIDENTS OF THE MARSH HOUSE

? ········ OLD LADY   NAN

? takes care of

ANNA ← swear eternal friendship → MARNIE

tells about Marnie

acquaintances   finds her diary

HISAKO

thinks she's Marnie ← SAYAKA

MOVED TO THE MARSH HOUSE

■ Anna, staying with relatives by the seaside because of her asthma, meets Marnie at the abandoned Marsh House.

■ Always closed-off to others, Anna starts to open up to Marnie as they spend the summer together.

■ When they go to the silo, Marnie leaves Anna behind, and she feels betrayed.

■ Anna learns the truth about Marnie from Sayaka, the new resident of Marsh House, and starts to feel better.

TRIVIA

Toichi originally had lines demonstrating his concern for Anna, like, "Watch out for high tide." But Yone-bayashi felt the kindness of adults was a source of stress for Anna, that it would make it harder for her to open up, so he turned Toichi into a completely silent character.

POSTERS

Two posters were created for *When Marnie Was There*, with very different feels: one animation and the other illustration.

■ Poster 2 showed Marnie and Anna together, emphasizing the fact that this was Ghibli's first film with two female leads.

■ Poster 1, using director Hiromasa Yonebayashi's imageboard, was created before the film's release date was determined. After the release date was set, the tagline "There is a magic circle in this world no one can see" was changed to "I love you very much."

NEWSPAPER ADS

Ads started running on July 4th, and focused on the film's dual heroines and dreamlike feel.

■ The first ad was this full-page color one featuring the image from Poster 2, which ran in the *Asahi Shimbun* and *Yomiuri Shimbun* on July 4, 2014.

■ This 1/3-page ad from July 25, about a week after the release, centered the copy around the phrase "Marnie's secret."

■ The August 1 *Asahi Shimbun* and *Yomiuri Shimbun* ads used a different picture of Marnie, and tweaked the copy to make it even more intriguing.

■ Chilean and Peruvian poster.

■ Korean poster.

■ Taiwanese poster.

■ Thai poster.

■ Norwegian poster.

■ This ad, which ran in the *Asahi Shimbun* and regional papers on August 8 and 15, kept the same keywords but replaced Marnie with a closeup of Anna crying, emphasizing the moving nature of the film.

■ The ad that ran in the *Asahi Shimbun* and *Yomiuri Shimbun* on August 29 showed a smiling Anna from the final scene, creating a new impression of the film.

■ This August 22 follow-up ad, which used a still of Marnie and Anna embracing, ran in the *Asahi Shimbun* and *Yomiuri Shimbun*.

BEHIND THE SCENES

During the initial stages of production, the plan was to base the exterior of Marsh House on a sketch Yonebayashi made of a vacation home in Karuizawa. When live-action veteran Yohei Taneda came on as art director, however, he suggested creating an original building with the characteristics of Western-style houses in Hokkaido, where the story is set.

Ten years in the making, Ghibli's first collaboration is a fable about a man's relationship with nature on a deserted island

THE RED TURTLE   2016

Release date: September 17, 2016
Running time: Approx. 81 minutes
© 2016 Studio Ghibli, Wild Bunch, Why Not Productions, Arte France Cinéma, CN4 Productions, Belvision, Nippon Television Network, Dentsu, Hakuhodo DY Media Partners, Walt Disney Japan, Mitsubishi, Toho

Deeply impressed with the work of Dutch-born animator Michael Dudok de Wit, producer Toshio Suzuki put together this Japanese/French/Belgian coproduction with the film company Wild Bunch, Ghibli's French distributor. Also a big fan of Dudok de Wit's work, Isao Takahata represented Studio Ghibli and took on the role of artistic producer, providing various ideas and supporting the director across the board. Though based in the UK, Dudok de Wit spent a month in Japan at Studio Ghibli's invitation to work on the screenplay and storyboards.

This striking film tells the story of a man stranded on a deserted island, not as a survival tale, but as a universal story of one person's lifetime, the beauty and severity of nature, and the unbroken chain of life passed down through the generations. In addition to the pale colors and simple drawings, the sound design drew critical acclaim, using only human cries and breath, birdsong, sounds of nature like the lapping of waves, and gorgeous music to tell an otherwise wordless tale. Known for highly artistic short films like *Father and Daughter,* for which he won the 2000 Academy Award for Best Animated Short, this was Dudok de Wit's first feature. It took a full ten years from the initial planning stage, including eight years of production. Unusually for an animated film, *The Red Turtle* was shown in the Un Certain Regard section of the prestigious Cannes Film Festival, and won the Special Jury Prize in that category.

Original Story, Screenplay Written
and Directed by ·············· Michael Dudok de Wit
Screenplay ······················ Pascal Caucheteux
Artistic Producer ·············· Isao Takahata
Music ···························· Laurent Perez Del Mar
Production Committee ········ Studio Ghibli
                                Wild Bunch
Producers ······················· Toshio Suzuki
                                Vincent Maraval

Studio Ghibli
Wild Bunch
Why Not Productions
Arte France Cinéma
CN4 Productions
Belvision
Nippon Television Network
Dentsu
Hakuhodo DY Media Partners
Walt Disney Japan
Mitsubishi
Toho

Illustration:
Michael Dudok de Wit

STORY

A man is thrown overboard into the raging seas during a storm, narrowly escaping death and washing up on a deserted island. He builds a raft and tries to paddle away, but an unseen force destroys the raft, forcing him back to the island. He tries again, but the result is the same. Undaunted, he tries a third time, and catches sight of a giant red turtle when his raft is destroyed once more.

Believing it was the red turtle that had destroyed his previous rafts, he gives in to his anger and strikes it with a pole, flipping it over and leaving it on the beach. When he sees the seemingly dead turtle lying motionless, he is struck with remorse. Then a woman appears...

Co-Production ·············· Japan
                            France
                            Belgium
Production ···················· Prima Linea Productions

Illustration:
Michael Dudok de Wit

FATHER

Washed up on a deserted island with no way to escape, he leads a solitary life until he meets a woman and lives out the rest of his days with her on the island.

CHARACTER RELATIONSHIPS

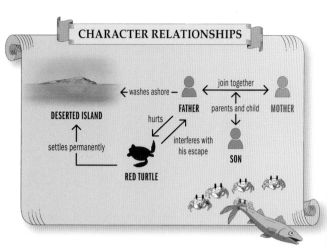

DESERTED ISLAND

FATHER — washes ashore →

join together

parents and child

MOTHER

settles permanently

hurts

interferes with his escape

SON

RED TURTLE

■ Having washed ashore on a deserted island, the man builds a raft and tries to return to his old life, but...

■ A woman suddenly appears and shows kindness to the man, who is instantly mesmerized by her.

MOTHER

She appears suddenly and begins living alongside the man.

SON

A child born to the man and woman. As a young child, he hears about the wider world from his father.

RED TURTLE

A large sea turtle with a red shell that the man sees when his raft is destroyed.

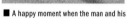

■ A happy moment when the man and his grown-up son run through a field together.

■ The family spends time drawing in the sand. The man draws the world he used to live in, and shows it to the boy.

■ There was only one Japanese poster, which was also used for the newspaper ads.

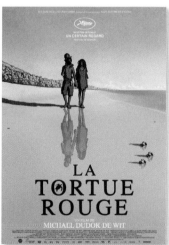

LA TORTUE ROUGE

UN FILM DE MICHAEL DUDOK DE WIT

■ The French poster used a still of the family walking on the beach.

■ The September 17, 2016, ad from the *Asahi Shimbun*.

■ September 16, 2016, *Asahi Shimbun* ad.

NEWSPAPER ADS

A horizontal ad ran on the release day, and a vertical one the day before. Both included comments from Naoki Matayoshi, writer and member of comedy duo Peace, and a poem by Shuntaro Tanikawa.

TRIVIA

There's something humanlike about turtles, able to come ashore as they are. Yet these ancient and solitary creatures are sometimes thought to be immortal, the polar opposites of human beings. The director decided to make the turtle red because it's a color associated with both danger and love, which he felt epitomized the story.

BEHIND THE SCENES

As artistic producer, Isao Takahata's main role was to review the screenplay and animatics (videos consisting of a series of successive storyboards) he received from director Dudok de Wit, and give his opinion as a creator. He put himself in the director's shoes, and tried his hardest to really grasp what Dudok de Wit wanted to accomplish.

■ The interior of the Sea of Decay is blanketed with an eerie fungus.

■ The Sea of Decay has swallowed up the fallen Giant Warrior, and continues to propagate.

Nausicaä of the Valley of the Wind

In the future, the planet is covered by a poisonous forest called the Sea of Decay. The fossils of the Giant Warriors who destroyed civilization are scattered about, and the interior of the forest is ruled by massive insects and fungi. The Sea of Decay is a terrifying presence seemingly inimical to human life, but is in fact purifying the air underground, and has the power to revive nature.

GHIBLI DRAWS
NATURE AND SCENERY

Ghibli's talented art department is famous for their backgrounds, and for natural landscapes in particular. This is largely the fruit of location scouting and on-the-ground research, but it's more than just a realistic expression of color or the contrast between light and shadow: it's also about choosing the right approach for each film to reflect its particular theme or worldview, which sometimes means being accurate down to the smallest detail and other times using dramatically simplified lines and colors. Such backgrounds help the viewers immerse themselves in the story, and make the characters seem all the more real.

■ The house is a blend of Japanese and Western architecture, with a well out back.

Only Yesterday

Toshio picks Taeko up at Yamagata Station, and she heads out to help with the safflower harvest. As they leave the center of town, the scenery outside the car window becomes more and more rural, until finally the stunning safflower fields come into view. The depictions of the early morning light and the mist and morning dew are not to be missed.

■ Mei runs between the rice paddies on her way to try and see her mother.

My Neighbor Totoro

The setting is based on the Tokyo suburbs of the 1950s, when fields and paddies were still numerous. The rich natural landscape, centered around a forest of massive old trees, invites nostalgia, and the house Satsuki's family moves into is surrounded by greenery, with a path leading to Totoro's forest.

Pom Poko

The tanuki aren't the only ones who appreciate the idyllic Tama Hills, blessed as they are with the beauty of the four seasons—but as the humans begin residential development, this rich natural environment starts to disappear. After Operation Specter fails, the tanuki use their final shapeshifting skills to bring back the former beauty of the landscape.

■ The tanuki look enviously at the humans' lifestyle.

■ They're driven out when the abandoned house is demolished.

■ The once-beautiful landscape is revived through their shapeshifting skills.

■ Shadowlike people wait at the train crossing.

Spirited Away

Chihiro takes the seaside train to Zeniba's house in Swamp Bottom to ask her how to save Haku. The train runs over the ocean leading out of the bathhouse, and the other passengers and the parent and child who wait at the train crossing appear as shadows. The memorable, mysterious landscapes are reminiscent of surrealism.

■ Swamp Bottom station, where Chihiro and her friends disembark.

■ Lit by the setting sun, the clouds are tinted a beautiful madder red.

■ Sosuke and Ponyo go to look for Lisa in a pop-pop boat.

■ Boats float like kites in the underwater town.

■ The water is filled with ancient creatures.

■ A giant jellyfish envelops Sunflower House.

■ A debonekus, a prehistoric fish created by director Hayao Miyazaki.

Ponyo on the Cliff by the Sea

Using the Water of Life her father has collected, Ponyo turns into a human and goes to see Sosuke, but the water leaks out and submerges the entire town. In this landscape where land and sea have become one, a parade of unique creatures including ancient fish and giant jellyfish appear.

■ The bamboo forest that plays a crucial part in the story.

■ After helping Koroku and the other injured people by the river, Ashitaka encounters the Deer God on his way to Iron Town.

■ The mountain hamlet, rendered in watercolors.

The Tale of The Princess Kaguya

Having seen the natural beauty of Earth and known human love, Princess Kaguya laments her return to the moon. The mountain hamlet she longs for is the embodiment of her memories of the old couple who raised her and of her first love, Sutemaru. The landscape was based mostly on the scenery around Kyoto.

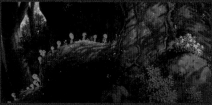

■ The lovable kodama tree spirits.

Princess Mononoke

Ancient spirits live deep within the Deer God's forest, where the land remains as it was long ago before the humans came, and clusters of mushrooms and wildflowers grow among the huge moss-covered trees and rocks. The virgin forests of Yakushima in Kagoshima Prefecture were used as a reference for this landscape.

DIRECTOR PROFILES

HAYAO MIYAZAKI

ISAO TAKAHATA

Born January 5, 1941, in Tokyo. After graduating with a degree in political economy from Gakushuin University, Miyazaki went to work at Toei Doga (now Toei Animation) in 1963. He worked as scene planner and key animator on *The Little Norse Prince Valiant* (1968), then moved to A Production, where he was responsible for the original concept, screenplay, layouts, and key animation for 1972's *Panda! Go Panda!* The following year, he moved to Zuiyo Eizo with Isao Takahata and others, then Nippon Animation and Telecom Animation Film, after which he co-founded Studio Ghibli in 1985. In the interim, he worked on scene planning and layouts for *Heidi, A Girl of the Alps* (1974), directed episodes of *Conan, The Boy in Future* (1978), and made his theatrical feature directorial debut with *The Castle of Cagliostro* (1979). In 1984, he wrote and directed *Nausicaä of the Valley of the Wind*, based on his manga of the same name serialized in the magazine *Animage*.

At Studio Ghibli, he directed theatrical feature-length animated films including *Castle in the Sky* (1986), *My Neighbor Totoro* (1988), *Kiki's Delivery Service* (1989), *Porco Rosso* (1992), *Princess Mononoke* (1997), *Spirited Away* (2001), *Howl's Moving Castle* (2004), and *Ponyo on the Cliff by the Sea* (2008). He also developed and wrote the screenplays for *Arrietty* (2010), directed by Hiromasa Yonebayashi, and *From Up on Poppy Hill* (2011), directed by Goro Miyazaki. In July 2013, he released *The Wind Rises*.

Spirited Away won the Golden Bear at the 52nd Berlin International Film Festival, and Best Animated Feature at the 75th Academy Awards. *Howl's Moving Castle* won a Golden Osella Award at the 61st Venice International Film Festival, and the following year, Miyazaki received the honorary Golden Lion for Lifetime Achievement at the same festival. In 2012, he was selected as a Person of Cultural Merit by the Japanese government, and in November 2014, he received an Honorary Award from the Academy of Motion Pictures Arts and Sciences. In July of that same year, he was inducted into the Hall of Fame of the Will Eisner Comic Industry Awards, one of the most prestigious U.S. comics awards.

Miyazaki also wrote the project draft and acted as producer for the Ghibli Museum, Mitaka, which opened in 2001. He is currently the museum's honorary director.

His publications include *Shuna's Journey, What is a Movie?* (conversations with Akira Kurosawa), *Princess Mononoke, Starting Point,* and *Magnifying Glasses and Anime Eyes* (conversations with Takeshi Yoro), all published by Tokuma Shoten; *Turning Point, The House Where Totoro Lives—Revised and Expanded Edition,* and *The Door to Books,* all published by Iwanami Shoten; and *Kazutoshi Hando and Hayao Miyazaki's Cowardly Patriotic Talks,* published by Bunshun Ghibli Bunko.

Born October 29, 1935, in Ise, Mie Prefecture, Takahata grew up in Okayama. In 1959, after graduating from Tokyo University with a degree in French literature, he went to work for Toei Doga. His first directorial work was for the TV series *Ken, The Wild Boy,* and he made his theatrical feature directorial debut with *The Little Norse Prince Valiant* (1968). After leaving Toei, he worked on television programs like *Heidi, A Girl of the Alps* (1974), *Marco, From the Apennines to the Andes* (1976), and *Anne of Green Gables* (1979), and directed the films *Downtown Story* (1981) and *Gauche the Cellist* (1982).

In 1985, he co-founded Studio Ghibli, where he directed *Grave of the Fireflies* (1988), *Only Yesterday* (1991), *Pom Poko* (1994), and *My Neighbors the Yamadas* (1999). In 2013, he released a long-awaited new opus, *The Tale of The Princess Kaguya.* It won the Mainichi Film Award for Best Animation Film, and the Los Angeles Film Critics Association Award for Best Animated Feature, and was nominated for an Academy Award for Best Animated Feature.

Takahata also produced *Nausicaä of the Valley of the Wind* (1984) and *Castle in the Sky* (1986), and acted as artistic producer for 2016's *The Red Turtle.*

In 1998, he received a Medal with Purple Ribbon from the Japanese government, and a Leopard of Honor at the 2009 Locarno Film Festival. Other awards and honors include a 2010 Anime Award Achievement Award, an honorary doctorate from the Rhode Island School of Design in 2012, an Anime D'Or from the Tokyo Anime Award Festival in 2014, and a Cristal d'honneur from the Annecy International Animation Film Festival. In April 2015, France made him an Officer of the Order of Arts and Letters, and in February 2016 he won a Winsor McCay Award.

His publications include *Things I Thought About While Making Movies* and *Animation in the 12th Century,* both published by Tokuma Shoten; a translation of Jacques Prévert's *Paroles,* as well as *Jacques Prévert, Greetings to a Bird,* both from Pia; *From One Painting—Japan Edition, From One Painting—Overseas Edition,* and *Animation, On Occasion,* all published by Iwanami Shoten.

Isao Takahata passed away on April 5, 2018, at the age of 82.

(English titles of most publications provisional)

TOMOMI MOCHIZUKI

Born in 1958 in Hokkaido. Mochizuki's first directorial work was for the program *Tokimeki Tonight* (1982), and he directed *Ocean Waves* for Studio Ghibli in 1993.

His major works include *Here is Greenwood* (1991), *Brave Command Dagwon* (1996), *Twin Spica* (2003), *Zettai Shonen* (2005), *House of Five Leaves* (2010), and *Battery* (2016). In addition to his directorial work, he has worked as script supervisor, screenwriter, and sound director for many animated films and series.

YOSHIFUMI KONDO

Kondo was born in Gosen, Niigata Prefecture in 1950. After graduating from Muramatsu Public High School in Niigata in 1968, he began working at A Production. As an animator, he worked on *Star of the Giants*, *Lupin the 3rd*, *The Gutsy Frog*, and *Panda! Go Panda!*, among others.

He joined Nippon Animation in 1978 to work on *Conan, The Boy in Future*, and in 1979 was selected to work as character designer and supervising animator for *Anne of Green Gables*, directed by Isao Takahata.

In 1980, he joined Telecom Animation Film. After working on *Sherlock Hound*, he was preparing to co-direct the Japanese-American coproduction *Little Nemo: Adventures in Slumberland* (1989), but dropped out of the project.

He joined Studio Ghibli in 1987, and worked as character designer and supervising animator on 1988's *Grave of the Fireflies*. Isao Takahata and Hayao Miyazaki put great store in his abilities, and Kondo went on to work with them on films including *Kiki's Delivery Service* (1989), *Only Yesterday* (1991), *Porco Rosso* (1992), and *Pom Poko* (1994). He made his theatrical feature directorial debut with 1995's *Whisper of the Heart*.

Yoshifumi Kondo passed away in 1998. He was only 47.

The high degree of skill he brought to everything from well-paced action sequences to detailed scenes of everyday life, and his uncompromising work ethic, influenced a great many animators.

HIROYUKI MORITA

Born in Fukuoka Prefecture in 1964. After working as an animator on many films including *Akira* (1988), *Perfect Blue* (1998), and *My Neighbors the Yamadas* (1999), he made his directorial debut with Studio Ghibli's *The Cat Returns* (2002). He went on to direct the TV series *Bokurano* (2007), and was assistant director for the 2017 3DCG film *Godzilla: Planet of the Monsters* and 2019's *NiNoKuni*.

Morita is an adjunct professor at Tokyo Zokei University and a lecturer at Nihon Kogakuin College, Hachioji Campus. He is one of the authors of *The Psychology of Animation*, in the *Japanese Psychological Association Series* (Seishin Shobo).

YOSHIYUKI MOMOSE

Born in Tokyo in 1953, Momose joined Studio Ghibli as a key animator on director Isao Takahata's *Grave of the Fireflies* (1988). Momose also worked as storyboard artist on *Only Yesterday* (1991) and *Pom Poko* (1994), was in charge of CG for *Princess Mononoke* (1997), and worked on storyboard and layout design for *My Neighbors the Yamadas* (1999). After making his theatrical directorial debut with *the GHIBLIES episode 2* (2002), he directed House Foods' "Let's Eat at Home" series of commercials (2003), as well as music videos for CAPSULE and Yui Aragaki, and was in charge of scene design for *The Tale of The Princess Kaguya* (2013).

For Studio Ponoc, he directed JR West's "Summer Train" commercial and the "Life Ain't Gonna Lose" segment from the animated anthology *Modest Heroes* (2018). He also directed *NiNoKuni* (2019), the film adaptation of the video game for which he acted as animation director and character designer, as well as the short film "Tomorrow's Leaves," a co-production with the Olympic Foundation of Culture.

GORO MIYAZAKI

Goro Miyazaki was born in Tokyo in 1967. After graduating with a degree in forest engineering from Shinshu University's Faculty of Agriculture, he worked as a construction consultant in park and urban garden planning and design. In 1998, he helmed the design of the Ghibli Museum, Mitaka, and served as its managing director from 2001 to June of 2005. He was also in charge of the creation of "Satsuki and Mei's House," which opened in 2005 in Aichi Earth Expo Memorial Park.

He made his debut as a director with Ghibli's *Tales from Earthsea* (2006), and went on to direct his second film, *From Up on Poppy Hill*, in 2011. He directed his first animated television series, *Ronja, the Robber's Daughter*, for NHK BS Premium (production and copyright: NHK, Dwango), which ran from fall of 2014 to spring of 2015. He also acted as production supervisor for the Japanese-language version of the Chinese animated film *Monkey King: Hero is Back* (released in Japan in 2018).

His most recent film is the feature-length 3DCG film *Earwig and the Witch*, released on August 27, 2021. He is also involved in Ghibli Park, scheduled to open in 2022 in Aichi Earth Expo Memorial Park in Nagakute.

In 2004, he received an Art Encouragement Prize for New Artists from the Ministry of Education, Culture, Sports, Science and Technology.

In 2016, *Ronja, the Robber's Daughter* won an International Emmy Award, presented to the world's best TV shows, in the Kids: Animation category.

HIROMASA YONEBAYASHI

Yonebayashi was born in 1973 in Nonoichi, Ishikawa Prefecture. After majoring in commercial design at the Kanazawa College of Art, he joined Studio Ghibli in 1996 and worked as an animator on *Princess Mononoke* (1997) and *My Neighbors the Yamadas* (1999). His first outing as key animator was on *Spirited Away* (2001), and he subsequently worked as key animator for *the GHIBLIES episode 2* (2002), *Howl's Moving Castle* (2004), and *Ponyo on the Cliff by the Sea* (2008). He was the assistant supervising animator on *Tales from Earthsea* (2006), and was selected to direct 2010's *Arrietty*. The film became the top-grossing Japanese film of the year, with an audience of 7.65 million and a box office of ¥9.25 billion. His second film, *When Marnie Was There* (2014), was nominated for Best Animated Feature at the Academy Awards.

After leaving Ghibli, he directed Studio Ponoc's first feature film, *Mary and the Witch's Flower* (2017), and the segment "Kanini & Kanino" for *Modest Heroes* (2018).

MICHAEL DUDOK DE WIT

Dudok de Wit was born in 1953 in the Netherlands. He studied etching and animation at art colleges in Switzerland and the UK, and in 1978, made *Interview* as his graduation project. After working in Spain as an animator, he settled in the UK in 1980. He worked as a freelancer for a number of studios throughout the 80s and 90s, including Disney, where he was a storyboard artist for *Beauty and The Beast* (1991) and an animator on *Fantasia 2000* (2000). He has also produced award-winning commercials for companies around the world, including United Airlines, AT&T, Nestlé, Volkswagen, and Heinz.

Starting in the 1990s he became acclaimed for his animated short films, including *Tom Sweep* in 1992 and *The Monk and the Fish*, which was completed in 1994 and nominated for an Academy Award for Best Animated Short. His most famous work, *Father and Daughter* (2000), won the 73rd Academy Award for Best Animated Short and the Grand Prix at the Annecy International Animation Film Festival. He completed *The Aroma of Tea* in 2006, and his 2016 feature film debut *The Red Turtle* was nominated for Best Animated Feature at the Academy Awards, after having won the Un Certain Regard Special Jury Prize at the Cannes Film Festival. He also writes and illustrates children's books, and teaches at art colleges in Europe and North America.

IN THEIR OWN WORDS

What hopes and feelings did Studio Ghibli's directors, including Hayao Miyazaki and Isao Taka-hata, pour into their films? What were they thinking during the filmmaking process? Here we present directors' unaltered planning documents and other comments from the time the movies were being produced.

Nausicaä of the Valley of the Wind

Hayao Miyazaki (Original story, screenplay, director)

From the theatrical pamphlet (1984)

A film people unfamiliar with the original manga can enjoy...

"A film to free the hearts and minds of a generation of young people made neurotic by overprotection, suffocated by a controlling society, with no path to independence"—in recent years I've submitted movie proposals like this, but to no avail. So I harnessed that feeling and started drawing a manga for the monthly magazine *Animage*.

Nausicaä of the Valley of the Wind is set on Earth during the twilight of humanity, and tells the story of a girl who learns to see more broadly even as she gets caught up in human strife. Having said that, it's not about the battle itself. The central theme will be the relationship humans have with nature itself,

which surrounds us and which we depend on.

—Can we find hope even in the twilight of civilization? And what viewpoint do we need in order to look for it? I intended to slowly reveal the answers in the manga, which should continue to be serialized over several years.

I didn't create the manga with animation in mind, and when I was asked to adapt it for film, I was honestly conflicted. But if a film *could* digest that central theme, I indeed felt compelled to make it.

In addition to expressing my gratitude to the people at Tokuma Shoten and Hakuhodo who gave me the opportunity to make the film, I want to say that I approached my original manga with humility, and I think I succeeded in creating a film that people who never read it can enjoy.

Castle in the Sky

Hayao Miyazaki (Original story, screenplay, director)

From the theatrical pamphlet (1986)

I want to speak to children's hearts

Can you tell an adventure story with a classical framework in the language of today?

Precisely in this age when justice has become an expedient and love a game, when dreams are mass produced, an age without uninhabited islands, when the universe has been devoured and treasures converted into currency, children

long more than ever for tales of passionate departures, where discoveries and amazing encounters wait just around the corner—for tales of hope.

Why do we hesitate to talk about the bonds that can only be won through self-sacrifice and devotion?

I want nothing more than to make a story that speaks directly to children's hearts, hidden as they are under layers of pretense, irony, and resignation.

This is the origin of Laputa!

(From the planning and production notes)

There was a model for Laputa, the floating island Swift writes about in Part III of *Gulliver's Travels*: Laputaritis, which Plato wrote about in his lost work of geography, *On the Sky*.

Laputaritis was founded by a people who, despising war, fled to the sky during the flourishing of the first great technological civilization (ours being the second). Their civilization advanced too far, however, and the Laputians lost their vitality, the population waning until eventually they were wiped out by the sudden outbreak of a mysterious disease around 500 BCE.

It is said that some Laputians survived by descending to the surface and hiding themselves among the people there, but the details are unknown.

Laputa's palaces are abandoned, protected by robots who await the king's return. But the kingdom has suffered a great deal of damage over the long years, and now only a small part of it still floats through the sky. The island creates a low-pressure system and is hidden by a ridge of clouds, moving with the westerlies, and has consequently never been spotted from the surface.

A few people still espouse the theory that before our current civilization, there was a technological civilization so advanced that it used even nuclear energy however it saw fit. Based on the Sanskrit epics the *Rāmāyana* and the *Mahābhārata*, this theory is particularly popular in India.

My Neighbor Totoro

Hayao Miyazaki (Original story, screenplay, director)

From the theatrical pamphlet (1988)

I want to create a fun, wonderful film set in Japan

My goal for the animated feature *My Neighbor Totoro* is to create a happy, heartwarming film, one that lets you go home feeling joyful and refreshed. Lovers' hearts grow fonder, parents recall treasured childhood memories, and children start climbing trees and exploring behind shrines because they want to meet Totoro—that's the kind of film I want to make.

Until very recently, when asked what Japan could boast of, adults and children alike would answer, "The beauty of nature and the four seasons." But no one says that anymore. We who live in Japan, and are undeniably Japanese, avoid setting our animations in Japan as much as possible. Has this country become such a shabby, dreamless place?

In this age of globalization, when we know full well that the most national things can become international, why don't we try to create fun, wonderful films set in Japan?

We need new approaches and fresh discoveries to answer this simple question. The film we make has to be light, lively entertainment, not just nostalgia or homesickness.

What we've forgotten;

What we haven't noticed;

What we're convinced we've lost;

I want to make *My Neighbor Totoro* from the bottom of my heart, believing these things still exist.

Totoro

This is the name that four-year-old Mei, one of the protagonists, gives them. No one knows their real name.

From a long, long time ago, when there were virtually no people in Japan, they've dwelled in our woods, and they seem to live for at least a thousand years. Large Totoro can be over six and a half feet tall. Covered in fluffy fur, Totoro could perhaps be considered a kind of monster, somewhere between a huge horned owl or badger or a bear, but they live a relaxed, carefree life, and aren't interested in threatening human beings. They reside in caves in the woods or the hollows of old trees and can't be seen by humans, but for some reason are visible to the young siblings Mei and Satsuki.

Totoro hate noise and have never had dealings with humans in the past, but they open their hearts to Satsuki and Mei.

Grave of the Fireflies

Isao Takahata (Director)

From the press release (1987) / theatrical pamphlet (1988)
Grave of the Fireflies and today's children

1

A 14-year-old boy takes his four-year-old sister to live in a tunnel dug into the hillside by a pond. Somewhere between playing at adventure and playing house, he brings in a charcoal brazier and a mosquito net, collects twigs to cook rice, and draws water from the sea when they need salt. They wash themselves in the pond, and catch pond snails as they swim.

It's summer. The sun beats down, rain patters on the surface of the water and flows down like a waterfall. Steam rises and sweat flows. Night falls on this world of blinding light, and a massive swarm of fireflies dance in the summer grass. The siblings release a hundred or more fireflies inside the mosquito net. In the pale light, their memories of long ago come back to them like a dream. In this case, though, "long ago" is only a month prior…

Such is the strange, heartbreaking life this brother and sister fashion for themselves. A mysterious aura surrounds them.

But this isn't a deserted island they've washed up on after a shipwreck—they're surrounded by fields and paddies, and there are people, and plenty of stately houses. When they look down the embankment from the pond, the city spreads out beneath them all the way to the sea. Burnt fields alternate with quiet, old-fashioned residential blocks under the blazing sun. The stark disconnect between the two is akin to the disconnect in the siblings' minds between before and after their sudden misfortune. Follow the river down from the city, where only the elevated tracks stand out, and cut across three sets of train tracks and a highway, and you'll find yourself on a sandy beach shimmering in the heat of summer.

For the month and a half between July 6 and August 22, 1945, even after the war has ended, Seita and Setsuko live in a hillside bomb shelter beside a reservoir. Having lost their mother during an air raid while their father was off at war, this town is their turf, their neighborhood.

How does the very young sister tell the difference between real life and playing house? Relentless hunger will teach her that.

This isn't a deserted island. There are lots of people. The siblings even interact with them. They get their ration of rice. The brother takes the kimono their mother left behind and goes to lay in supplies, with a bunch of ten-yen bills from her savings account shoved into his pocket. But even if the neighbors run into the siblings by the town well, they don't come by the bomb shelter where the two are living. Are they hesitant to interfere because they see the older brother, in his third year of middle school, as a full-fledged adult? They're probably just busy with their own lives and families, and don't have the wherewithal to worry about the siblings. Never mind worrying about them—when the brother raids the fields for even the smallest scrap of food, they beat him and call the police.

Every time he hears an air raid siren, the brother rushes to a part of the city that's still standing. Racing through the deafening explosions and strafing machine gun fire, he bursts into houses whose residents have fled and steals food or whatever clothing he might be able to trade. Even when he sees the glint of a B-29 in the sky, he's no longer scared; he almost feels like waving to them.

2

If war suddenly broke out today, and the same kind of destruction was visited on Japan, how would children who lost their parents survive? And how would adults treat other people's children?

I can't help feeling that Seita, the older brother in *Grave of the Fireflies*, is like a contemporary boy who accidentally time traveled back to that miserable era. And the almost inevitable outcome is that he lets his little sister die, and then dies himself a month later.

Back then, the third year of middle school was an age at which some children entered the naval aviator prep course or military academy prep school and became child soldiers. While Seita is a navy lieutenant's firstborn son, though, he doesn't seem at all like the child of a nation at war. When their house burns down in an air raid and his little sister asks, "What are we gonna do?" all he can say is, "Dad'll get revenge for us." He shows no spirit of self-sacrifice to the nation or the emperor, and the shock of the air raid erases whatever normal hostility he may have felt toward the enemy.

He grew up relatively affluent for the time, and enjoyed an urban lifestyle. He certainly never had to face adversity, and never had to help strict parents with their work or clench his teeth to put up with humiliation. He never had to grovel, and even though it was wartime, he would have been one of those leading a comparatively carefree life.

But Seita loses his mother and his home, and goes to live at a distant relative's house. Whether she had a grudge against her late husband's cousin (their father, the naval lieutenant) or had simply always lacked compassion, she soon starts treating the siblings as a burden. Seita can't stand her harassment and sarcasm, he can't bring himself to kneel before the hysterical widow and beg for her forgiveness in order to protect his sister and himself. From her perspective, she must not have found Seita endearing at all.

The widow is cruelty incarnate, telling the children, "Okay, let's each take care of our own meals. Surely then you can't complain," and, "If you're that afraid for your life, go live in a bomb shelter," but she can't have believed they would ever actually do it. Seita, however, can't bear to remain in this bitter relationship that requires him to curry favor and surrender himself completely. He chooses to remove himself from the situation, moving to the bomb shelter and fending for himself just as she suggested. The widow must have hated this child who wouldn't abase himself and come crawling back to her, and her conscience probably didn't bother her after he was gone.

Seita's actions and emotions put me in mind of the materially comfortable modern youths and children who make pleasure their major criterion for dealing with other people, and who dislike complicated or difficult relationships. Not that the adults are any different.

In this modern age, we're protected by double and triple layers of social protection and control in seemingly direct proportion to our loosening family bonds and decreasing solidarity with neighbors. We make mutual noninterference the basis for social interaction, and confirm our kindness to each other through a playful solicitude that never gets at anything authentic. If there were a major disaster—it doesn't have to be war—and society unraveled, devoid as it is of principles of mutual aid or cooperation, people's relationships would be laid bare and man would become wolf to man even more than in the immediate post-war years. I shudder to think that I could be on either side of that. And if they were to flee from human interaction and try to make it on their own with just a little sister in tow, how many boys, how many *people* could succeed

in providing for her to the extent Seita does?

Although the story is tragic, Seita isn't a miserable figure. He holds his head up high, and even strikes the viewer as a brave young man standing on his own two feet. Like a woman, like a mother, this 14-year-old boy indefatigably dedicates himself to the most basic human need: feeding himself and his sister.

Their solitary life in the bomb shelter is the heart of the film, and its salvation. For a fleeting moment, light shines into the lives of these two children, who have been saddled with a terrible fate. A young child's smile, the very essence of innocence.

Seita provides for his little sister on his own and works to keep them both alive, but of course this is beyond him. They both perish.

3

"Grave of the Fireflies" was written as the period of post-war reconstruction, when standing strong and surviving were paramount, gave way to an era of rapid economic growth. Even as they were moved to pity, some readers at the time didn't want to accept such a tragic ending.

But "Grave of the Fireflies" emits a powerful light that illuminates our present world, and makes us tremble. In the forty-plus years since the war ended, Seita's life and death have never felt less distant or more resonant than they do now.

Which is why I really want to make this film now.

In our animations, we have always portrayed admirable boys and girls who courageously face hardship, find a way through, and bravely survive. But in reality, there are some circumstances you can't find a way through, when cities and villages become battlegrounds and people's hearts are consumed by strife. The ones that will die in that situation are the gentle youth of today, half of us. It is of course important to portray courage and hope and resilience in animation, but we also need to make films that force us to consider how we are connected to one another.

Kiki's Delivery Service

Hayao Miyazaki (Producer, screenplay, director)

From the theatrical pamphlet (1989)
The hopes and hearts of modern girls

The excellent children's novel *Kiki's Delivery Service* by Eiko Kadono (Fukuinkan Shoten) lovingly portrays the hopes and hearts of modern girls as they stand at the crossroads of dependence and independence. For the protagonists of past

stories, hard-won financial independence was itself mental independence. But as we can see from current Japanese buzzwords like *free arbeiter* (serial part-timer), *moratorium* (putting off joining the rat race), and *travaille* (job-hopping), financial independence no longer necessarily means mental independence. Nowadays we need to be talking about emotional poverty more than material poverty.

In a time when leaving the nest is too easy to be called a rite of passage and a convenience store can provide everything necessary to live among others, the independence girls must face has become a thornier problem—how to discover their talent, how to manifest it, how to achieve self-actualization.

Thirteen-year-old witch Kiki has only one magical ability: she can fly. In this world, witches are no longer rare, and as part of her training Kiki must live for one year in a strange town and get the people there to accept her as a witch.

Her situation is like that of a young woman who moves by herself to the big city with dreams of becoming a manga artist. There are said to be 300,000 young would-be manga artists in Japan today. It's not even a particularly rare profession: making one's debut is relatively easy, and it's perfectly possible to scrape together a living. But what happens these days is that, in the course of their everyday routine, these manga artists hit a wall for the first time. With her mother's favorite broom for protection, the radio her father bought her for diversion, and her black cat familiar by her side, Kiki's heart is nevertheless filled with loneliness and a longing for the company of other people. She represents all those girls who, cherished and even financially supported by their parents, long for the glamour of the city and go there to seek their independence. Kiki's naivete and hasty resolve reflect society today.

In the novel, Kiki overcomes difficulties through her inherent good nature, which spreads into a widening circle of friends and allies. For the film adaptation, we have to make some changes. Although it's nice to see Kiki's talent blossom, the hearts of young girls who live in our current cities are more warped. For all too many of them, nothing could be more difficult than overcoming the hurdles to independence, and they don't feel they've ever received anyone's blessing. I think we have to do more to address the issue of independence in the film. Movies end up creating a sense of reality whether you want them to or not, which means Kiki will probably experience a stronger sense of loneliness and discouragement than in the book.

The first thing we imagined when we encountered Kiki was a little girl flying above a city at night. There are lots of glittering lights, but none of them welcome her… Flying is isolating. The power to fly means liberation from the bounds of the earth, but freedom also means insecurity and loneliness. This girl who decides to be true to herself by flying is our protagonist. There have been many "magical girls" in TV animation, etc., but magic was never more than a means to realize their dreams. They became idols without any struggle. The magic in *Kiki's Delivery Service* is not such a convenient power.

In this film, magic is a limited ability that represents the talents, whatever they may be, that all real-life girls have.

We plan to put together a happy ending where, as Kiki flies over the rooftops, she feels strongly connected to the people beneath them, and at the same time has a heightened awareness of her own identity. We're prepared for the fact that the happy ending can't be mere wish fulfillment; it has to be earned by everything that comes before.

Neither criticizing their youthful exuberance nor being blinded by it, I believe we have to finish this film as a message of solidarity with a young audience who stand at the crossroads of dependence and independence (because we were young once, and our young staff face these very problems even as we speak). And for that same reason, I believe this film has what it takes to win the hearts of its audience as a work of top-notch entertainment.

Only Yesterday

Isao Takahata (Director and screenplay)

From the theatrical pamphlet (1991)
Production notes

——I went on a journey with my fifth-grade self.

As the old saying goes, "Make the beloved child take a journey."

The efficiency of modern travel means it lacks hardship, and so we lose the opportunity to experience the kindness of others. And yet, it's still a unique opportunity to learn about life and take a close look at oneself.

Some journeys take us from place to place, others take us through time. If you send the "beloved child"—yourself—on a journey through both, you may be able to find out who you are, to come out of your shell, to find the real you.

The film *Only Yesterday* is the interim statement (a reportage) from Taeko Okajima, a 27-year-old office worker who goes on just such a journey.

1. The Original Work

Only Yesterday is an animated adaption of the manga of the same name.

Over the course of twenty-odd stand-alone chapters, the

manga details the seemingly insignificant experiences of a fifth-grade girl through her adult reminiscences.

It's 1966, the year the Beatles came to Japan. The narrator Taeko Okajima is ten at the time, and the youngest of three sisters who live in a suburb of Tokyo with their parents and grandmother.

While some of the episodes include things specific to the moment, the manga isn't retro per se—it's mostly composed of the kind of compelling girlhood experiences common across the generations.

There's nothing special to speak of about the girl, our protagonist. She's a totally average, normal child who doesn't seem to have much in the way of individuality. She's good at writing, and bad at math. Her family and her class aren't particularly special either. Her parents are an old-fashioned couple: the wife obeys her husband, no doubt a fervently devoted company man during this period of rapid economic growth. They are upper middle class, no different from the families of Taeko's classmates.

The chapters are about the kinds of things that could happen to anyone in the course of normal everyday life, told in an extremely simple, matter-of-fact way. The blink-and-you'll-miss-it humor and pathos are enjoyable, but the events themselves are neither particularly moving nor invested with lessons to be learned.

I suspect it would be hard for people who haven't read the manga to imagine how this would be fascinating.

And yet it clearly is.

Why?

First off, because the memories are sliced out with such panache.

People only remember events that were momentous for them, and end up forgetting the rest. Even our memories of what led up to those big events are influenced by the results and the emotions we feel at the time, often taking root in our minds in a distorted form, and our adult emotions and interpretations warp them even further. It's really these distorted things that we call "memories." As a result, memories, even bittersweet ones, tend to become hazy and nostalgic.

But in the manga *Only Yesterday*, the ten-year-old protagonist's reality and way of experiencing the world are presented as-is, in vivid detail. It's like going back in a time machine, the protagonist returning to the world of her ten-year-old self as if it was only yesterday. What's so moving about it isn't the events themselves, but the sensory experience of that world.

That doesn't mean that what we're presented with is the objective reality of that time; we see and hear and feel only what the ten-year-old Taeko saw, heard, felt. This subjective experience is bound to be slightly different from "objective" reality.

While at the same time bringing us into the realm of this ten-year-old's sensibilities and observations—assuring us through this subjectivity that these are indeed "memories"—*Only Yesterday* holds firmly to a standard of objectivity in its presentation, which allows these strangely raw and vivid memories to take root in the form of manga.

If "memories" are what we see when we look back at the past with eyes clouded by sentimentality, *Only Yesterday* is like reportage by someone who went back in a time machine to the time and place where their memories were created.

This is its greatest appeal.

Secondly, because the memories in question are all of things that could happen to anyone.

Some outstanding literary works vividly portray memories very much worth the telling. But the reason the memories in *Only Yesterday* feel so vivid to everyone is that they're everyone's memories, things so common they could happen to any of us.

Many people who read *Only Yesterday* say, "I was like that when I was that age," or, "It's like I'm back in elementary school." They feel like these memories are their own, and the manga triggers their memories and experiences to come flooding back to them.

These people didn't feel like their memories were worth the telling. In fact, they had forgotten them completely. And now *Only Yesterday* has brought them back.

The third reason is that these memories are so plausible as the reportage of an average ten-year-old.

Is anything really trivial to a ten-year-old girl? Adults only think so because they see things through an adult's value system. They've forgotten that for a ten-year-old girl, every day is a fresh experience. Most everything that happens in *Only Yesterday* would be very serious or even painful for an ordinary girl.

The average ten-year-old girl is still passive most of the time, and doesn't act against her circumstances or take control of situations through her words or actions. Life doesn't work like it does for the protagonists of anime or children's books.

The growing ego creates friction with the protection and restrictions of parents and schools, but most of the time this friction in fact promotes the ego's further growth and merely lays the groundwork for the onset of adolescence. Adolescence is the time of ordeals that establish the ego, and because of the magnitude of these ordeals, most people forget the small frictions that came before.

In a way, forgetting is the same thing as overcoming, so it's only natural that it should be hard to see what children this age are really like. Their egos are underdeveloped, and their individuality isn't yet clear enough to come to the surface. Even if their inner sensibilities have blossomed, all we see on the outside is a ten-year-old blur.

The manga *Only Yesterday* is groundbreaking in its vivid portrayal of a young girl at this age.

Girls around the age of ten will see themselves reflected in this manga, and after going back and forth between sympathy and resistance, will, if nothing else, come to appreciate that grown-ups used to be the same as them.

2. The Title

Only Yesterday uses an antiquated phonetic character to write its title, which seems to be connected to the retrospective mood so common among young people today. And it certainly has the power to appeal to this sensibility, packed as it is with references to the Beatles' visit, miniskirts, girls' manga magazines like *Friend* and *Margaret*, Barbie dresses, the TV show *Pop-Up Gourd Island*, flipping up girls' skirts, and the popular punchline "You scared the hell out of me!"

People now start having class reunions young, where they get fired up talking about the past. Even in small groups, the old days is everyone's favorite topic. And they all get to feel secure knowing they were all the same. *Only Yesterday* is perfect for providing that sense of security.

3. Where does this retrospective mood come from?

As traditional value systems crumble, every kind of human relationship is destabilized, from society to family to romantic pairings. We no longer even talk about "human relationships" when we want to create unity, strengthen our bonds, or comfort each other. It only brings the word "fraying" to mind.

Based on our own value systems, other people seem selfish, which means that we're all selfish, and friction is the result. Even when it comes to recreation, or rather precisely because it's recreation, we avoid things like mahjong that involve people with different personalities coming together. Now there are plenty of machines that allow us to play alone, however we want. We don't interfere with other people, and we don't want them to interfere with us. You're you, I'm me, never the twain shall meet… But that's not really true. We're all extremely uncomfortable around strangers, yet long for company. We so badly want to let ourselves depend on someone, but we can't because we don't let others depend on us.

We're surrounded by things, information, freedom, pleasure, but we're all lonely. We're all uneasy. We're unable to discern what's truly important to us, what's really worthwhile enough to support ourselves with. We haven't established our own identities. We aren't able to say, *This is who I am, no matter how other people are or how the world is*. If the prosperity of others, of the world, fell apart, we feel like we would automatically be gone too. Which is why we seek reassurance by affirming our similarities with other people, however small they may be.

Avoiding human relationships doesn't mean we like to be lonely. Watching TV by yourself doesn't mean you're soli-

tary. In fact, we love to gather in places we know will be friction-free. There are plenty of hobby clubs and class reunions. We even engage in trendy "things to do by yourself" in groups. Though even when we're in groups, we don't engage with each other. We don't form a circle. We sit in a row, facing the same direction, like when we're watching TV. What we share isn't within us but in front of us. And we feel a little bit relieved that it's the same for all of us.

In reality, retro is just another manifestation of the same phenomenon. We look back on the past, enumerate the details, and feel secure in the knowledge that everyone had the same experience. Assuming that a sense of belonging and identity is necessary for humans to feel emotionally secure, do we really need to cling to such feeble things? Unfortunately, it seems we do.

4. Structuring the film *Only Yesterday*

We start by recognizing that in modern life, this retrospective mood is a kind of anti-anxiety drug. Let's admit that making a film of *Only Yesterday* is partially about appealing to this feeling, which will happen naturally if we're going to try to capitalize on the appeal of the original manga. (We'll use around ten chapters of the manga for the film.)

But I don't think we want to make the film with the goal of appealing to that retrospective mood. In fact, it's the reverse. That kind of nostalgia makes it difficult for us in these modern times to establish our sense of self, and I don't want to encourage that tendency.

To cure mental illness, first you dig through the patient's past, all the way down to their subconscious. The patient steps back and makes themself an object of study, and once their self-analysis is complete, they're cured. So looking back on the past probably isn't a bad first step, whatever form it takes.

Whether the world is in a retrospective mood or not, *Only Yesterday* has such an enduring appeal because it brings the past back to life so vividly.

Building on this foundation, I want to envision the protagonist, Taeko Okajima, as she would be at 27, and have her look back on her ten-year-old self. There's nothing wrong with 27-year-old Taeko; she's grown into a nice young woman, cheerful around other people.

As someone who grew up in the era of women's independence, Taeko went to college and got a job that isn't just something to do until she gets married. She works hard, and has managed to fit in a romantic relationship or two around her job. But now she's 27 and single.

Work doesn't feel as fresh and engaging as it did when she was first learning the ropes. Her mother pressures her to go to a formal marriage interview, saying it's her last chance. Taeko has never gone along with that stuff, though, feeling like it would take away her agency.

On the surface, she's working as cheerfully as ever, and

has even more fun after work than the men do, but she feels that she can't move forward with confidence unless she clears her mind and makes some decisions.

Like the ten-year-old Taeko, I want the 27-year-old version to be an ordinary person. She's having a hard time establishing her identify, just like the rest of us.

What would happen if that Taeko suddenly recalled herself at ten? This is half of the concept for the film. The other half involves sending grown-up Taeko to the countryside to experience life on a farm. (There's a basis for this: Taeko was born and raised in Tokyo, and has never spent time in the countryside. She was always envious of friends who had family outside the city. If we add in the premise that her older sister's husband is from the country, Taeko can go to visit and be excited about having a new rural "hometown.")

We live in the city and wait for food to be brought to us. We've lost sight of the fact that we're animals. Likely driven by instinct, we want nature and greenery and water, but we want a made-up nature that's pretty, hygienic, harmless, 100% pure, and a fantasy. And we want occasional contact with that untouched nature to refresh our spirits. But intrinsically, animals can only live in nature. Exposed to its threats, they take from it, receive from it, eat, live. This was also the root of human endeavor. And only those who lose their sense of reality or fail to establish their identity in the midst of this endeavor would be the mentally ill.

It goes without saying that in the modern day, farmers are the ones who live closest to that root.

I'll send Taeko out to the countryside and have her meet a young man who's thrown himself into farming. This is because I'm certain that the most fundamental litmus test for stepping outside yourself and establishing your identity lies in the countryside, where the root of human endeavor persists.

Preparation notes for *Only Yesterday* (January 8, 1990)

Porco Rosso

Hayao Miyazaki (Original story, screenplay, director)

From the press release
Production memo

● Manga film revival

Porco Rosso is a film even businessmen exhausted from international flights, their brains number than ever from lack of oxygen, can enjoy. It also has to be a film that boys, girls, and middle-aged women can enjoy, but we can't forget that first and foremost, this is "a manga film for middle-aged men who are so exhausted their brains have turned to tofu."

It's jolly but not riotous.

It's dynamic but not destructive.

There's plenty of love, but we don't need lust.

It's a simple story without subplots, filled with honor and freedom, and the characters' motivations couldn't be clearer.

All the men are jovial and lighthearted, the charming women are enjoying what life has to offer, and the world is endlessly bright and beautiful. That's the film we want to make.

● Bear in mind that what we see of the characters is just the tip of the iceberg

Porco, Fio, Mr. Curtis, Master Piccolo, Gina, the Mamma Aiuto gang, the other air pirates—these main characters should all feel real, like they've carved a path through life. Their hijinks stem from past suffering, and simplicity is a sign of hard-won maturity. We have to value every one of these characters. We should love their foolishness. We mustn't cut corners in the portrayal of the background characters either. We absolutely cannot make the common mistake of thinking that manga is about drawing people stupider than ourselves. Otherwise, the film won't satisfy the oxygen-starved middle-aged men.

● Instead of more detail, more frames to make it dynamic

Rather than adding more lines to the ocean, the spray from the waves, the flying boats, the people, let's show them through movement. Keep the forms simple, the drawings easy, and put all that energy toward movement instead. Let's find the cheerfulness, the joy of movement.

● The colors

Vivid but tasteful, not overdone.

Cheerful and lively, but balanced so the eyes don't get tired!!

● Backgrounds

A town you'd want to visit. Skies you'd want to fly through. A secret hideaway you'd want for yourself. A carefree, bright, invigorating world. Earth was once beautiful.

Let's make a film like this.

Ocean Waves

Interview with director Tomomi Mochizuki

From the pamphlet (1993)
I'd always wanted to do an anime adaptation of one of Himuro's books

—How did you end up working on this film?

Mochizuki: I actually proposed an anime adaptation of *Ocean Waves* back when the novel was still being serialized. I was already a Saeko Himuro fan, and I'd read pretty much all her books—the way the stories unfold in novels like *Nante Suteki ni Japanesque* [How Wonderfully Japanesque] and *Nagisa Boy* is so masterful. So I'd always wanted to do an anime adaptation of one of her novels. I proposed *Ocean Waves* partly because it was still being serialized, so the timing was good, but also because the magazine serializing it was *Animage,* so I thought I might have a better chance (laughs). It didn't end up happening at the time, though…

It's a complete coincidence that Ghibli asked me to work on the film. It was encouraging that Katsuya Kondo, who drew the novel's illustrations, would be so thoroughly involved. I couldn't imagine doing it without him.

—The novel's portrayal of adolescence feels so authentic, but how do you as the director see it?

Mochizuki: It's definitely a realistic coming-of-age story, and I tried to be nuanced about it. With realistic content, some people will always say you should do it as live action, but I don't subscribe to that way of thinking. I don't necessarily think live action is always better for telling realistic stories. Drawings are compelling in a different way than shooting with a camera.

In *Only Yesterday,* for example, there's a scene of safflowers swaying in the breeze, and I think that scene is able to be *more* moving than the real thing because it's done with animation. I think it's things like that which make realistic animated stories compelling. I'm not at all drawn to animation with stories that are too far removed from reality. For *Ocean Waves,* I'm trying to present things with a sense of realism. The depiction of the characters is key in this film.

—Which character are you most drawn to?

Mochizuki: Rikako, I suppose. She's the type of person you can't describe in just a few words. Real people are complex and multi-dimensional, so I think portraying someone like her is appealing. Plus she's pretty (laughs).

Pom Poko

Isao Takahata (Original story, screenplay, director)

Production notes (from the theatrical pamphlet, 1994)
The life of the modern tanuki

One day, the bamboo grove behind a landowner's house near where I live suddenly disappeared, replaced by a vacant lot. Everyone used to call the bamboo grove "the Sparrow's House," because every evening the sparrows would return to their nests there and make a huge racket. When I saw the grove was gone, the first thing I thought was, "Where did those sparrows go?"

The so-called "new towns" like Tama, Senri, and Tsukuba, and the golf courses springing up everywhere, require large-scale clearing of mountains and forests, and the topography changes completely in a very short period. It goes without saying that creatures lose their habitats, and many of them perish, but wouldn't the surrounding areas also be affected by this kind of disaster? Wouldn't those creatures be forced into fierce competition to survive, away from human eyes? Species would fight each other, yes, but there would also be fierce intraspecies battles over territory. Many lives lost, many lines extinguished.

Tanuki, who have been living around human settlements since time immemorial and who have close contact with humans, are just as susceptible to these disasters. There are reports from across Japan of tanuki haunting villages and even cities to stubbornly hang on, getting hit by cars as they scrounge for scraps and look for handouts from children. Buffeted by the rough seas of development, what other choice do they have if they want to survive?

Through *Pom Poko,* I want to explore how the tanuki have lived and died during this time of rapid change and devastating wars; how they've struggled against their cruel fate by means of their shapeshifting abilities; whether insensitive modern humans have had the slightest inkling of what was happening to the tanuki; and if love can blossom even in such times, enabling the tanuki to propagate the species.

Whisper of the Heart

Hayao Miyazaki (General Producer, screenplay, storyboards)

From the press release (1994) / theatrical pamphlet (1995)
Why girls' manga now? —This film's aim—

As the chaos of the 21st century slowly comes into view, Japan's social structure begins to judder and creak. We are definitely living in a time of transition, and yesterday's common sense and received wisdom are rapidly losing their hold. Thanks to our level of material accumulation, young people may not have been exposed to this wave yet, but the signs are definitely there.

What kind of films do we make in times like these?

Returning to the true essence of living.

Finding your own starting point.

Turning your back on ever more rapidly changing trends.

We want to make a film that boldly trumpets the need to expand our view and look further down the line.

This film isn't trying to win favor with young audiences by showing them that we understand their lives. Nor does it raise questions or reveal an awareness about what young people are going through today.

It's a kind of challenge to young people, from some middle-aged men with lingering regrets about their own youths. It tries to arouse the thirst of the audience, who tend to give up on making themselves the protagonists in their own stories—just as we did when we were younger—and show them the importance of really yearning for something.

This film is about meeting someone of the opposite sex who raises you up—all of Chaplin's films were about this—and the miracle of how this encounter revives you.

The original comic is nothing more than the kind of commonplace love story you find so often in girls' manga. In that world, nothing comes between the two characters. The protagonist is a girl who dreams of her own tale beginning, but there are no restrictions or adults who don't understand, and any setbacks

or detours are still far, far off. As with other current girls' manga, the only important thing is the two characters' feelings for each other, and nothing particularly eventful happens. The two confirm their mutual love, but the story doesn't go beyond that. Girls' manga always end there, which is why people have kept reading them.

The boy in the story dreams of becoming an illustrator, which is also typical of girls' manga. He's not interested in making urgent, intense art. The girl, who dreams of being a writer, creates fairytales set in some indeterminate country, and like the boy, stays in safe territory where there's no risk of being hurt.

So why do I propose adapting *Whisper of the Heart*?

Because no matter how forcefully a bunch of middle-aged men argue that it's a fragile and unrealistic dream, we can't deny that the longing for such an encounter and the innocent yearning this manga so honestly and soundly portrays are a crucial truth of adolescence.

It's easy to ironically point out that such soundness is just fragility under the protection of others, or that true love can't exist in an age without impediments. In that case, couldn't we express the beauty of soundness even more powerfully, overwhelmingly even?

A soundness so strong as to blow reality away… Why couldn't Aoi Hiiragi's *Whisper of the Heart* form the kernel of such an attempt?

What if the boy wanted to become a craftsman? What would happen to the story if he decided to go to Cremona as soon as he graduated junior high to become a luthier?

The fact is, the film adaptation of *Whisper of the Heart* all started from this idea.

A boy who loves woodworking, and who himself plays the violin. His room in his grandfather's attic becomes a basement workshop, and the grandfather, an antique dealer in the original, becomes a furniture and art restorer who also enjoys playing music… And in that basement workshop, the boy fosters his dream of becoming a violin maker.

While his peers are instead doing everything they can to avoid the future (many of these kids believe that nothing good will happen to them once they grow up), this boy has his eyes fixed firmly on the future and is advancing steadily towards his dream. If our heroine met a boy like that, what would happen?

The moment we asked these questions, a run-of-the-mill girls' manga instantly transformed into the raw material for a

work about today—a rough stone that would become a gleaming gem if we polished it.

We should be able to retain the pureness of the world of girls' manga, while asking how we can live a rich life in our own.

The challenge of this film is to take an idealized encounter and add as much reality as we possibly can to it, while shamelessly singing the praises of being alive.

Princess Mononoke

Hayao Miyazaki (Original story, screenplay, director)

From the press release (1995) / theatrical pamphlet (1997)
A battle between humans and savage gods —This film's aim—

In this film, the warriors, feudal lords, and peasants who usually feature in historical dramas hardly appear at all. Even when they do, they're the most minor of minor characters.

Along with the ferocious mountain gods, the central figures in the film are the kind of people who rarely appear on the stage of history: members of an iron-producing community called Iron Town—engineers, laborers, blacksmiths, iron-sand gatherers, charcoal makers, with teamsters and cattlemen to transport their goods. They've armed themselves and formed a unique system of industrial handicrafting, so to speak.

The gods, meanwhile, take the form of wolves, boars, and bears. The pivotal Deer God is a totally imaginary creature, with a human face, the body of a beast, and antlers made of tree branches.

The protagonists are a young man descended from the Emishi, who disappeared long ago after being crushed under the heel of the dominant Yamato people, and a young woman not unlike some clay figurines of the prehistoric Jomon period.

The main locations are the deep, foreboding forest of the gods, and the fortress-like Iron Town. The castles, towns, and rice farming villages where period dramas are conventionally set form nothing more than a distant backdrop. Instead we want to recreate a purer natural landscape of Japan from an age when the population was much smaller, when the forests were dense and there were no dams, a Japan of tall mountains and deep valleys, clear rushing streams, narrow dirt roads, and plentiful birds, beasts, and insects.

Our goal in all this is to shape a freer group of characters, unbound by the conventions, preconceptions, and biases of traditional historical films. Recent research in history, ethnology, and archaeology has shown that our country's history is

far richer and more diverse than we've been led to believe. The lack of imagination in historical drama has come almost entirely from film. Disorder and fluidity were the norm in the Japan of the Muromachi period, when this film is set. Modern Japan developed out of the chaos of this time, with its social upheaval, flamboyant styles, rampant brigands, and new art forms. It differed from the subsequent Warring States period, when organized battles were fought between standing armies, and also from the preceding Kamakura period, with its fierce and earnest warrior class.

It was a more unpredictable and fluid time, with less clearcut class distinctions between warriors and peasants, and more freedom for women, as depicted in contemporaneous drawings of craftspeople. In such a time, the contours of life and death were very clear. People lived, loved, hated, worked, and died. Life was not ambiguous.

That's why, as we face the imminent chaos of the 21st century, I want to make this film.

I'm not trying to solve all the world's problems. There can never be a happy ending in the battle between ferocious gods and humans. But even amid hatred and carnage, life is still worth living. Wonderful encounters and beautiful things can still exist.

I will depict hatred, but only to show that there is something more precious.

I will depict the bondage of a curse in order to show the joy of liberation.

What I want to show is the boy reaching an understanding of the girl, and the girl opening her heart to the boy.

In the end the girl will say to the boy, "I love you, Ashitaka. But I can never forgive the human race."

The boy will smile and say, "That's okay. I still want to share my life with you."

That's the kind of film I want to make.

My Neighbors the Yamadas

Isao Takahata (Screenplay and director)

Production notes (from a manuscript on a flyer
included in the press release, 1997)
Part II of the "My Neighbor" series

Studio Ghibli brings you part two of the "My Neighbor"
series. No, really, I'm not joking. This is a special project of the
utmost seriousness.

We all want Totoro to live in the trees or forest next door.

When we sense Totoro nearby, it makes us happy. Surrounded by nature, we feel like we can become good people.

But we'd also be thrilled if the Yamadas lived next door.

When we sense the Yamadas nearby, for some reason we
feel relieved. It cheers us up, our faces relax into smiles, we can
catch our breath. We feel like somehow we'll make it through
another day.

The Yamada family are the protagonists of *My Neighbors the
Yamadas* (later retitled *Nono-chan*), a comic strip serialized in
the *Asahi Shimbun*. I hear that a lot of subscribers can't leave the
house without reading it every morning, even if they don't have
time for any of the articles.

Producer Toshio Suzuki is a huge fan, and for quite a while
he's been asking everyone in sight to do an adaptation of the
strip as part two of the "My Neighbor" series, but everyone
took it as a joke. Besides, it wasn't a project that appealed to us.
So no one seriously considered it.

Of course it didn't. Sure, *My Neighbors the Yamadas* is a
masterpiece, head and shoulders above all the other strips in
the newspaper these days, but an adaptation would be too far
removed from Studio Ghibli's image. And just think about it—
the project wouldn't give Ghibli's staff much of an opportunity
to put their particular strengths and abilities to use. Besides,
making a compelling animation (especially a feature-length
one) out of a four-panel gag comic is a Herculean task. It'd be
practically impossible. There are other strips that have been extended and combined into animated shows and movies, like
the popular *Sazae-san* and the successful *Ganbare!! Tabuchi-kun!!*
(a.k.a. *There Goes Our Hero*), but sadly, they sacrificed the originals' concise appeal.

So why have we decided to brave these dangers and take on
My Neighbors the Yamadas as a "special emergency project"? Is
there any hope of success?

First and foremost, it's because we realized that Mr. Suzuki's concept of the "My Neighbor" series was neither a play
on words nor a joke, and in fact could be timely and relevant.
The jokey bit of wordplay's "Encouragement of Unseriousness"
might seriously be the very thing we needed. In other words, as
I said at the beginning, I started to believe that now more than
ever, everyone could use neighbors like the Yamadas.

Spirited Away

Hayao Miyazaki (Original story, screenplay, director)

From the theatrical pamphlet (2001)
Chihiro in a strange town
—This film's aim—

While it may not have weapons brandished left and right
or a showdown involving supernatural powers, this film is still
very much an adventure story. It's not about the confrontation
between good and evil, however, but about a girl thrown into
a world where heroes and villains are all intermingled, where

she uses her wits to survive, and along the way learns about
discipline, friendship, and dedication. She comes through, slip-
ping through, and returns to her normal life, at least for the
time being. But just as the world isn't destroyed, it's not because
evil has been obliterated; it's because she has acquired the ability to live.

The primary goal of this film is to use the form of fantasy
to throw our world into sharp relief, a world that has become
hazy and ambiguous, and yet seeks to consume us despite that

ambiguity.

In a world where children are sheltered and protected, where life feels like a distant blur, all they can do is shore up their fragile egos. Chihiro's spindly limbs and sullen, bored expression symbolize this. But when reality hits and she finds herself trapped in a sticky situation, she taps into her dormant ability to adapt and persevere, and realizes she has the vitality to take decisive action.

In her situation, most people would probably panic and simply try to pretend it wasn't happening, but then they'd be killed or devoured more or less right away. Chihiro gets to be the protagonist not because she's pretty or a rare saint, but because she has the strength *not* to be devoured. This is the film's strong suit, and the reason it can be a film for ten-year-old girls.

Words are power. In the world Chihiro wanders into, uttering a word is a weighty act that can't be taken back. At Yubaba's bathhouse, if even once Chihiro were to say, "I don't like it here," or, "I want to go home," the witch would throw her out on the spot, and she would wander aimlessly until she expired, or be turned into a hen and lay eggs until she was eventually eaten. When Chihiro says, "I want to work here," on the other hand, even the witch can't ignore her declaration. Today, words are taken all too lightly. They're like froth, you can say anything you want to, but that's just a reflection of our hollow reality. Words are still power, even today. It's just that the world is filled with empty ones, which have no meaning, and no power.

Stealing a name isn't just about changing what someone is called; it's a way of controlling them completely. Sen is horrified when she realizes she's starting to forget that her name is Chihiro. And each time she goes to the pigsty to visit her parents, she becomes less concerned about their new appearance. In Yubaba's world, you have to live with the ever-present risk of being devoured.

In this world of hardship, Chihiro starts to come alive. This sullen, listless character's expression will be transformed into a stunningly vibrant one by the time we reach the grand finale.

The true nature of the world hasn't changed at all. I intend to use this film to argue persuasively that words are will, they are ourselves, and they are power.

This is also why I wanted to make a fantasy set in Japan. Even though it's a fairy tale, I didn't want it to be a Western one, full of escape routes. This film may seem like an imitation of the tales of other worlds you see all the time, but I like to think of it as a direct descendent of folktales like "The Sparrow's House" and "The Mouse Palace." Even if they aren't quite parallel worlds, our ancestors still made bad choices at the homes of sparrows, and enjoyed banquets at the palaces of mice.

I decided to render Yubaba's bathhouse in the *giyofu* style of pseudo-Western architecture (built with Japanese techniques but a Western appearance) to evoke a dreamlike sense of familiarity and uncertainty, but also because traditional Japanese design is a repository of such diverse images. People simply don't know how rich and unique our folkloric space is: tales, oral tradition, observances, design, from religious ritual to sorcery. It's true that "Firecracker Mountain" and "Momotaro" have lost some of their oomph. But stuffing the whole of our tradition into the cozy little world of folktales is terribly unimaginative. Surrounded by tech and superficial mass-produced products, children are losing their roots more and more. We have to show them just how rich our tradition is.

By introducing traditional design into a story for our time, placing it like a piece in a vivid mosaic, we can make the world of film fresh and compelling and at the same time refresh our awareness of ourselves as residents of this island nation.

In this borderless age, people without a place to call their own will be looked down upon more than anyone else. A place is a past, a history. Peoples without a history or who have forgotten their history will vanish like the dew, or become hens fated to lay eggs until they are devoured.

I want this to be a film where an audience of ten-year-old girls can encounter their own true hopes and dreams.

The Cat Returns

Hiroyuki Morita (Director)

From the press release (2002)
What Haru felt

Everyone wants to enjoy their life. They want an attractive lover, a rewarding job, status and glory, to feel like they've succeeded.

But our heroine, Haru Yoshioka, just can't seem to get anywhere. A high school girl should at least have a boyfriend, be really into sports or studying to achieve a dream… She should feel more fulfilled. Instead Haru thinks, "Maybe the Cat Kingdom is the place to be. You get to lie around all day and forget your worries. Sounds like paradise."

Jeez, what a slacker. Is this the kind of thing a teenage girl should be saying? Is she hopeless? Sad and desperate?

No, that's not it at all. Haru thinks about all kinds of things, just like everyone else; she wonders if there's something more interesting to do, she thinks there must be a way for her to shine.

When she thinks about a good-looking boyfriend or rewarding job, though, they all feel somehow empty, like cookie-cutter dreams. Forget all that real-world stuff—maybe the key to true happiness lies in a heart that can feel like the Cat Kingdom might be paradise.

Baron, proprietor of the Cat Bureau, seems to find Haru interesting. This mysterious cat statuette who lives in a tiny dollhouse may have nothing, but he does have style. (Weird?!)

Protecting Haru from the ignorant and foolish adventure that unfolds in the Cat Kingdom (though what else would you expect from cats?) is easy for a nice guy like Baron. During it all, Baron keeps sending Haru the message, *Why don't you try living a dashing life like this?*

Everything Haru experiences seems pointless—dancing, swordfights, escaping from a maze. But figuring out how you want to live is hard, and there's a 0% chance you'll ever get anywhere if you stay shut up in your room. Maybe the coolest thing to do is to start running toward something like Haru does, thinking, "This could be great!"

The feeling of loving someone is precious, but we aren't born just to fall in love. We have to study hard and work hard, we have to grow, but we're not all going to become great. Growing is hard, not being able to grow is natural, and if you're just going to do it the easy way, maybe it's better not to. First off, we should forgive ourselves for being immature, should value our consideration and good intentions, and be ready to take in the scents and feel the wind.

In fact, the hardest thing is to wake up feeling good, enjoy your morning tea, and feel the warm air. If you can just do that, you should be able to find a new tomorrow!

The Cat Returns is that kind of movie.

the GHIBLIES episode 2

Yoshiyuki Momose (Director)

From the press release (2002)
A message

The point of *the GHIBLIES* is to put characters based on caricatures of normal people (who aren't especially famous) front and center, and use them to depict the everyday lives of so-called normal people. We started by asking ourselves how we could put together an animated film based on this premise.

The film is a collection of shorts, and we changed the drawing style and music to fit each segment. The idea was to use everything on the screen to express the characters' feelings by proxy, since their facial expressions tend to be somewhat lacking. We made the style resemble watercolors, oil paints, or doodles, depending on the story. And rather than finishing the characters with flat surfaces of color as in traditional cel animation, we added texture to these terribly simple and intense characters, so they would have the same feel as the backgrounds and the whole thing could move cohesively as a single picture. We figured this might help draw the audience more seamlessly into the story.

Changing art styles for each segment might sound like some kind of technical experiment, but we did this only because we thought it was the most effective way to get across the liberated atmosphere of *the GHIBLIES*' world. We chose this technique because it was necessary for telling a universal story in a movie consisting of shorts. The fact that we were able to combine this type of experimental visual expression with entertainment is all thanks to meeting the Ghiblies themselves.

The film we made isn't normal, and the characters aren't normal, but all we ever wanted to show was the normal everyday lives of characters who would be considered totally normal. My hope is that because of this film, people will take another look at their unchanging everyday lives, and feel like they might be able to become the slightest bit more colorful.

Howl's Moving Castle

Hayao Miyazaki (Screenplay and director)

From the film production materials (2002)

Preparatory memo for
Howl's Moving Castle

◎ Junko Nishimura, the novel's translator, provides an excellent summary of the story, so I'll use that here with some revisions and additions.

"Sophie, the eldest daughter of a milliner, is turned into an old woman by the Witch of the Waste. To make matters worse, the spell leaves her unable to tell anyone about it. Seeking a way to break the curse, she leaves home and works her way into the castle of the infamous wizard Howl, where she becomes his housekeeper.

"The castle is filled with mysterious things and strange doings. Views of cities that should be too far away to see are right outside the window, and the doors seem to connect to many places. Not to mention that a fire demon living in the hearth is lending Howl his power!

"At a certain point Sophie secretly falls in love with Howl, who himself is under threat from the Witch of the Waste. War breaks out, and the king demands Howl's cooperation.

"Can Sophie find a way to break the curse and attain happiness?"

○ The Original Novel

One gets the sense this was originally conceived as a Christmas play for children. Tradition might be too strong a word, but there seems to be a custom in England of children enjoying Christmas plays. This novel's structure bears some similarity to *The Silver Curlew* by Eleanor Farjeon, which I believe was originally written as a script for a Christmas play. *Howl's* is easy to understand if we look at it as a Christmas play, but it's not necessarily helpful for adapting it to film. Just the opposite, in fact:

What would Howl's castle be like? Calcifer's fireplace takes center stage, where someone in a flame costume speaks and stretches up to make the flames leap. There are a window and four doors to left and right, opening onto a succession of different worlds. On the stage, exposition (including plenty of soliloquy) moves the story along. The many characters enter and leave through the many doors, talking in loud voices, mocking each other, laughing, crying. For the grand finale, the entire cast comes on stage to fight and hug each other on their way to a big slapstick happy ending. It's no exaggeration to say this novel is more suited to vaudeville than it is to film.

Sophie's and Howl's lives have a very immediate relevance. Sophie feels somehow trapped, almost cursed by her youth, while Howl lives in virtual reality (magic) and can only play at fashion and love. With no purpose or motivation, he is in a sense a typical young man. But that doesn't necessarily mean the novel is relevant or worth adapting. Time marches on, ruthlessly crushing many Howls and Sophies beneath its feet. I have a hard time believing the world of 2004, when this film is scheduled for release, will accept this vaudevillian fantasy.

○ So, what to do?

This is a kind of domestic drama. Before Sophie falls in love with Howl, she establishes herself as a sort of housewife.

Sophie is the key that brings the fire demon, the apprentice Markl, the dogman, the scarecrow, and Howl himself together and makes them a family. The moving castle becomes a home. Then, war breaks out. Not a fairy-tale war, not a conflict with personal courage and honor at stake, but an all-out war between modern nations.

Howl seems to evade the draft, but is required to cooperate with the war. This is not a request but a demand.

Howl wants to be free, to be true to himself and live as he pleases without being involved with others. But the nation won't allow this. Howl and Sophie are forced to take sides. In the meantime, the horrifying reality of total war shows its face: fire rains from the sky and explosions wrack the port town onto which one of the castle's doors opens, Sophie's hometown, the royal palace, even the wastelands themselves.

What will Sophie and Howl do? If we can unflinchingly depict this, *Howl's Moving Castle* will become a film that can endure in the 21st century. If we have Howl and Sophie join forces to stop the war or save mankind, however, that would make the story ring even more hollow. They have to face this difficulty while asking themselves how they'll live their lives from there on out.

① Setting (place, time period)

The setting will be largely informed by the near-future fantasy drawings of Robida, a French caricaturist active around the time of the Meiji Restoration. Magic and science coexist in the irony-laden mechanized civilization he created during the latter part of the 19th century.

This was the peak of patriotism, when cheering crowds threw bouquets at the feet of soldiers as they marched off to war, their guns decorated with flowers.

The houses in Sophie's hometown have an Alsatian feel, the main road is lined with pavilions for the world fair, and steam engines belch black smoke everywhere you look.

While people have turned the skies over their towns grey with soot, the skies over the deserted wastelands are clear and blue—but they're cold, with blustery winds and constantly drifting clouds, like Patagonia in South America.

② The Moving Castle

The moving castle in the novel simply moves as a magical door, but doesn't have substance. That's what you would have to do for a play, probably, but it doesn't make for an engaging movie. Our moving castle will be a weird amalgamation of bits of machinery and fragments of buildings, staggering through the wastelands on ten iron legs. Howl's house exists inside it. So when Calcifer is freed from his contract and leaves through the chimney, Howl's house will appear—it'll probably roll out onto the wastelands in its true form: a shabby structure with missing pieces of roof and wall, patched with junk like scrap iron poles and boards.

I'm not clear on the story itself yet, but I think I'd like to take things in this direction.

October 28, 2002

Tales from Earthsea

Goro Miyazaki (Screenplay and director)

From the flyer
Production notes:

"People have lost their minds"

I first read Ursula K. Le Guin's *Earthsea Cycle* more than twenty years ago, when I was still in high school. At the time, I found volumes 1 and 2 the most compelling. I saw myself in Sparrowhawk's arrogance and frustration in volume 1, along with his unification with his own shadow, and I felt both joy and sorrow at Tenar's liberation from the darkness of the Tombs in volume 2.

When I reread the whole series to prepare for this film, however, I was surprised to find myself drawn more strongly to volumes 3 and 4, and to *Tales from Earthsea*. Part of it was surely that I had changed as I got older, but I think the biggest reason was that the world had changed dramatically in the interim.

We're living in Hort Town, a place that has lost its sense of reality

The world we now live in is like Hort Town or Lorbanery, places that appear in volume 3. Everyone is desperately bustling around, but to no obvious purpose. We just seem to be afraid of losing everything—both the things we can see and the things we can't. It's like everyone has lost their minds.

I won't go into detail, but this is clearly due to drastic changes in social conditions both here and abroad. But no one seems to be able to show us how to make society better, or what direction we should move in. Adults have lost their pride, tolerance, compassion, and thoughtfulness, while young people see no hope in the future and are assailed by feelings of helplessness.

As a result, life and death have lost their sense of reality. If your own existence feels diluted, it only makes sense that other people's existence will feel vague as well. The steady rate of suicide and the increase in senseless murder strike me as manifestations of this.

A story of life and death, and also of rebirth

Development started on the *Earthsea* film even as I was pondering how we should live in times like these, and that's why I decided to base the film on volume 3 of the series. The world is losing its equilibrium, and the cause lies within us. If we follow it back to the source, we arrive at the question of life and death, and I felt like this was the most important theme we could tackle right now.

Sparrowhawk and Arren have many conversations in volume 3, and Arren's questions are the same as mine, while Sparrowhawk's responses really struck a chord with me. Maybe Sparrowhawk answered just as I would. After all, I'm directly between the two in age. I understand Sparrowhawk's words better than I did when I was young, but because of my age, I can also understand Arren's feelings. I think another reason I chose volume 3 was that it's the story of a man approaching old age, trying to pass the baton to a young man.

I was also deeply moved by the rebirth of humanity depicted in volume 4 and the *Tales from Earthsea* collection. Having lost his magic, Sparrowhawk begins a new life with Tenar; a wounded girl recovers; a formerly arrogant mage finds a new beginning; and two young characters meet and start out afresh. These volumes share a life-affirming view: men and women support each other as equals, and young and old alike can recover and begin

again. In addition, there's a sense that life is lived in harmony with the earth.

I suspect we lost our way because, amid increasing urbanization and the overdevelopment of civilization, we came to believe we could predict and control the entire world. It seems to me that by understanding and accepting that there are forces of nature we're powerless to control, we can live richer lives.

Take a journey with Sparrowhawk and company

"What does it mean to live authentically now?" I tossed this question at *Tales from Earthsea*, listened to the voices of Sparrowhawk and the many other characters, and then kept on asking questions. This is without a doubt the main subject of the film.

Production will wrap up soon. I have the strange feeling that I've been talking with Sparrowhawk and Arren and the others, that we went on a long journey together. I hope all of you who see this film enjoy it, and if possible, take this same journey with Sparrowhawk and company.

Ponyo on the Cliff by the Sea

Hayao Miyazaki (Original story, screenplay, director)

From the theatrical pamphlet (2008)
A small seaside town

This is the story of a fish girl who comes from the sea, and won't let go of her willful desire to live with a human boy named Sosuke. At the same time, it's the story of five-year-old Sosuke sticking to his promise.

The film transplants Hans Christian Andersen's "The Little Mermaid" to modern Japan, gets rid of the Christian overtones, and depicts a story of adventure and love between two little children.

A small seaside town and a house on a cliff. A small cast of characters. An ocean that's like a living creature. A world where magic is no big deal. The ocean outside connects with the ocean we all carry within our own subconscious, which is why we can distort space and play with the art style, and depict the ocean as a central character rather than a simple background.

A girl and a boy, love and responsibility, the ocean and life— depicting such primal things without hesitation is an attempt to face up to this age of neurosis and anxiety.

Arrietty

Hayao Miyazaki (Planning and screenplay)

From the proposal / production committee materials (2010)
Feature-length film proposal (*Little Arrietty*) 80 minutes

From Mary Norton's *The Borrowers*.
Change the setting from 1950s England to Japan in 2010. The location can be the Koganei area we're all used to.
A family of Borrowers—14-year-old girl Arrietty and her

parents—live under the kitchen floor of an old house.

These little Borrowers "borrow" everything they need to live from the humans upstairs. They don't use magic and they're not fairies. Plagued by cockroaches and termites, battling mice, they evade bug bombs, insecticide, roach motels, and boric acid balls. They live a humble, cautious life, and studiously avoid being seen or noticed.

This is a traditional family: the brave, patient father who goes on dangerous hunts, the responsible mother who creatively manages and protects her household, and Arrietty, a girl with an untrammeled sensibility and curiosity.

The banal world we're all so used to looks fresh once more when seen through the eyes of the four-inch-tall Borrowers. The appeal of the animation lies in seeing these little people move and work with their entire bodies.

The film shows us the Borrowers' lives, and follows Arrietty and a human boy as they meet, develop a relationship, and part ways. In the end, the Borrowers escape the hullabaloo caused by cold-blooded humans and make their way into the wild.

My hope is that this film soothes and encourages people living in these chaotic and uncertain times…

July 30, 2008

From Up on Poppy Hill

Goro Miyazaki (Director)

From the theatrical pamphlet (2011)
Nothing comes of resignation and calculation

I was born in 1967, so I grew up during the period of rapid economic growth and came of age smack dab in the middle of the bubble. It was a carefree time of consumption and hedonism. In the 80s, when I was a teenager, hit songs had lyrics about "rebelling against adults," "freedom," "dreams," and "revolution."

There was the hope that with everything completed, something might change. But when the bubble popped, this turned into hopelessness. We felt that nothing would change. There had been endless calls for reform, but they were all a sham. Twenty years on, hopes and dreams had at some point been replaced by money and a desire for stability.

For people of my generation, who have been consumers for as long as we can remember, everything was given to us and nothing was of our own making. Literature, films, music, manga, animation, even jobs. Everything we saw had been created by the previous generation.

There was no way to create something new and original. I think that's why we were so overly attracted to words like "individuality," "freedom," and "dreams" within the existing framework. I think somewhere deep down, I've always had a sense of resignation.

I have a confession to make. *From Up on Poppy Hill* was the first time I ever really gave it my all. I've worked hard at every job I've ever had, I think, but I always made sure not to cross a certain line. I protected myself through calculation and resignation. This was even true while I was working on *Tales from Earthsea*.

Last summer, a combination of things was making me feel cornered. The pressure of my sophomore film, setbacks with the project, my father's screenplay, a tight schedule, the success of *Arrietty*, etc. etc. But I didn't have time to think about any of that. I had to keep forging ahead.

My father had written the screenplay, and I didn't want to be the one to drop the ball. The one thing I wanted to avoid was people saying the film didn't live up to the screenplay. I had to rid myself of the usual attitude of "This'll have to do."

When I was drawing the storyboards, my body was in worse shape than ever before. Part of it was probably age. My teeth got bad, my hair thinned out, my eyes started to go, and I threw out my back for the first time in my life. But no matter what I did, I didn't feel like I was getting any closer to the goal.

Even when the storyboards were finished and production was in full swing, I was consumed with doubt. Was the film even the slightest bit better? Was it becoming something that wouldn't compare unfavorably with the screenplay? I fervently wished I could draw better, that I had more knowledge and more experience. I couldn't help feeling like something was always missing. I hadn't felt any of these things during the production of *Tales from Earthsea*.

In May, production finally entered the homestretch and we started on the additional dialogue recording. I went to the studio where Masami Nagasawa, Junichi Okada, and the other members of the cast were recording, and as I watched them, I felt strangely moved. Before I knew it, *From Up on Poppy Hill* had become something more than I'd imagined. How did I make something like this?

The film that was developing seemed like something beyond my abilities. During the dubbing process, I kept asking myself that question: how was I able to make a film like this? It probably sounds stupid, like I'm singing my own praises, but I couldn't help the thought. The truth is, it might just have been luck. A wonderful screenplay, a great staff, Satoshi Takebe's beautiful score, and those actors. So much good fortune helped me get to this point. The producer kept telling me, "You're lucky," and I think he was right.

But that's just fine. Because it brought me here. "You can do it if you try," I decided to think.

For me, *From Up on Poppy Hill* was a path to remembering something I'd forgotten, and facing something I'd given up on. During an interview where I was being thoroughly grilled, I remembered something: When I was young, I dreamed of working in animation. But faced with the enormity of my father's presence, the adolescent me gave this up and tucked it away somewhere deep in the recesses of my mind.

I blamed it on the times and my generation, but the resignation and cowardice were all my own. Maybe it was just a personal problem, but I can't help thinking it wasn't that simple. This is a problem that plagues both my generation and subsequent ones. What the previous generation built was big and solid, and we might not be able to compete. But that doesn't mean they're insurmountable.

1963, when Umi and Shun's story is set—I expect the sky was wide, and you could look up as you walked. Now our sky is hidden most of the time; that expansive view is gone. But if you keep climbing, that wide sky should still be there. I feel like Umi and Shun are saying from the screen, "Nothing comes of resignation and calculation."

The Wind Rises

Hayao Miyazaki (Original story, screenplay, director)

From *The Wind Rises* film production notes (2011) / theatrical pamphlet (2013)

Proposal: **"Airplanes are a beautiful dream"**

A friendship between Jiro Horikoshi, designer of the Zero, and his like-minded Italian predecessor Gianni Caproni that transcends time and space. Both overcame endless setbacks and pushed themselves to achieve their boyhood dreams.

In the Taisho period (1912-1926), a rural boy decides to become an airplane designer. He dreams of creating an airplane like a beautiful wind.

The boy grows up to attend university in Tokyo, becomes an elite engineer in the massive arms industry where his talents blossom, and ultimately creates a beautiful aircraft that will go down in history: the Mitsubishi A6M1, which will become the Navy Type 0 carrier fighter, known simply as the Zero. For three years beginning in 1940, the Zero was the world's most outstanding fighter plane.

From boyhood to adolescence, our protagonist lived in a Japan where the sense of stagnation and helplessness was even more severe that it is now—the Great Kanto Earthquake, the Great Depression, unemployment, poverty and tuberculosis, revolution and fascism, suppression of free speech and war after war. At the same time, popular culture blossomed, and modernism, nihilism, and hedonism were rampant. It was a time when poets fell ill and died in the course of their travels.

The Japanese Empire was rushing headlong toward destruction and ultimate collapse during the time our protagonist Jiro was designing airplanes. But this film isn't trying to condemn war or inspire Japan's youth with the superiority of the Zero. Nor do I intend to defend the character by saying that all he really wanted was to make civil aircraft.

My goal is to depict someone who stayed true to his dream. Dreams harbor madness, and that poison shouldn't be hidden. Aspiring to something too beautiful can be a trap. The cost of beauty is high. Jiro is torn apart, discouraged, and his design career is cut short. But regardless, his inventiveness and talent were unsurpassed, and that's what I want to show.

The title of the film, *The Wind Rises*, comes from the title of a Tatsuo Hori novel. Hori translated a line from Paul Valery's poetry as "The wind has risen; we must try to live." The film's protagonist "Jiro" is a mixture of the historical Jiro Horikoshi and the author Tatsuo Hori, who lived during the same period. It's an unusual work that depicts youth in a completely fictionalized 1930s, with the birth of the now legendary Zero as the warp, the meeting and separation of young engineer Jiro and his tragic love Nahoko as the weft, and Caproni transcending space and time to add some extra color.

■ Note on the Visuals

I want to render the abundant greenery of Japan's landscape from the Taisho to the early Showa periods as beautifully as possible. The sky was not yet smoggy, the clouds were white, the waters were clear, and there wasn't a speck of litter in the countryside. The cities, on the other hand, were poor. I don't want to dull the buildings with sepia tones; instead, we'll flood them with the colors of East Asian modernism. Bumpy roads, chockablock signs, and a chaotic forest of telephone poles.

We need to structure this film as a critical biography, from boyhood to adolescence and then to middle age, but the daily life of an engineer is probably about as dull as it gets. While doing our best to minimize audience confusion, we'll have no choice but to make bold jumps through time. I think this film will be comprised of three types of visual:

Daily life will be an accumulation of plain scenes.

Dreams will provide a free and sensual space. Time and weather blur, the earth swells, flying objects float gently in the sky. This should serve to express Caproni and Jiro's monomania.

Technological explanations and meetings should be carica-tures. I don't want to get into the weeds of aviation technology, but when we have to, we'll make it as cartoonish as possible. The proliferation of meetings and conferences in this type of film is a chronic flaw of Japanese cinema. An individual's fate is decided at a meeting. This film should not have any scenes of meetings. If it must, we'll make it as cartoonish as possible and cut down the dialogue. What we must depict are the individuals.

I want to make a realistic
dreamlike,
sometimes cartoonish,
and overall beautiful film

January 10, 2011

The Tale of The Princess Kaguya

Isao Takahata (Original concept, screenplay, director)

Director's message from *The Tale of The Princess Kaguya* official website (2013)

Over half a century

Once upon a time, almost 55 years ago, a company called Toei Doga planned an animated adaptation of *The Tale of the Bamboo Cutter,* to be directed by the great Tomu Uchida. It didn't end up happening, but partly at Uchida's behest, the company performed a groundbreaking experiment: they asked all employees to submit plot ideas for the adaptation. A few of the best ones were selected and made into a mimeographed booklet.

I didn't submit anything. New hires who hoped to become producers or directors had been asked to submit proposals beforehand, so my proposal had already been rejected. Instead of adapting the story itself, I had written a prologue exploring the premise that this whole strange tale is based on, a scene of dialogue between the Moon King and Princess Kaguya before she leaves the lunar world.

In the original tale, when Princess Kaguya tells the bamboo cutter she has to go back to the moon, she says, "I came down to this land because of an 'ancient vow.'" And the messengers who come to bring her back say to the bamboo cutter, "Princess Kaguya committed a crime, so we sent her down to this land and left her for a while in the keeping of lowly people like you. Her penance is over, and we've come to take her home."

What kind of crime had Princess Kaguya committed on the moon, and what was the "ancient vow," this promise she had made there? And if she had been sent down to Earth as a pun-ishment, why had it ended? Why isn't she glad? What crimes even *could* exist on the pure and unsullied world of the moon? In other words, how did she end up on Earth?

If I could answer these questions, all the incomprehensible aspects of the Princess's character in the original tale would suddenly make sense. I got excited, believing I'd found a clue, but this "ancient vow" concept lay gathering dust until I picked it up half a century later.

Even now, I can see this scene on the moon between Princess Kaguya and her father so clearly. The Moon King is saying something very important about her crime and punishment, but Princess Kaguya isn't listening at all. Her eyes are bright with excitement as she fixes them on the Earth, where she's about to be sent…

But I didn't put this scene at the beginning of the film. As long as I had discovered the "true story of Princess Kaguya," the part not depicted in *The Tale of the Bamboo Cutter,* I didn't need the prologue. I could make it into a captivating film filled with both comedy and tragedy, without changing the basic story at all. And I should be able to make Princess Kaguya a truly memorable character you could even identify with. I started work on *The Tale of The Princess Kaguya* with this grandiose ambition in mind.

In truth, I have absolutely no idea whether this kind of story has any relevance in today's world. But at the very least, I can say with confidence that this film is worth seeing. The talent and competence of the staff who came together to make this film, and the level of artistic expression they were able to accomplish, are a revelation. *That's* what I want people to see. That's my earnest desire.

When Marnie Was There

Hiromasa Yonebayashi (Screenplay and director)

From the project plan (movie production documents) /
theatrical pamphlet (2014)
A message

Two years ago, Mr. Suzuki gave me a book called *When Marnie Was There*. It was a classic masterpiece of British children's literature that Mr. Miyazaki also recommended, and Mr. Suzuki asked me what I thought about making a film based on it.

After I finished reading it, I thought it would be difficult to adapt. As a work of literature, I enjoyed it thoroughly, and I found it moving. It was just that the story seemed difficult to tell through animation, since Anna and Marnie's conversations are really what's so great about it. They bring about subtle emotional changes in both characters. That's the most engaging thing about the book, but how would you show this in animation? At the very least, I wasn't confident in my ability to depict this in an engaging way.

But after I read the novel, an image remained imprinted on my mind: Anna and Marnie standing together in the backyard of a stone mansion on a beautiful marsh, holding hands. They could even waltz under the moonlight. As they connect emotionally with one another, they're constantly surrounded by the beauty of nature, pleasant breezes, and familiar music from the past. As I tried my hand at a few sample illustrations, I decided I wanted to take on the challenge of making this film.

The story is set in Hokkaido. Anna is a 12-year-old girl with a lot of pain locked away in her small body. Then she meets Marnie, a mysterious girl with a tragic past. Could I make a film that would save the souls of these young girls, left behind by a modern world only interested in adults?

I don't think I can change the world with this one film like Mr. Miyazaki. But after *The Wind Rises* and *The Tale of The Princess Kaguya*, the most recent films by the two great maestros, I want to make another Studio Ghibli film for children. I want to make a film for the Annas and Marnies in the audience, one that sits quietly beside them and keeps them company.

The Red Turtle

Interview with Michael Dudok de Wit (Director)

From the theatrical pamphlet (2016)
I wasn't interested in the story of how a man would survive on a deserted island. With this film, I wanted to show something beyond that.

The inspiration for this film
In November of 2006, I received an email from Studio Ghibli containing two questions. The first was, "Does *Father and Daughter* have a Japanese distributor? If not, we would very much like to distribute it." The second was, "Do you have any interest in making a feature-length film?" I answered the first question, but the second made me think, "What on earth is happening here?" It all started with this exchange. I was so honored that for months I couldn't believe it. I mean, I'm a huge Ghibli fan! I thought about it for a week or so, then responded that I'd really like to meet with them and talk it over.

Back and forth with Studio Ghibli
In February 2007, I met with someone from Ghibli's international division at my home in London. They said they would like me to write a synopsis first. I didn't have any feature film proposals, but I did have some themes in mind, one of which had to do with a castaway on a southern island. In July of that year, I finished a synopsis and sent it to Ghibli along with some drawings. They responded immediately, and said, "This looks interesting, please start on the screenplay." So I did. After location scouting in the Seychelles, I finished the first draft in April 2008, and took it to

Ghibli. I went to Japan again in March and April of 2010. On that third April trip, I stayed near Studio Ghibli and was there for about four weeks, including the Japanese May holidays. During that time, I was able to finish an animatic (a video consisting of a series of successive storyboards in order, used for verification purposes. The storyboards are swapped out for completed scenes as you go).

Why I wanted to make a film about a castaway

A man on a deserted island was something I'd been mulling over for a while. It's such a common theme, but I like that kind of archetypal story. I wasn't interested in the story of how a man would survive on a deserted island, however. With this film, I wanted to show something beyond that.

Location scouting in the Seychelles

The Seychelles consists of an archipelago of small islands. I spent ten days there with the locals, experiencing their simple way of life. I wandered on my own, observing every nook and cranny of my surroundings and taking tons of photographs. I didn't need the kind of beauty found in a travel brochure. The castaway I was envisioning couldn't love the island where he was stranded. He had to want to return home no matter what, because the island wasn't the kind of place that welcomes visitors. All it offered was danger, extreme isolation, rain, and insects.

Writing the script

I made a classic mistake with the script: it was way too detailed. The movie would have been incredibly long. But the foundations of the story were solid. I moved on to the next step and created the animatic. Through this process, I realized that translating my story into the language of film wouldn't be easy. I met with Pascale Ferran and discussed the film with her in depth. She helped me understand what the problem was, and made the story clearer and more powerful.

The film's sense of time

The scenes of trees, sky, clouds, and birds that I depict in this film are pure and simple moments, deeply familiar to us. There is no past or future there. Time stands still. This film tells us its story in both linear and circular ways. Just as music highlights silence, time is used to narrate the absence of time. This film also addresses the true nature of death. Humans resist death, they fear it and fight against it, which is all totally healthy and natural. And yet we also beautifully and instinctively understand the purity of life, and that there's no need to resist death. I hope the film can communicate that sense.

The film's mystique

I had the idea of bringing a giant turtle into the film at quite an early stage. We thought long and hard about how much mystique to maintain. The film has no dialogue, so we needed to employ that mystique cleverly, without depending on words. Without dialogue, the characters' breathing naturally becomes richer.

Eliminating dialogue

Initially, there were a few lines of dialogue. When I showed Isao Takahata an almost complete cut of the film, he suggested I go even bolder and cut the dialogue entirely. I was so satisfied with the animation itself that I'd had the same thought. I discussed it with producer Toshio Suzuki as well, and he said, "Go ahead and get rid of the dialogue. That way we can focus more on the drawings." So I decided to do it.

Coexisting with nature

Two years after the script was completed, the big Tohoku earthquake occurred. I agonized over whether I should take out the tsunami scene, and discussed it with Ghibli. They said, "It's definitely a delicate issue, but this film isn't about man vs. nature. It's about man being a part of nature, so I think you can leave the scene as is." Based on their response, and the fact that I thought it was necessary for the story, I kept it in the film.

The music

Because the film has no dialogue, the music is an especially critical element. Initially, I didn't have a specific musical style in mind. Laurent Perez Del Mar composed some pieces featuring exquisite melodies that were perfect for a main theme, and made the whole thing a real pleasure. He quickly came up with suggestions for where the music should go, including scenes I hadn't even considered, and led me down the right path. He really did surprise me so many times.

Relationship with Studio Ghibli and Isao Takahata

I went to Japan in 2004 as a member of the international jury for the Hiroshima International Animation Festival. During that trip, I visited Studio Ghibli and met Isao Takahata and Toshio Suzuki. When they proposed this feature film idea to me, I asked Mr. Takahata and Studio Ghibli to work with me, as a precondition. I talked with Mr. Takahata and other Studio Ghibli staff about everything from creating the script to the animatic, the sound effects, and the music. It was a wonderful experience. We sent letters and emails back and forth, but they always respected my opinion and never pressured me into anything. I am so grateful to Isao Takahata and the rest of the Ghibli staff.

Working with Isao Takahata

Mr. Takahata and I thoroughly discussed what we wanted to express with this film. Sometimes we debated details like a character's clothing, but we spent most of the time discussing the story, symbolism, more philosophical points. Occasionally, our cultural differences were noticeable. The symbolic value of the fire scene, for example, was slightly different for each of us. But thankfully we were on the same basic wavelength, so we were able to have passionate yet subtle conversations. Mr. Takahata worked very enthusiastically on this project, and was deeply involved as artistic producer.

*Excerpted from multiple interviews.

SELECTIONS FROM "EVERYTHING GHIBLI!"

THERE'S ALWAYS MORE GHIBLI TO ENJOY! LET GHIBLI CAPTIVATE YOU WITH ITS BOOKS, DVDS, CDS, AND RECORDS. HERE ARE SOME OF THE NEWEST AND BEST BOOKS AND MORE!

BOOKS

HAYAO MIYAZAKI AND THE GHIBLI MUSEUM

¥27,500 / 978-4-00-024893-8
Iwanami Shoten

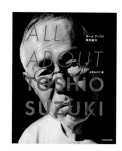

ALL ABOUT TOSHIO SUZUKI

Edited by Akiko Nagatsuka
¥4,620 / 978-4-04-680245-3
KADOKAWA

GORO, WHERE DID YOU COME FROM, WHERE ARE YOU GOING?

Interview: Chizuko Ueno   Photographs and words: Kanyada
¥1,650 / 978-4-19-865212-8, Tokuma Shoten

THE GHIBLI MUSEUM STORY

Photographs: Kanyada
¥4,180 / 978-4-7993-2580-3
Discover 21

THE ART OF SERIES

Collections of character and
machine art, image boards, and more.
¥2,724 - ¥3,410, Tokuma Shoten

ROMAN ALBUM SERIES

Guidebooks that reveal the charms of each film
through staff interviews and other content.
¥1,257 - ¥3,300, Tokuma Shoten

ANIME PICTURE BOOK SERIES

Easy-to-read picture books for children
telling the stories of Ghibli films.
By Hayao Miyazaki et al.
¥1,870 each, Tokuma Shoten

STUDIO GHIBLI STORYBOARDS COLLECTION SERIES

Collecting all the storyboards from each film,
including insights into the filmmaking process and
exclusive details that didn't make it into the films.
By Isao Takahata, Hayao Miyazaki et al.
¥2,640 - ¥3,960, Tokuma Shoten

BUNSHUN GHIBLI PAPERBACK CINEMA COMIC SERIES

All the fun of Studio Ghibli in
comic book form, illustrated with
actual stills from the movies.
By Hayao Miyazaki et al.
¥1,485 - ¥2,200, Bungei Shunju

BUNSHUN GHIBLI PAPERBACK GHIBLI TEXTBOOK SERIES

Understanding the world of Ghibli's films
through conversations with staff and critics.
By Isao Takahata, Hayao Miyazaki et al.
¥715 - ¥1,518
Bungei Shunju

*As of March 29, 2021. Retail prices include sales tax. Books shown within the ☐ are examples from series.

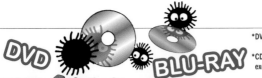

THE EVERYTHING GHIBLI! COLLECTION

Nausicaä of the Valley of the Wind
¥5,170

Castle in the Sky
¥5,170

My Neighbor Totoro
¥5,170

Grave of the Fireflies
¥5,170

Kiki's Delivery Service
¥5,170

Only Yesterday
¥5,170

Porco Rosso
¥5,170

Ocean Waves
¥5,170

Pom Poko
¥5,170

Whisper of the Heart
¥5,170

Princess Mononoke
¥5,170

My Neighbors the Yamadas
¥5,170

Spirited Away
¥5,170

The Cat Returns / the GHIBLIES episode 2
¥5,170

Howl's Moving Castle
¥5,170

Tales from Earthsea
¥5,170

Ponyo on the Cliff by the Sea
¥5,170

Arrietty
¥5,170

From Up on Poppy Hill
¥5,170

The Wind Rises
¥5,170

*The Tale of The
Princess Kaguya*
¥5,170

When Marnie Was There
¥5,170

The Red Turtle
¥5,170

THE EVERYTHING GHIBLI! COLLECTION SPECIALS

*Everything Ghibli! Special
Short-Short 1992-2016*
¥4,180

*Here's How the One CD Hayao Miyazaki
Ever Produced Came to Be*
¥4,180

*Hayao Miyazaki and
the Ghibli Museum*
¥4,180

*Kazuo Oga—Ghibli's Image Artisan Exhibition:
The Man Who Drew Totoro's Forest.*
¥4,180

*Ghibli's Landscapes
Japan as Drawn by Hayao Miyazaki
A Journey Through Europe with Miyazaki*
¥5,170

*The Kingdom of
Dreams and Madness*
¥5,170

**Studio Ghibli
Hayao Miyazaki & Joe Hisaishi Soundtracks Box Set**
¥22,000

**Studio Ghibli
Isao Takahata Soundtracks Box Set**
¥16,500

**Studio Ghibli Songs
New Edition**
¥4,180

Earwig and the Witch
Soundtrack
¥2,750

**Studio Ghibli
7-inch Box Set**
¥6,600

CHARACTER INDEX

THIS IS AN ALPHABETICAL INDEX OF THE STUDIO GHIBLI CHARACTERS WHO APPEAR IN THIS BOOK.

IF MULTIPLE CHARACTERS HAVE THE SAME NAME, THE FILM TITLE FOLLOWS IN PARENTHESES. WHERE NECESSARY, FURTHER DETAILS FOLLOW IN SQUARE BRACKETS.